D0113978

A special issue of
Cognition and Emotion

Development of Emotion-Cognition Relations

Edited by
Carroll E. Izard
Department of Psychology,
University of Delaware, U.S.A.

LEA LAWRENCE ERLBAUM ASSOCIATES, PUBLISHERS LEA
Hove and London (UK)   Hillsdale (USA)

Copyright © 1989 by Lawrence Erlbaum Associates Ltd.
All rights reserved. No part of this book may be reproduced in any
form, by photostat, microform, retrieval system, or any other
means without the prior written permission of the publisher.

Lawrence Erlbaum Associates Ltd., Publishers
27 Palmeira Mansions
Church Road
Hove
East Sussex, BN3 2FA
U.K.

British Library cataloguing in Publication Data

Development of emotion-cognition relations.
1. Children. Cognitive development
I. Izard, Carroll E. (Carroll Ellis),, 1923- II.
Cognition & emotion, ISSN 0269-9931

ISBN 0-86377-143-2

Typeset by Acorn Bookwork, Salisbury
Printed and bound by BPCC Wheatons, Exeter

Contents

Editorial: Studies of the Development of Emotion-Cognition
Relations
Carroll E. Izard   257

Cognitive-Emotional Interactions in the Brain
Joseph E. LeDoux   267

Infants' Expectations in Play: The Joy of Peek-a-boo
W. Gerrod Parrott and Henry Gleitman   291

Talking with Feeling: Integrating Affective and Linguistic
Expression in Early Language Development
Lois Bloom and Richard Beckwith   313

The Causal Organisation of Emotional Knowledge:
A Developmental Study
Nancy L. Stein and Linda J. Levine   343

Young Children's Theory of Mind and Emotion
Paul L. Harris, Carl N. Johnson, Deborah Hutton,
Giles Andrews and Tim Cooke   379

Understanding the Motivational Role of Affect:
Lifespan Research from an Attributional Perspective
Bernard Weiner and Sandra Graham   401

Subject Index   421

COGNITION AND EMOTION, 1989, 3(4), 257–266

Editorial: Studies of the Development of Emotion–Cognition Relations

Carroll E. Izard

Department of Psychology, University of Delaware, U.S.A.

This issue of *Cognition and Emotion* is devoted to studies of the development of emotion–cognition relations, children's knowledge of the causes of emotions, and the relations of that knowledge to expectations or anticipations of emotion experiences. The studies show that infants of seven months display different expressive behaviours to confirmed and disconfirmed expectations; that the first words of 13-month-olds are not coordinated with expressions of joy or negative emotions and 19-month-olds vocabulary spurts contain very few emotion labels; that 3- to 7-year-olds can label their emotions and understand relations among beliefs, desires, and emotion experiences; and that understandings of relations among causal attributions and emotion experiences are stable over the life span. These findings suggest interesting possibilities for research on developmental processes that integrate emotion, cognition, and action.

INTRODUCTION

Perhaps the most critical issue in the domain of emotion–cognition relations is the question of the distinctiveness or separability of the two phenomena. One of the contributors to this volume (LeDoux) describes a separate neural circuit for affective computations—rapid, automatic processing of the emotionally relevant information in a stimulus. In his view, cognitive computations involve different brain structures and pathways and take longer to complete. Evidence for separate systems for emotion-information processing and traditionally defined cognitive-information processing has important implications for all areas of psychology.

The assumption of different neural substrates for affective and cognitive processing raises especially interesting questions for developmental

Requests for reprints should be sent to Dr C. E. Izard, Department of Psychology, 220 Wolf Hall, University of Delaware, Newark, Delaware 19716, U.S.A. This work was supported in part by NSF Grant No. BNS8706146 and NIMH Grant No. MH4205003.

© 1989 Lawrence Erlbaum Associates Limited

psychology. For example, evidence reviewed by LeDoux suggests that the substrates for affective computations mature earlier than do the substrates for cognitive computations.

Another issue in the development of emotion–cognition relations is the question of how and when particular cognitive attainments influence emotion experiences and vice versa and how these interactions relate to memory. Parrott and Gleitman's experiments show that infants of seven months react with different emotions to confirmed and violated expectations. Of special interest is the fact that both confirmation and violation of expectation elicit emotion responses. This raises the question as to what really distinguishes the two kinds of events in the infant's memory, the different discriminating features that were detected or the different emotions that were experienced.

A third issue is that of the coordination and integration of the emotions system and the cognitive system. If there are distinct neural and mental processes in emotion and cognition, then there must be developmental processes whereby the two systems are interrelated. Complex adaptive actions of the organism require the harmonious interaction of its subsystems. Bloom and Beckwith's paper addresses an aspect of this problem in their study of the relations among emotion expressions and early uses of language. Their results suggest that expressive behaviour (a component of the emotions system) and language (an index of cognition) are indeed separable phenomena and that their interaction can be studied rather precisely at different stages of development.

A fourth issue in the emotion–cognition domain is the development of knowledge about emotions and the development of adaptive applications of this knowledge. The paper of Harris, Johnson, Hutton, Andrews, and Cooke; that of Stein and Levine; and that of Weiner and Graham address this topic. Harris and his colleagues' demonstration of three- to seven-year-old children's ability to anticipate emotional reactions of others and themselves has implications for the development of empathy and the use of cognition in the self-regulation of emotion experiences. Stein and Levine's theory of emotion knowledge offers a description of the cognitive-affective processes that enable children to label their feelings and understand the conditions that lead to different emotions. Weiner and Graham show that certain relations among attributional processes and conceptions of emotion experiences hold over the life span.

Separate Neural Basis for Emotional and Cognitive Processes

LeDoux's paper provides exciting possibilities for conceptualising the relations among neural and mental processes in emotion. Unlike some neuroscientists and many behaviourally oriented psychologists, LeDoux acknowledges that the principal aim of emotion theory is to explain emotion experience.

LeDoux holds that there are two neural circuits for the activation of emotions—one subcortical, the other involving neocortex. The subcortical (thalamo-amygdala) circuit evaluates the emotional significance of events via rapid, automatic processing of sensory data. At the mental level, this can be described as minimal information processing that leads only to the detection of certain features of the stimulus. Thus human infant's smile at a face as soon as it is capable of detecting its contours. LeDoux's scheme provides a basis for viewing this smile as a function of affective computations.

The emotion-activation circuit involving neocortex (cortico-amygdala circuit) evaluates the details of the stimulus. The cortico-amygdala circuit participates in all higher order cognitive antecedents of emotion—appraisal, comparison, categorisation, attribution, inference. At this level, emotions are a function of cognitive computations.

LeDoux's conception of a neural basis for automatic, unconscious information processing that leads to emotion experiences could provide a basis for inferring emotion experiences/feelings in the young infant. The thalamus and amygdala may be sufficient for generating emotion feelings, and they mature relatively early. The cortex and hippocampus, which are so critical to memory and locale/context learning, mature later than the thalamus and amygdala.

Extrapolating from LeDoux's model, one could conceive of affective computations as the initial neural/mental response to any event. Any resulting emotion would then influence the subsequent cognitive computations required by complex events. If this position is correct, one could argue that emotion influences the cognitive processes elicited by all events and situations that have affective features.

Emotion Expressions and Cognitive Processes

Since the resurgence of research in emotional development that began in the early 1970s, there has been an interest in the relations among certain cognitive attainments and emotion processes. Haviland (1976) showed that infants' emotion expressions are critical cues in the assessment of infant intelligence, even when standardised scales are used. Ramsay and Campos (1978) found that smiling is an effective index of transition from stage 5 to stage 6 of sensorimotor development. As compared to infants at stage 5, infants who had reached stage 6 (considered to be capable of fully representing an absent object) were more likely to smile if they found a toy that had been hidden in a complex sequence of manipulations. Lewis, Sullivan,

Stanger, and Weiss (in press) have shown that self-recognition, as indexed by an infant touching or covering his or her rouge-covered nose when seen in a mirror, is associated with behaviours indicative of shame or embarrassment. These self-recognition and associated shame behaviours rarely occur before 15 months of age but are present in over 75% of infants between 21 and 24 months of age.

The foregoing experiments do not show precisely the relation between a particular cognitive attainment and a particular emotion expression. They do indicate that emotion-expressive behaviours can serve as markers of item comprehension on intelligence tests, stages of sensorimotor development, and levels of self-knowledge.

In their contribution to this volume, Parrott and Gleitman showed how the smile and brow-lift relate to six-, seven-, and eight-month-old infants' inferred cognitive processes during a peek-a-boo game. The peek-a-boo game included trick trials—after the infant had seen one person in three trials, a different person appeared from behind the screen; and in another experiment, the familiar person on early trials reappeared in a different location. They found that infants of all three ages smiled more on trials when the familiar person reappeared and lifted their brows more frequently on the person-switch and location-switch trials. There was a tendency for the effect of smiling to increase with age.

In Parrott and Gleitman's experiments, the infants' emotion responses were apparently affected by their ability to store an image of the experimenter and develop an expectation about his or her appearance. The reappearance of the same person in the same place elicited the greatest amount of smiling, and violation of expectations in terms of person or place elicited more brow lifts. The authors make the reasonable inference that infants experience more enjoyment of the familiar and expected in the traditional peek-a-boo game and more surprise to the trick trials. They suggest several possible explanations of the finding that young infants', in contrast to older children and adults, did not show greater enjoyment of deviations from their expectations. However, it seems that the brow-lift, which may signal surprise *or* interest depending on the total pattern of facial movements (Izard, 1979), might be elicited at any age by the novelty of the violation of an expectation.

The authors noted the implications of their method and findings for studying the development of emotion–cognition relations. They showed very clearly that the smile and brow-lift are useful markers of different perceptual-cognitive processes—in this case the smile marked recognition of the familiar through relatively easy comparison and matching of image and percept. The brow-lift marked the somewhat more difficult cognitive processes of assimilating novel aspects that were introduced in the ongoing events (peek-a-boo).

Parrott and Gleitman's findings are also consistent with the notion that there is correspondence between the discrete expressive behaviours and underlying emotion experience or feeling states. The causal events (stimuli) predicted expectable emotion responses with considerable regularity. Further, smiling was shown to be greater for the climax of the peek-a-boo game (reappearance of experimenter) than for other aspects of the face-to-face interaction.

Infants' Emotion Expressions and First Verbalisations

Bloom and Beckwith's study of relations between emotion expressions and verbalisations is an important addition to the earlier work of Bloom and her colleagues on this topic. Previously they had shown that expression relating to emotion-eliciting events facilitates the child's learning of the language of causality. In this study they discover a number of interesting relations (and lack of them) between aspects of linguistic and facial expression.

Children's First-Words (mean age 13 months) are typically uttered with what Bloom and Beckwith called "neutral affect". The results of their particular coding scheme reliably identified negative emotion and the positive emotion of enjoyment (smiling, laughing). The coding scheme did not attempt to identify signals of interest, considered by a number of theorists as the most frequently expressed positive emotion (Campos & Barrett, 1984; Izard & Malatesta, 1987). Thus the results tell us clearly that First-Words are typically uttered when there are no signs of joy or negative emotion, but they did not determine whether interest signals were present.

The co-occurrence of interest signals and First-Word utterances would not be inconsistent with Bloom and Beckwith's interpretation of the events. The emotion of interest has been shown to facilitate attention focusing and performance (Renninger & Wozniak, 1985). Further, emotion theorists have suggested that interest facilitates cognitive processes (Tomkins, 1962). Thus the pre-verbalisation suppression of expression may not, and perhaps need not, apply to the expression of interest.

One other factor should be considered in interpreting Bloom and Beckwith's findings regarding the temporal relations among emotions and speech. Apart from the possibility that interest *expression* may occur during First-Word and vocabulary spurt (VS) utterances, the *experience* or *feeling* related to other emotions may be occurring. Emotion theorists have suggested that emotion experiences/feelings outlast expressions (Izard & Malatesta, 1987); and theorists of different persuasions have argued that in later stages of development, emotion feelings may occur without *expressions* (see, for example, Scherer & Ekman, 1984). In any case, the absence of smiling, laughing, and negative emotion expressions during First-Words (or speech at any age) does not necessarily mean absence of emotion feelings. Nevertheless, Bloom and Beckwith have convincingly demonstrated that early speech and nonverbal emotion expression, particularly intense expressions, are not integrated.

By the time children exhibit a VS (mean age 19 months), language and nonverbal emotion expression overlap a significant amount of time, but even at this age words at VS are more likely to be said with low intensity positive emotions. The authors suggested that this may be so because positive emotion requires less cognitive work than negative emotions. An alternative, or possibly complementary, explanation is that the 19-month-old's capacity to self-regulate intense emotions, particularly intense negative emotions, is not sufficient to enable the child to engage in both nonverbal emotion expression and speech. At 19 months the child is far more proficient in nonverbal expression than in language, and the difference in fluency in the two communication systems probably stems from the child's relatively greater command of nonverbal expression.

It is especially interesting that First-Word and VS utterance do not consist of emotion labels. Bloom and Beckwith note that for an infant expressing emotion with facial and bodily movements, emotion labels, even if they are in the infant's vocabulary, would be redundant. This finding should be a caveat to investigators who study children's comprehension of emotion or the organisation of emotion knowledge.

Bloom and Beckwith made an important point when they said that language, with all its power and flexibility as a system of communication, can by no means express all the aspects of emotion feelings. This is undoubtedly true at all stages of development.

The Development and Applications of Emotion Knowledge

Harris and his colleagues present three experiments that examined the influence of three- to seven-year-olds' beliefs and desires on their understanding of the emotional reactions of animal characters which were portrayed in various situations. They found that children as young as three years understood that the character's emotional reaction to an event would be a function of the character's beliefs and desires. In predicting how the character would feel after a particular event, the children not only took the characters beliefs and desires jointly into account, but they also considered the relation between beliefs and desires. They also seemed to understand that emotion is more a function of the relation between desire and expected reality than that between desire and actual reality. The authors discuss the cognitive processes that young children use when they reason about relations among beliefs, desires, and emotions. They conclude that children have a working theory of mind and emotion that enables them to attribute emotion experiences to others and to anticipate their own emotional reactions.

The authors' findings have important implications for the development of empathy and emotion regulation. When children have the ability to take others' beliefs and desires into account and thereby understand and predict their emotional experiences, they should have the capacity for empathic feelings. As Harris and his colleagues note, children's understanding of belief–desire–emotion relations also suggests that children can simulate future events in imagination and anticipate their own emotional reactions. This sort of imaginary role-playing in anticipatory scenarios gives the child practice in choosing among actual events on the basis of their anticipated emotional impact. Undoubtedly, children accomplish this sort of emotion regulation, at least to some extent, in pretend play. Perhaps the better the growing child's make-believe script stimulates the belief–desire–emotion sequences in real situations and events, the greater becomes his or her ability to anticipate and thereby regulate emotion experiences.

Stein and her colleagues (Stein & Jewett, 1986; Stein & Levine, 1989) have proposed a theory of emotion knowledge in which the attainment and maintenance of goals is the primary focus for explaining emotion experiences and the wishes and plans that follow. They hold that awareness of "want-have" states enable children to label their feelings about different events. Thus wanting a particular state and attaining it is likely to lead to joy, whereas wanting and not attaining is likely to lead to sadness or anger. Anger is more likely when the subject focuses attention on the conditions that caused the failure to attain the goal, and sadness is more likely when the subject focuses on the consequences of the failure. The model suggests that peoples' knowledge about emotions includes awareness of (a) a valued state that may undergo change, (b) the conditions that lead to change, (c) the consequences of the change for goal-related behaviour, and (d) available plans that would maintain or re-instate the change.

In the study reported in this issue, they hypothesised that happiness, joy, sadness, and anger would be differentiated in terms of (a) goal achievement or failure, (b) the focus of attention once goal failure has occurred, (c) the animate/inanimate nature of the agent that caused goal failure, and (d) an assessment of the possibility of reinstating goals following failure. Their subjects were preschool and first grade children and college students. The stimulus materials were vignettes illustrating different combinations of goals and outcomes on want-have states. The vignettes and the relevant questions about thoughts, feelings, and actions were presented to subjects in individual interviews.

Their results generally confirmed their hypotheses and confirmed their expectation regarding a causal link between emotion experiences and perceptions of changes in the likelihood of attaining or maintaining goals or valued states. They also found some expectable age differences in understanding emotions. Preschool children, unlike first graders and college students, were just as likely to infer sadness as anger when intentional harm was inferred. The older groups were more likely to associate anger with intentional harm. They concluded that even three- to four-year-olds have considerable knowledge of the causes and consequences of emotions.

Attributions as Causes and Explanations of Emotions

Weiner and his colleagues have developed an attributional theory of emotion (Weiner, 1985) and emotional development (Weiner & Graham, 1984) that provides the conceptual framework for their contribution. The thrust of the theory is that the structure of thinking plays a key role in the activation of certain common emotional experiences such as anger, pity, pride, and shame. Whether an event elicits anger, pity, or some other emotion depends on the subject's perceived causes of the event. Perceived causes can be analysed in terms of common features, principally, locus (internal vs. external), stability, and controllability. Once an emotion is activated, the emotion experience and the accompanying expectations guide subsequent behaviour. The theory sets some limits for itself in recognising that a number of emotions such as excitement, joy, disgust, and contempt are not necessarily or primarily elicited or influenced by the properties of causal attributions.

Much of the earlier work of Weiner and his colleagues has focused on middle-school children and young adults, and the explanatory concepts of attribution were applicable to both groups. In studies of five- to nine-year-old children, however, they found that causal connections between certain combinations of perceived causes and particular emotions change with age.

For this issue, Weiner and Graham investigated changes over the life span in relations among causal attributions, the emotional experiences of anger and pity, and altruistic behaviours. They presented 5- to 80-year-old subjects with vignettes about a person needing help and varied the controllability of the persons' needy condition. The subjects rated the controllability of the event, the degree of anger or pity they would feel for the needy persons, and the likelihood that they would help these persons.

As predicted, persons in a predicament with uncontrollable causes elicited reports of less anger, more pity, and greater likelihood of being helped. For both controllable and uncontrollable conditions, increasing age was associated with decreasing anger and increasing pity and altruism.

CONCLUSION

The studies reported here, together with those reviewed by the authors, demonstrate that we have made a good beginning in research on the development of emotion–cognition relations. They also suggest interesting questions for future research. How does coordination or co-occurrence of emotion expressions and cognitive processes in preverbal infants affect memory? More generally, what are the functions of emotion expressions in cognitive development?

Given that certain cognitive processes and emotion expressions are well coordinated (or occur in predictable sequences) in early infancy, what processes create the apparent independence between emotion expressions and first words and between children's first vocabulary spurt and emotion labels? How do children come to look angry and sound angry at the same time? How do they eventually learn to separate feelings from nonverbal and verbal communication? Does the emergence of first words, vocabulary spurts, and the later appearance of emotion labels indicate special achievements in the child's ability to self-regulate emotions?

Can levels or types of emotion knowledge be related to levels of emotion regulation? How do cognitive attainments and the child's growing knowledge about emotion inform us about the functions of emotion experiences? To what extent will the study of emotions, language, and emotion knowledge strengthen inferences about the assumed organisational and motivational properties of emotions? With these and numerous other questions before us, research on the development of emotion–cognition relations should flourish.

Manuscript received 28 February 1989
Manuscript revised 27 April 1989

REFERENCES

Campos, J. J. & Barrett, K. C. (1984). Toward a new understanding of emotions and their development. In C. E. Izard, J. Kagan, & R. B. Zajonc (Eds), *Emotions, cognition, and behavior*. Cambridge University Press, pp. 299–263.

Haviland, J. (1976). Looking smart: The relationship between affect and intelligence in infancy. In M. Lewis (Ed.), *Origins of intelligence*. New York: Plenum Press, pp. 353–377.

Izard, C. E. (1979). *The maximally discriminative facial movement coding system (Max)*. Newark, Delaware, University of Delaware, Office of Academic Computing and Instructional Technology.

Izard, C. E. & Malatesta, C. Z. (1987). Perspectives on emotional development. I: Differential emotions theory of early emotional development. In J. D. Osofsky (Ed.), *Handbook of infant development*, 2nd edn. New York: Wiley-Interscience, pp. 494–554.

Lewis, M., Sullivan, M. W., Stanger, C., & Weiss, M. (in press). Self development and self-conscious emotions. *Child Development*

Ramsay, D. & Campos, J. (1978). The onset of representation and entry into stage 6 of object permanence development. *Developmental Psychology, 14*, 79–86.

Renninger, K. A. & Wozniak, R. H. (1985). Effect of interest on attentional shift, recognition, and recall in young children. *Developmental Psychology, 21*(4), 624–632.

Scherer, K. R. & Ekman, P. (1984). *Approaches to emotion.* Hillsdale, N.J.: Lawrence Erlbaum Associates Inc.

Stein, N. L. & Jewett, J. (1986). A conceptual analysis of the meaning of negative emotions: Implications for a theory of development. In C. E. Izard & P. Read (Eds), *Measurement of emotion in infants and children, Vol. 2.* Cambridge University Press, pp. 238–267.

Stein, N. L. & Levine, L. J. (1989). The causal organisation of emotional knowledge: A developmental study. *Cognition and Emotion, 3*(4), 341–376.

Tomkins, S. S. (1962). *Affect, imagery consciousness, The positive affects.* New York: Springer.

Weiner, B. (1985). An attributional theory of achievement motivation and emotion. *Psychological Review, 89*(4), 548–573.

Weiner, B. & Graham, S. (1984). An attributional approach to emotional development. In C. E. Izard, J. Kagan, & R. Zajonc (Eds), *Emotions, cognition, and behavior.* Cambridge University Press.

COGNITION AND EMOTION, 1989, 3(4), 267–289

Cognitive–Emotional Interactions in the Brain

Joseph E. LeDoux

Centre for Neural Science, New York University, New York, NY, USA.

Emotion and cognition are mediated by separate but interacting systems of the brain. The core of the emotional system is a network that evaluates (computes) the biological significance of stimuli, including stimuli from the external or internal environment or from within the brain (thoughts, images, memories). The computation of stimulus significance takes place prior to and independent of conscious awareness, with only the computational products reaching awareness, and only in some instances. The amygdala may be a focal structure in the affective network. By way of neural interactions between the amygdala and brain areas involved in cognition (particularly the neocortex and hippocampus), affect can influence cognition and cognition can influence affect. Emotional experiences, it is proposed, result when stimulus representations, affect representations, and self representations coincide in working memory.

INTRODUCTION

One of the most consuming issues in the study of emotion is the relation between cognitive and emotional processes. Is cognition a necessary link in the causal chain leading to emotion? Is emotion just a subset of cognition or is affect processed separately and independently of cognition? If emotion and cognition are separate functions, what types of interactions, if any, take place between them? These are questions about the psychological mechanisms of emotion and answers to them are most often sought through psychological experimentation. However, it is also possible to address such questions through studies of brain mechanisms. If two psychological processes, such as emotion and cognition, can be shown to have different neural correlates or to involve different neural systems, the

---

Requests for reprints should be sent to Dr Joseph E. LeDoux, Centre for Neural Science, New York University, 6 Washington Place, NY 10003, U.S.A.

© 1989 Lawrence Erlbaum Associates Limited

case for their independence is strengthened, if not proven. Alternatively, if the neural mechanisms of cognition and emotion cannot be differentiated, the argument that these are closely related, perhaps inseparable, functions would be supported. The aim of this article is to illustrate that emotion and cognition are mediated by separate but interacting neural systems and that emotional and cognitive processes and distinct but sometimes interacting functions of the brain.

THE NEUROBIOLOGY OF EMOTION: HISTORICAL CONSIDERATIONS

William James (1884) raised the question of whether the brain contains a special emotional system or whether emotion might simply be just another function of the then recently discovered sensory and motor areas of the cortex. James preferred the latter idea, which was the basis of his renowned theory. According to James, the perception of an exciting event (by sensory cortex) produces bodily changes (through motor cortex). These bodily changes then flow back to the brain, where they are perceived (by sensory cortex). The perception of the bodily changes, combined with the continuing perception of the exciting event, gives rise to a feeling about the stimulus. This feeling is the emotion. He contrasted his view (that bodily changes precede and determine emotional experiences) with the common sense notion that emotional experiences are the precursors of the bodily expressions of emotion.

James's theory was subsequently criticised by Cannon (1927, 1931), who argued that, among other factors, bodily changes were not specific enough and were too slow to account for emotional experience. On the basis of studies from his laboratory (Cannon & Britton, 1925; Bard, 1929), Cannon argued that the brain did indeed possess a special emotional system and that the hypothalamus was the integrative structure of this system (Cannon, 1927, 1931).

Papez (1937), building upon the ideas of cannon, postulated a circuit theory of emotion centered on the hypothalamus. The emotional system of the brain, in his view, involved the relay of sensory inputs to the hypothalamus and from there to the anterior thalamus, cingulate cortex, and hippocampus, which then connected back with the hypothalamus. The flow of information through this loop was viewed as essential to emotional functions.

MacLean (1949, 1952), inspired by the Papez circuit theory, postulated the existence of a visceral brain or limbic system. According to MacLean, the limbic system consists of a group of phylogenetically old cortical structures located in the medial walls of the cerebral hemispheres, as well as several subcortical nuclei associated with these areas of the limbic cortex. These structures were viewed as forming an integrated neural system involved the mediation of all aspects of emotion.

The limbic system hypothesis has been extremely influential and remains to this day the dominant view of how the brain mediates emotion. Nevertheless, the validity of the limbic system hypothesis as an account of the neurobiology of emotion is highly questionable. In the first place, although some areas traditionally included in the limbic system have been implicated in emotional processes, there is little evidence to support the idea that limbic areas function as a unified network in the mediation of emotional processes. Secondly, the morphological concept on which the limbic system was built (phylogenetically old areas of the cortex) has been questioned (Swanson, 1983). This leaves no structural criterion for determining which brain areas should be included in the limbic system (Brodal, 1982). Moreover, key limbic areas, such as the hippocampus, have now been shown to be much more involved in cognitive than in emotional functions, a point to which we will return.

The failure of the limbic system hypothesis to provide an adequate account of how the brain mediates emotion does not necessarily discredit the more general idea that a special emotional system exists in the brain. We are not, in other words, necessarily thrown back 100 years to James' idea that no special emotional system exists. However, in searching for the emotional system, or any other system in the brain, it helps to have a clear idea of what to look for. One of the difficulties of the early neurological theories is their vague descriptions of what they meant by emotion. Before proceeding, it will thus be useful to briefly describe what we mean by emotion.

THE PSYCHOLOGY OF EMOTION: THEORETICAL CONSIDERATIONS

What is it that a theory of emotion needs to explain? A survey of the psychological literature on emotion strongly suggests that emotional experience is the primary factor that a theory of emotion needs to explain. Common sense suggests the same. After all, what are emotions if not affectively charged conscious experiences? While emotional experience is certainly an important part of what a theory of emotion needs to explain, the focus on experience has, to a large extent, obscured a more fundamental mechanism.

The psychology of emotion has, for the past 20 to 30 years, been dominated by cognitive and facial feedback theories and emotional experience. Cognitive theories claim that one's perceptions, thoughts, and beliefs about a situation can determine the emotional state that is experienced (see Schachter & Singer, 1962; Mandler, 1975; Bem, 1972; Lazarus, 1982; Laird, 1974; Frijda, 1986). For example, a common argument is that in an emotional situation a state of bodily arousal, usually of the peripheral autonomic nervous system, is evoked. Contrary to James and in line with Cannon, cognitive theories assume that the physiological arousal is emotionally ambiguous (i.e. is the same across different emotional situations). The organism is required to interpret the physiological condition with respect to the physical and social environment in order to make sense of it. Cognitive interpretation allows the organism to label the state and thus to differentiate different emotional experiences. Facial feedback theories agree that physiological signals from the autonomic nervous system lack the specificity to differentiate emotions. These theories argue, though, the feedback from the facial musculature does have the required specificity (e.g. Tomkins, 1962; Ekman, 1984; Izard, 1977). Facial feedback theories are thus consistent, in principle, with James' more general feedback hypothesis.

Cognitive and feedback theories of emotion fail to explain a critical factor. How is it that the initial state of bodily arousal or facial expression is evoked? Not all stimuli and situations lead to such expressive conditions. Cognitive theories require that the brain has a mechanism for distinguishing emotional from mundane situations prior to activating the autonomic nervous system. Feedback theories have an even more stringent requirement. The brain must have a mechanism for judging not just the difference between emotional and non-emotional situations, but must also identify the exact nature of the emotional situation, prior to initiating facial responses specific to that situation. In either case, the brain must perform some emotional computation prior to producing physiological (autonomic, humoral, or somatic) responses that subsequently contribute to (in the case of cognitive theories) or determine (in the case of facial feedback theories) the emotional experience. The mechanism required in both instances is one which computes the affective significance of stimuli and produces responses appropriate to the computed significance.

While cognitive and feedback theories assume that emotional experience results after information is relayed back to the brain from the periphery, another possibility exists. This possibility was suggested in the early neurological theories of Cannon and Papez. In these theories, sensory stimuli activated the hypothalamus, which discharged to the periphery to produce emotional responses and to the cortex to produce emotional experiences. In contrast to the cognitive and feedback theories, the neurological theories thus assumed that emotional experiences were generated centrally, by way of hypothalamic activation of the cerebral cortex. However, for these theories to work, the hypothalamus must compute stimulus significance prior to activating the cortex. Otherwise, all stimuli would produce emotional experiences.

Regardless of whether one favours a cognitive, feedback, or central theory of emotion, the core of the emotional system is thus a mechanism for computing the affective significance of stimuli. As this mechanism is the precursor to conscious emotional experience, it operates, by definition, outside of conscious awareness.

It is now widely accepted that mental information processing takes place largely outside of conscious awareness, with only the end-products reaching consciousness and being represented as conscious content (Jackendoff, 1987; Kihlstrom, 1987). As Lashley (1956) argued, we are never aware of processes but only of the consequences of processes. The suggestion that affective information processing occurs without conscious awareness of the processing itself is thus an idea that sits comfortably within contemporary information processing psychology. This suggestion is also consistent with psychoanalytic views of affect (see Rapaport, 1950; Bowlby, 1968) and with the affective primacy views of Zajonc (1980) and Izard (1981).

The idea that there exists a basic emotional processing system that determines but operates independent of conscious emotional experience has important implications. Specifically, it clears at least some of the confusion about whether it is possible to study emotion in animals. Regardless of the extent to which non-human creatures have full-blown conscious emotional experiences of the types that humans have, non-human animals do have the basic neural mechanism of emotion, a system for computing the affective significance of stimuli and for producing emotional responses appropriate to the computed significance.

In some instances, which are most prevalent in lower mammals and non-mammalian vertebrates, the computation of stimulus significance is genetically built into the brain. Key stimulus elements in the environment can trigger or release instinctive emotional responses. In other instances, particularly in primates and higher mammals, the brain has a striking capacity to learn and remember the emotional significance of stimuli and events. Affective learning and memory allow us to assign emotional valence to novel stimuli and to change the value that was previously assigned to a stimulus.

The processes involved in stimulus evaluation could, if one chose, be called cognitive processes. The meaning of the stimulus is not given in physical characteristics of the stimulus but instead is determined by computations performed by the brain. As computation is the benchmark of the cognitive, the computation of affective significance could be considered a cognitive process.

If the computation of stimulus significance is a cognitive process, then emotion, we must conclude, is just a class of cognition. However, it is important to distinguish two classes of computations on the basis of their computational consequences. For example, the computations that determine that a snake is a vertebrate, that it is biologically closer to an alligator than to a cow, and that its skin can be used to make belts and shoes, have very different consequences than the computations that determine that a snake is likely to be dangerous. The former, called here cognitive computations, yield information about the stimulus itself and its relationship to other stimuli. These tend to lead to further information processing about the stimulus. The latter, called here affective computations, yield information about the relation of the stimulus to the individual. These often lead directly to motor responses (behavioural, autonomic, and humoral responses) rather than to more elaborate processing of the stimulus and its semantic associations. Stimulus elaboration may also follow, but reaction (behavioural and physiological) is the primary consequence of affective processing. In the presence of danger it is more important to emit appropriate escape or defence responses than to ruminate over cognitive attributes of the stimulus. As we shall see later, the affective processing system receives sensory inputs from early stages of sensory processing. Consequently, emotional responses can be rapidly initiated on the basis of crude stimulus properties prior to and independent of more complex stimulus transformations, such as those involved in the recognition of objects as semantic entities.

This theoretical perspective strips both affect and cognition of the mystical veil of consciousness and places them on equal conceptual footing as companion (somewhat parallel) processing systems of the brain. The systems receive and operate on information from the same stimulus sources, but they differ in what they do with the information.

In summary, the core of the brain's emotional system is the network that computes the affective value of the stimuli an organism encounters. Emotional responses and conscious emotional experiences are consequences of affective computations performed on these stimuli. Affective computations are distinct from cognitive computations, but the two computational systems often interact. Both affective and cognitive computations occur without conscious awareness, with only the computational products reaching consciousness.

The foregoing characterisation of emotional processes in terms of affective computations applies mainly to relatively simple emotional reactions coupled to specific stimuli. This over-simplification restricts the generality of the view put forth but allows an approach to the neurobiology of emotion that would otherwise be impossible. It is the hope that by focusing on relatively simple emotional computations, such as those underlying fear processing, we may learn general principles of affective organisation that might help shed light on more complex processes as well.

NEURAL COMPUTATION OF STIMULUS VALUE

One job of the emotional system of the brain is to compute the affective significance of immediately present stimuli. The definition of stimuli used here is broad, and includes events originating in the external environment (exteroceptive stimuli), within the body (interoceptive stimuli), or within the brain (thoughts and memories).

Affective Processing of Exteroceptive Stimuli

The most important discovery in the history of neurobiological studies of emotion was made in 1937 by Kluver and Bucy. These investigators found that large lesions of the temporal lobe of monkeys produced a striking behavioural syndrome that involved changes in motivated and emotional behaviours. The monkeys were no longer threatened by the presence of humans and other previously feared stimuli, attempted to copulate with animals of their own sex or even of different species, and ate their faeces, raw meat, and just about any other object placed in front of them. Kluver and Bucy described the animals as having a "psychic blindness". That is, the animals were not blind to the sensory properties of stimuli but only to their affective significance. Accordingly, later investigators have described the problem as involving a neural disconnection of sensory processing areas from the affective system (Weiskrantz, 1956; Geschwind, 1965; Jones & Mishkin, 1972; Mishkin & Aggleton, 1981).

The neuro-anatomical basis of the Kluver–Bucy syndrome was disco vered through studies which attempted to determine which parts of the temporal lobe were essential to the production of the disturbances. Studies by Weiskrantz (1956) showed that lesions restricted to the amygdaloid nuclei buried deep within the temporal lobe are responsible. Subsequent work demonstrated that select lesions of the amygdala in a variety of vertebrates render animals incapable of guiding their behaviour on the basis of the affective significance of sensory stimuli (e.g. Jones & Mishkin, 1972; Goddard, 1964; Ursin and Kaada, 1960; Cohen, 1980; Fonberg, 1972; Blanchard & Blanchard, 1972; Kapp, Frysinger, Gallagher, & Haselton, 1979; Davis et al., 1987; LeDoux, Sakaguchi, Iwata, & Reis, 1986; Iwata et al., 1986).

Recordings of the electrical activity indicate that some amygdaloid cells respond preferentially to the affective significance of sensory stimuli (Fuster & Uyeda, 1971; Jacobs & McGinty, 1972; Halgren, 1981; Rolls, 1981; Sanghera, Rolls, & Roper-Hall, 1979; Nishijo et al., 1988). Amygdala neurons appear to be less sensitive to physical features of stimuli than to their affective significance (Nishijo et al., 1988; Ono et al., 1983; Sanghera et al., 1979). In a recent study, amygdala neurons responded to novel better than familiar stimuli and better to stimuli with affective significance than to neutral stimuli; some amygdala neurons differentiated stimuli with positive and negative affective significance (Nishijo et al., 1988). Although relatively few of the latter type of neurons were found, this could be due to sampling problems, which are enormous in this type of work, or to the possibility that significance is not coded by individual neurons but across populations of amygdala neurons. The amygdala thus appears to be a key structure in the neural network that computes stimulus significance. The amygdala essentially performs the functions that were suggested for the hypothalamus by Cannon (1927, 1931) and Papez (1937).

Considerable work has focused on the question of how sensory stimuli normally activate the amygdala. It has been shown, for example, that each exteroceptive sensory processing area of the cortex sends fibre projections to the amygdala (Turner, Mishkin, & Knapp, 1980; Jones & Powell, 1970; Aggelton et al., 1980; Mehler et al., 1981). Thus, the amygdala receives afferents from the visual, auditory, somatosensory, gustatory, and olfactory areas of the cortex. Moreover, interruption of connections between modality-specific cortical areas and the amygdala produces a modality-specific Kluver–Bucy syndrome (Downer, 1960; Horel & Keating, 1969). For example, disconnection of the visual cortex from the amygdala makes monkeys tame in the presence of visual stimuli but the animals exhibit normal fear reactions when touched.

Traditionally, it was assumed that the major if not the only projections of thalamic sensory relay structures was to sensory areas of the neocortex. However, recent anatomical studies have shown that thalamic relay nuclei, in addition to projecting the sensory cortex, also send projections to the amygdala (e.g. LeDoux, Sakaguchi, & Reis, 1984; LeDoux, Ruggiero, & Reis, 1985). And recent behavioural studies, using classical conditioning techniques, have shown that when simple sensory cues are used as conditioned stimuli, the thalamo-amygdala projections are necessary and sufficient for the conditioning of fear responses (LeDoux et al., 1984; 1986; Iwata et al., 1986). Although these mechanisms are best established for the auditory system, they are also operative in the visual system (unpublished observation), and probably other systems as well.

Thus, the amygdala receives sensory inputs from the thalamus both directly and by way of the cortex. The thalamo-amygdala projections appear to be involved in the processing of the affective significance of relatively simple sensory cues, whereas the cortico-amygdala projections are necessary when complex stimuli are processed.

In real life, simple stimuli of the type processed by the thalamo-amygdala circuits are seldom encountered in isolation. Most stimuli are complex conglomerations. However, complex stimuli are composed of simpler elements. As complex stimulus information is being relayed to the cortex for perceptual processing, the simpler components are capable of activating the emotional circuits of the amygdala by way of projections from the thalamus. As the projection to the amygdala from the thalamus is monosynaptic, and thus several synapses shorter than the projections to amygdala through cortex, the thalamo-amygdala projection may make up in processing time what it lacks in processing quality. The rapid arrival of crude stimulus information from the thalamus could prepare amygdala neurons to receive more complex stimulus information from the cortex. Even though the thalamic system is probably not capable of full object recognition, it can inform the amygdala of the sensory modality that is being activated and of basic stimulus properties. This may facilitate subsequent affective processing based on a more complete perceptual analysis by way of cortical projections to the amygdala.

In primitive vertebrates, which lack a well-developed neocortex, the primary sensory inputs to subcortical forebrain areas, such as the amygdala, are from subcortical sensory structures. The thalamo-amygdala projections in mammals should therefore be viewed not as an anomaly but as an evolutionarily primitive emotional processing system which has been embellished with the evolution of the neocortex and cortico-amygdala projections. Moreover, the thalamo-amygdala circuits may play a critical role in the processing of affective significance and the control of emotional responses early in life prior to the full maturation of the neocortex and its anatomical connections, as discussed later.

Affective Processing of Interoceptive Stimuli

In addition to receiving information about the external world, the amygdala also receives signals from within the body. Although we know considerably less about the pathways transmitting interoceptive information to the brain, one such system that has been well characterised is the vagus nerve and its second-order projections.

The vagus nerve, which is the tenth cranial nerve, is made up of fibres originating in the tissues of the abdominal cavity, including afferents from the gut, heart, blood vessels, and other organs. These afferents terminate in the nucleus of the solitary tract (NTS) in the medulla. The NTS, in turn, projects to several forebrain areas, including the amygdala (Ricardo & Kho, 1978) and electrical stimulation of the vagus nerve alters the activity of amygdala neurons (Radna & MacLean, 1981). Interruption of vagal activity disrupts performance in emotional tasks (Albiniak & Powell, 1981) and interferes with rewarding brain stimulation (Ball, 1974). Observations such as these led Kapp, Pascoe, and Bixler (1984) to suggest that the amygdala is critically involved in viscerosensory processing. Although present data do not yet prove that the amygdala is a critical site for the evaluation of the affective significance of viscerosensory inputs, the findings are totally consistent with this possibility.

Affective Processing of Cognitive Inputs

In addition to receiving exteroceptive and interoceptive sensory inputs, the amygdala receives afferents from the hippocampus (e.g. Ottersen, 1982; Amaral, 1987). This is significant because the hippocampus has come to be regarded as one of the most important structures of the brain for cognitive processing.

Although originally implicated in emotional functions in MacLean's limbic system theory, the evidence for a direct role of the hippocampus in emotional functions is less than convincing. For example, lesions of the hippocampus do not produce the emotional changes of the Kluver–Bucy syndrome (e.g. Weiskrantz, 1956; Jones & Mishkin, 1972; Alverez-Royo et al., 1988), nor do they interfere with conditioned emotional responses (Rickert, Bennett, Lane, & French, 1978). However, hippocampal lesions do interfere with performance in a variety of cognitive tasks, such as various long-term memory tasks (Squire & Zola-Morgan, 1983; Olton, Becker, & Handelmann, 1979) and tasks requiring the use a mental (cognitive) map of the spatial environment to solve a problem (O'Keefe & Nadel, 1978; Barnes, 1988). Although Gray (1982) argues that the hippocampus is the core of the anxiety system of the brain, it seems that the hippocampus may be more involved in the cognitive than in the affective aspects of anxiety (see LeDoux, 1987).

The hippocampus, like the amygdala, receives inputs from sensory processing areas of the cortex. Unlike the amygdala, the sensory inputs are integrated across sensory modalities in complex association cortex before reaching the hippocampus. As a result of the additional pre-processing, the hippocampus is slower to respond to sensory inputs than the amygdala, but the information it receives is far more complex. The hippocampus thus receives and operates on inputs regarding the same stimulus as the amygdala, but the inputs undergo considerably more processing before reaching the hippocampus. The hippocampus processes inputs that have largely transcended their initial input modality. This is exactly what would be expected of a brain structure involved in higher cognitive processes.

These observations suggest that connections between the hippocampus and amygdala may allow the amygdala to evaluate the affective significance of cognitive information processes in the hippocampus. If so, the role of the amygdala in assigning emotional significance would not be restricted to immediately present sensory stimuli arising from the external environment or from within the body, but would also apply to sensory-independent cognitive information generated centrally, perhaps in the form of images, thoughts, and memories.

Although the role of the amygdala in assigning affective significance to sensory stimuli is unshakable, two qualifications should be added. First, other brain areas may also play some role in evaluating affective qualities of stimuli (e.g. Pankseep, 1982; Butter, Mishkin, & Mirsky, 1968; Damasio & van Hoesen, 1983). Second, the computation of affect may not be the only function of the amygdala (Murray & Mishkin, 1985; Mishkin, 1982). These are minor pertubations of the hypothesis and should not detract from the abundant evidence implicating the amygdala as a major component of the brain's affective processing system.

INTERACTIONS BETWEEN AFFECTIVE AND COGNITIVE PROCESSING SYSTEMS

The argument so far is that the amygdala is critically involved in the processing of affect. The task now is to examine how neural interactions between the amygdala and areas involved in cognitive processing might mediate cognitive–emotional interactions. For the sake of simplicity, the emphasis will be on interactions between the amygdala and the hippocampus. However, it should be noted that the cognitive network involves many other areas of the cortex besides the hippocampus (e.g. Goldman-Rakic, 1987; Squire and Zola-Morgan, 1983; Barnes, 1988).

Cognitive Modulation of Affective Processing

Connections between the hippocampus and the amygdala, in addition to allowing the amygdala to evaluate the significance of cognitive information, may also allow cognitive information to modulate the processing of affect. For example, it has been shown that although hippocampal lesions do not interfere with emotional conditioning, the modulation of conditioned emotional responses by cognitive (contextual) information, as in the blocking paradigm, is interfered with (Solomon, 1977; Rickert et al., 1978). In a typical blocking experiment, one CS is paired with the US and, subsequently, a second CS is introduced along with the first CS and both are paired with US. Usually, the second CS does not acquire conditioned affective significance. The pairing of the first CS with the US appears to "block" the subsequent association of the second CS with the US. However, if the hippocampus is damaged, blocking is interfered with and conditioning to both stimuli occurs. The hippocampal animal is no longer able to filter out irrelevant or redundant stimulus information. The amygdala is thus required for the conditioning of affective significance to the first or relevant CS and the hippocampus for the prevention of conditioning to the irrelevant CS. Projections from the hippocampus to the amygdala may be required to prevent the amygdala from assigning affective weight to the irrelevant CS.

Another example of how cognitive information may modulate affective processing involves stress-induced gastric pathology. Amygdala lesions greatly reduce the development of ulcers following stress and ulcer formation may depend upon descending connections from the amygdala to the gut (Henke, 1982). In contrast, hippocampal lesions aggravate the development of stress-induced ulcer formation (Kim et al., 1976). The usual interpretation of the effects of hippocampal lesions on ulceration is that in the absence of the hippocampus the animals are less able to cope with stress (Henke, 1982). To the extent that coping is a cognitive process (Lazarus, 1982), projections from the hippocampus to the amygdala may allow cognitive information to modulate activity in the amygdala in such a way as to minimise the formation of ulcers through the descending connections of the amygdala.

Affective Modulation of Cognitive Processing

It seems obvious that our emotional states can influence the way we see the world and act in it. Our perceptions and thoughts, in other words, can be coloured by our emotions and moods. Experimental evidence for this comes from a variety of sources (Bruner & Postman, 1947; Clark & Teasdale, 1985; Bower, 1980; Derryberry & Rothbart, 1984; Isen, 1983). An interesting question is how the brain might use affective information to influence cognitive processing?

Although little data is available that directly addresses this question, one hypothesis is that projections from the amygdala to areas involved in cognitive processing might perform this function. For example, the amygdala projects to the hippocampus. These connections could allow the amygdala to modulate memory processing, influencing what gets stored in long-term memory or affecting the strength with which various items get stored. The amygdala also sends projections to a number of other regions of the cerebral cortex, possibly allowing it to affect cognitive processing occurring in these areas as well.

INDEPENDENCE OF EMOTION AND COGNITION

The discussion above has focused on interactions between affective and cognitive processing systems. In this section, we see that the systems can also function independently.

Affective Primacy

Although numerous instances of interactions between cognition and emotion are available, this should not imply that the systems always interact. Much of the experimental base of cognitive psychology, for example, has been built on the elimination of affect as a factor in cognition. Affect has generally been treated as a variable to be controlled rather than one to be studied in cognitive laboratories. Cognition (at least in the cognitive laboratory) does not require affect for its functioning. By the same token, affective computations can be performed without the assistance of cognitive computations.

Zajonc and his colleagues (see Zajonc, 1980) have amassed evidence that affect is processed prior to and independent of cognition. Affect, in this instance, means a judgement about how much the stimulus is liked and cognition means stimulus recognition. For example, when subjects are briefly shown nonsense shapes, their subsequent recognition scores are at chance when chosing between shapes that were presented and those that were not. Stimulus preference, however, is weighted towards shapes that were presented, reflecting the well-known phenomenon that people prefer familiar over unfamiliar stimuli. Zajonc uses evidences of this type to argue that affective judgements do not depend upon prior cognitions and in fact are performed unconsciously. Neurologically, these observations require the existence of pathways that transmit sensory inputs to the affective system (i.e. amygdala) without first transmitting the inputs to the cognitive system (i.e. hippocampus). As we have seen, this clearly occurs. Sensory inputs reach the amygdala from the thalamus and from the association areas of the cortex. In contrast, before reaching the hippocampus the inputs must first be transmitted beyond sensory association cortex to multimodal integrative areas. It thus makes sense that affective processing could occur faster than and independent of cognitive processing. The fact that the amygdala often operates on the basis of stimulus features rather than whole objects (see earlier discussion) suggests why stimulus recognition is not also possible through this system.

Developmental Dissociation of Emotion and Cognition

One of the most interesting phenomena of memory is infantile amnesia. The first two years of life are a time when a tremendous amount of learning takes place. Yet, we have little conscious recall of that information. Why is it so difficult to remember experiences from early childhood?

Jacobs and Nadel (1985) have proposed an intriguing explanation of infantile amnesia. They argue that infantile amnesia, the inability to consciously recall information acquired in early childhood, arises because the hippocampus, which is required for conscious, declarative, autobiographical memory, is not fully mature at birth. Other, early maturing systems, however, are able to form memories, but not declarative, autobiographical memories that depend upon the hippocampus. As memories laid down prior to the maturation of the hippocampus are laid down using memory codes that are indecipherable to the hippocampus, these memories are not available to the hippocampus once it matures, some time between 18 and 36 months in humans.

Jacobs and Nadel (1985) drew a parallel between infantile memories and fear/phobia learning in adults. They argued that fears and phobias learned by adults possess may of the characteristics of infantile memories, such as broad generalisation curves and resistance to extinction, and that these characteristics are imparted to fear and phobia learning by processes which essentially turn off the hippocampus. Specifically, they suggested that under certain stressful conditions, hormones are released that interfere with normal hippocampal function and return the organism to the infantile condition. In this state, all learning that takes place would be mediated by some non-hippocampal system. Recent studies provide support for part of their hypothesis, for hormones released during stress interfere with the development of long-term potentiation (Shors, Levine, & Thompson, 1988; Foy, Stanton, Levine, & Thompson, 1987), a form of neural plasticity that may significantly contribute to learning in the hippocampus (Teyler & Discenna, 1987).

Although the identity of the non-hippocampal system that mediates early learning was not specified by Jacobs and Nadel, it seems likely that the amygdala is critically involved in at least the affective aspects of such learning. As we have seen, in adults the amygdala is a key structure in the system underlying affective learning, which is a major form of learning present in infancy. Moreover, it is well established that the amgydala matures relatively early in life. In rodents, for example, the amygdala possesses most of its neurons by embryonic day 15 or 16 and after embryonic day 17 no additional neurons are generated (Ten Donkelaar, Lammers, & Gribnau, 1979; McConnell & Angevine, 1983). This contrasts strikingly with neurogenesis in the hippocampus (see Cowan et al., 1981). In the hippocampal dentate gyrus, which is a particularly important region for memory processes, the first neurons do not appear until embryonic day 14 and at birth only a small proportion of neurons are present. Although granule cell generation is greatest during the first postnatal week, neurogenesis continues in the dentate gyrus as long as three months postnatally. While the rodent hippocampus is basically inoperative in the early days and possibly weeks of life, the amygdala may well be functioning and could be involved in the formation of affective memories prior to the maturation of the cognitive memory functions mediated by the hippocampus. Although the developmental time scale is spread over a longer period, the lead–lag relation between the amygdala and hippocampus may be maintained in humans.

One problem with the notion that the amygdala is involved in the formation of infantile affective memories is that much of the sensory input to the amygdala comes from the neocortex, which like the hippocampus, matures postnatally (Jones, 1981). Even though the amygdala is relatively precocious, it may be stymied by the slower development of areas that relay information to it. But, as we have already discussed, in addition to receiving sensory inputs from the neocortex, the amygdala also receives sensory inputs directly from thalamic areas, which tend to mature earlier than the cortical areas. The evolutionarily and developmentally primitive thalamo-amygdala connections may therefore be very important in the early time of life prior to the maturation of the neocortex and hippocampus.

NEUROLOGISING EMOTIONAL EXPERIENCE

Cognition and affect have been treated here as independent but sometimes interacting computational functions of the brain. To the extent that information processing takes place outside conscious awareness (see earlier discussion), processing within and between cognitive and affective systems occurs without conscious awareness. The end-products of both affective and cognitive processing may reach conscious awareness, but neither affective nor cognitive processing is synonymous with or require the participation of phenomenal experience.

It is one thing to say that the products of affective and cognitive processing reach conscious awareness and quite another to explain how this occurs. A number of authors have suggested that we are consciously aware of the information content of short-term of working memory (Jackendoff, 1987; Kihlstrom, 1987; Dennett, 1981; Minsky, 1985). Kihlstrom (1987) has combined this notion with James' (1884) idea that the key to consciousness is self-reference. In James' words "The universal conscious fact is not 'feelings exist' and 'thoughts exist' but 'I think' and 'I feel'". Kihlstrom argues that in order for an experience to reach conscious awareness a link must be made between the mental representation of the event and a mental representation of the self as the agent or experiencer. These episodic representations, according to Kihlstrom, reside in short-term or working memory.

Kihlstrom's hypothesis can be extended to account for emotional experience. Emotional experience results when three types of representations coincide in short-term memory: event (stimulus) representations, affective representations activated by stimulus representations, and representations of self. We have no immediate hope of understanding the neural mechanisms underlying representations of self. However, as the earlier discussion indicates, we now know a great deal about how the brain generates representations of stimuli and their affective significance. If we can work out how representations of stimuli and their affective significance come to coincide in working memory, we may be well on the way to understanding how these then interact with representations of the self to generate emotional experience.

Short-term or working memory was for some time viewed as a unitary storage system. However, recent evidence favours the idea that several modality-specific short-term memory systems (slave systems) exist and that these are related to a central attentional control system (Baddeley, 1981). The central attentional system integrates information from the slave systems and from long-term memory. Anatomically, the central attentional system has been related to the frontal lobes (Shallice, 1982), whereas the slave systems are probably localised in the specific brain regions involved in processing the stimulus properties. Thus, for example, the slave system would involve areas of the visual cortex for visual stimuli, areas of the auditory cortex for acoustic stimuli, and language processing areas of the cortex for verbal stimuli. The central attentional system determines which slave system will occupy conscious awareness at a given time.

The foregoing attempts to explain how stimulus representations come to occupy working memory and thus consciousness. Can we now build into this an account of how affective representations come to coincide in working memory with stimulus property representations?

Consider an example. A threatening object appears in peripheral vision. Visual stimulus information is transmitted from the retina to the thalamus and then to the visual cortex (for simplicity we ignore the thalamo-amygdala projection), where stimulus property representations are constructed. These computations have two consequences. First, by way of cortico-cortical (including neocortical-hippocampal) networks, stimulus property computations are integrated and a representation of the object is constructed and related to the environmental context in which it occurs and to other object representations with which it is sematically or pragmatically (experientially) associated. Secondly, by way of cortico-amygdala connections, stimulus property representations activate affective representations linked to those stimulus properties. These, in turn, activate descending circuits and lead to motor (autonomic, humoral, and behavioural) responses and activate ascending circuits that project back to the same areas that initially activated the amygdala. At this point there would be a coincidence in visual association cortex of stimulus property and affective representations. However, because visual association cortex and amygdala both project to the frontal lobe, the representations would also coincide there. The frontal cortex would initially receive the stimulus property signal from visual association cortex and the affective computation from amygdala, but as processing continues would also receive the stimulus property representation integrated with the affective representation from visual association cortex. By integrating stimulus representations, affective representations, and stimulus-affect representations with a representation of self (which remains as mysterious a concept as ever), an affectively charged experience, a feeling about the significance of the stimulus, might result.

This is a central hypothesis of emotional experience in the tradition of Cannon (1927, 1931) and Papez (1937). Emotional experience, according to this hypothesis, can be generated completely within the brain without the participation of the peripheral nervous and humoral systems. This hypothesis does not necessarily exclude the peripheral systems. In fact, feedback from the periphery probably plays two very significant roles in emotion.

One role of peripheral feedback is to give the brain a second chance at emotional experience when the central mechanisms fail to produce such an experience. Suppose that sensory inputs to the amygdala activate the descending pathways controlling emotional responses, but because of the net balance of excitation and inhibition in the system, fail to send signals back to the cortex. In these situations, emotional experience would not be generated centrally because the affective significance of the event would not reach the working memory system. However, feedback from the periphery would reach the brain. What happens then is anyone's guess, partly because we don't really know what "feedback" means. For the sake of discussion, let us assume that feedback refers to signals picked up by baroreceptors located on blood vessels. When arterial pressure rises in the presence of a threatening stimulus, these receptors will be activated and send neural impulses to the NTS in the brainstem. This area, in turn, projects to the amygdala. The amygdala thus now has additional excitatory input and this is sufficient to overcome the inhibition that previously prevented cortical activation. If the initial stimulus is no longer being processed by visual receptors the affective representation would reside in working memory without the stimulus representation. The organism might then be motivated to search its environment for an explanation for the existence of an affective representation in working memory (although this statement obviously raises many questions about how motivation does this, no attempt will be made to provide an explanation).

A second role of peripheral feedback is that of amplifier. Cannon was no doubt correct in arguing that peripheral feedback from the autonomic nervous system and circulating hormones is too slow to determine the nature of emotional experience in many situations. These systems take several seconds to achieve their maximal response during emotional arousal. By this time, most emotional states have surely begun to be experienced. Although slow, responses of these systems have a lasting action and may serve to amplify (increase the intensity and duration of) the emotional experience. This could possibly be achieved by strengthening the cortical and amygdaloid synapses that are temporarily activated in the early moments of the emotional experience.

CONCLUSIONS

The main points of the paper can be summarised as follows. (1) affect and cognition are separate information processing (computational) functions mediated by different brain systems. (2) affective and cognitive computations are performed without conscious awareness. (3) both emotional responses and conscious emotional experiences are consequences of affective computations. (4) the amygdala is the core of the affective computational system. (5) by way of neural connections between the amygdala and cognitive processing areas (such as the hippocampus and neocortex), cognitive–emotional interactions take place. (6) the products of both affective and cognitive computations reach conscious awareness by way of entry into working memory. (7) emotional experience results when event, affective, and self-representations simultaneously coincide in working memory. (8) emotional experience can be mediated entirely within the brain, that is, without peripheral feedback. (9) peripheral factors make important contributions as amplifiers of the central network. (10) when the central network fails to generate an emotional experience in an emotional situation peripheral feedback gives the brain a second shot at an emotional experience.

The careful reader will find many gaps in this attempt to bridge the psychology and neurobiology of emotion. However, the aim was not so much to develop a grand unification theory of emotion as to illustrate that the two fields are not as far apart as one might at first think. Some may feel that I have hopelessly mixed levels of analysis from neurons to social interactions. I hope most readers instead found that the boundaries between levels are more fluid than is usually perceived.

Manuscript received 4 January 1989
Manuscript revised 9 March 1989

REFERENCES

Aggleton, J., Burton, M. J., & Passignham, R. E. (1980). Cortical and subcortical afferents to the amygdala of the rhesus monkey (Macaca mulatta). *Brain Research*, *190*, 347–368.
Albiniak, B. A. & Powell, D. A. (1981). Peripheral autonomic mechanisms and Pavlovian conditioning in the rabbit (*Oryctolagus cuniculis*). *Journal of Comparative Physiology and Psychology*, *94*, 1101–1113.
Alverez-Royo, P. et al. (1988). Independence of memory functions and emotional behavior:

separate contributions of the hippocampal formation and the amgydala. *Neuroscience Abstracts*, *14*, 1043–1043.

Amaral, D. G. (1987). Memory: anatomical organization of candidate brain regions. In F. Plum (Ed.), *Handbook of physiology. Section 1. The nervous system*. Vol. V, *Higher functions of the brain*. Bethesda: American Physiological Society, pp. 211–294.

Baddeley, A. (1982). The concept of working memory: A view of its current state and probable future development. *Cognition 10*, 17–23.

Ball, G. G. (1974). Vagotomy: effect on electrically elicited eating and self-stimulation in the lateral hypothalamus. *Science*, *184*, 484–485.

Bard, P. (1929). The central representation of the sympathetic system. *Archives of Neurology and Psychiatry*, *22*, 230–246.

Barnes, C. A. (1988). Spatial learning and memory processes: the search for their neurobiological mechanisms in the rat. *Trends in Neuroscience*, *11*, 163–169.

Bem, D. J. (1972). Self-perception: an alternative interpretation to cognitive dissonance phenomena. *Psychological Review*, *74*, 183–200.

Blanchard, D. C. & Blanchard, R. J. (1972). Innate and conditioned reactions to threat in rats with amygdaloid lesions. *Journal of Comparative Physiology and Psychology*, *81*, 281–290.

Bower, G. H. (1980). Mood and memory. *American Psychologist*, *36*, 129–148.

Bowlby, J. (1969). *Attachment and Loss*: Vol. 1, *Attachment*. New York: Basic Books.

Brodal, A. (1982). *Neurological anatomy*. New York: Oxford University Press.

Bruner, J. S. & Postman, L. (1947). Emotional selectivity in perception and reaction. *Journal of Personality*, *16*, 60–77.

Butter, C. M., Mishkin, M., & Mirsky, A. F. (1968). Emotional responses towards humans in monkeys with selective frontal lesions. *Physiology and Behavior*, *3*, 213–215.

Cannon, W. B. (1927). The James–Lange theory of emotions: A critical examination and an alternative theory. *American Journal of Psychology*, *39*, 106–124.

Cannon, W. B. (1931). Again the James–Lange and the thalamic theories of emotion. *The Psychological Review*, *38*, 281–295.

Cannon, W. B. & Britton, S. W. (1925). Pseudoaffective medulliadrenal secretion. *American Journal of Physiology*, *72*, 283–294.

Cicchetti, P., LeDoux, J. E., & Reis, D. J. (1987). The lateral amygdaloid nucleus: Sensory interface of the amygdala in fear conditioning. *Neuroscience Abstracts*, *13*, 643.

Clark, D. M. & Teasdale, J. D. (1985). Constraints on the effects of mood on memory. *Journal of Personality and Social Psychology*, *48*, 1595–1608.

Cohen, D. H. (1980). The functional neuroanatomy of a conditioned response. R. F. Thompson, L. H. Hicks, & B. Shvyrkov (Eds), *Neural mechanisms of goal-directed behavior*. New York: Academic Press, pp. 283–302.

Cotman, C. W. & D. T. Monaghan (1988). Excitatory Amino Acid Neurotransmission: NMDA Receptors and Hebb-Type Synaptic Plasticity. *Annual Review of Neuroscience*, *11*, 61–80.

Cowan, W. M., Stanfield, B. B., & Amaral, D. G. (1981). Further observations on the development of the dentate gyrus. In W. M. Cowan (Ed), *Studies in development neurobiology: Essays in honor of Viktor Hamburger*. New York: Oxford University Press, pp. 395–435.

Damasio, A. R. & van Hoesen, G. (1983). Emotional disturbances associated with focal lesions of the limbic frontal lobe. In K. M. Heilman & P. Satz (Eds), *Neuropsychology of Human Emotion*. New York: Guilford, pp. 85–110.

Davis, M., Hitchcock, J. M., & Rosen, J. B. (1987). Anxiety and the amygdala: Pharmacological and anatomical analysis of the fear-potentiated startle paradigm. In G. H. Bower (Ed.) *The Psychology of Learning and Motivation*. San Diego: Academic Press, pp. 263–305.

Dennett, D. (1981). *Brainstorms: Philosophical essays on mind and psychology*. Cambridge Mass.: Bradford Books.

Derryberry, D. & Rothbart, M. K. (1984). Emotion, attention, and temperament. In C. E. Izard, J. Kagan, & R. B. Zajonc (Eds), *Emotion, cognition, and behavior*. Cambridge University Press.

Downer, J. D. C. (1961). Changes in visual gnostic function and emotional behavior following unilateral temporal lobe damage in the "split-brain" monkey. *Nature, London*, *191*, 50–51.

Ekman, P. (1984). Expression and the nature of emotion. In K. Scherer & P. Ekman (Eds) *Approaches to Emotion*. NJ: Erlbaum, Hillsdale, pp. 319–343.

Fonberg, E. (1972). Control of emotional behavior through the hypothalamus and amygdaloid complex. In D. Hill (Ed.), *Physiology, emotion, and psychosomatic illness*. Amsterdam: Elsevier, pp. 131–162.

Foy, M., Stanton, M., Levine, S., & Thompson, R. F. (1987). Behavioral stress impairs long term potentiation in rodent hippocampus. *Behavioral Neural Biology*, *48*, 138–149.

Frijda, N. (1986). *The emotions*. Cambridge University Press.

Fuster, J. M. & Uyeda, A. A. (1971). Reactivity of limbic neurons of the monkey to appetitive and aversive signals. *Electroencephalography and Clinical Neurophysiology*, *30*, 281–293.

Geschwind, N. (1965). The disconnexion syndromes in animals and man. Part II. *Brain, 88*, 585–644.

Goddard, G. (1964). Functions of the amygdala. *Psychology Review*, *62*, 89–109.

Goldman-Rakic, P. (1987). Circuitry of primate prefrontal cortex and regulation of behavior by representational memory. In F. Plum (Ed.), *Handbook of physiology. Section 1. The nervous system*. Vol. V, *Higher functions of the brain*, Bethesda: American Physiological Society, pp. 373–418.

Gray, J. A. (1982). *The neuropsychology of anxiety*. New York: Oxford University Press.

Halgren, E. (1981). The amygdala contribution to emotion and memory: Current studies in humans. In Y. Ben-Ari (Ed.), *The amygdaloid complex*. Amsterdam: Elsevier, pp. 395–408.

Henke, P. G. (1982). Telencephalic limbic system and experimental gastric pathology: a review. *Neuroscience and Biobehavior Reviews*, *6*, 381–390.

Horel, J. A. & Keating, E. G. (1969). Partial Kluver–Bucy syndrome produced by cortical disconnection. *Brain Research*, *16*, 281–284.

Isen, A. M., Shalker, T. E., Clark, M., & Karp, L. (1978). Affect, accessibility of material in memory and behavior: A cognitive loop? *Journal of Personality and Social Psychology*, *36*, 1–12.

Iwata, J. et al. (1986). Intrinsic neurons in the amygdaloid field projected to by the medical geniculate body mediate emotional responses conditioned to acoustic stimuli. *Brain Research*, *371*, 395–399.

Izard, C. E. (1977). *Human emotions*. New York: Plenum.

Izard, C. E. (1981). Emotion-cognition relationships and human development. In C. E. Izard, J. Kagan, & R. B. Zajonc (Eds), *Emotions, cognition, and behavior*. Cambridge University Press.

Jackendoff, R. (1987). *Consciousness and the computational mind*. Cambridge, Mass.: Bradford Books.

Jacobs, W. J. & Nadel, L. (1985). Stress-induced recovery of fears and phobias. *Psychological Review*, *92*, 512–531.

Jacobs, B. J. & McGinty, D. J. (1972). Participation of the amygdala in complex stimulus recognition and behavioral inhibition: evidence from unit studies. *Brain Research*, *36*, 431–436.

James, W. (1884). What is emotion? *Mind, 9*, 188–205.

James, W. (1890). *Principles of Psychology*, New York: Holt.

Jones, B. & Mishkin, M. (1972). Limbic lesions and the problem of stimulus-reinforcement associations. *Experimental Neurology*, *36*, 362–377.

Jones, E. G. & Powell, T. P. S. (1970). An anatomical study of converging sensory pathways within the cerebral cortex of the monkey. *Brain*, *93*, 793–820.

Jones, E. G. (1981). Development of connectivity in the cerebral cortex. In W. B. Cowan (Ed.), *Studies in developmental neurobiology: Essays in honor of Viktor Hamburger*. New York: Oxford University Press, pp. 354–394.

Kapp, B. S., Frysinger, R. C., Gallagher, M., & Haselton, J. (1979). Amygdala central nucleus lesions: effects on heart rate conditioning in the rabbit. *Physiology and Behavior*, *23*, 1109–1117.

Kapp, B. S., Pascoe, J. P., & Bixler, M. A. (1984). The amygdala: a neuroanatomical systems approach to its contributions to aversive conditioning. In N. Buttlers & L. R. Squire (Eds), *The neuropsychology of memory*. New York: Guilford.

Kihlstrom, J. F. (1987). The cognitive unconscious. *Science*, *237*, 1445–1452.

Kim, C. et al. (1976). Influence of hippocampectomy on gastric ulcer in rats. *Brain Research*, *109*, 245–254.

Kluver, H. & Bucy, P. C. (1937). "Psychic blindness" and other symptoms following bilateral temporal lobectomy in rhesus monkeys. *American Journal of Physiology*, *119*, 352–353.

Laird, J. D. (1974). Self-attribution of emotion: the effects of expressive behavior on the quality of emotional experience. *Journal of Personality and Social Psychology*, *29*, 475–486.

Lashley, K. (1956). Cerebral organization and behavior. In H. Solomon, S. Cobb, & W. Penfield (Eds), *The brain and human behavior*, Baltimore: Williams and Wilkins, pp. 1–18.

Lazarus, R. S. (1982). Thoughts on the relation between emotion and cognition. *American Psychologist*, *37*, 1019–1024.

LeDoux, J. E. (1986). Sensory systems and emotion: a model of affective processing. *Integrative Psychiatry*, *4*, 237–248,

LeDoux, J. E. (1987). Emotion. In F. Plum (Ed.), *Handbook of physiology. Section 1. The nervous system*. Vol. V, *Higher functions of the brain*. Bethesda: American Physiological Society, pp. 419–460.

LeDoux, J. E., Sakaguchi, A., & Reis, D. J. (1984). Subcortical efferent projections of the medial geniculate nucleus mediate emotional responses conditioned by acoustic stimuli. *Journal Neuroscience*, *4*(3), 683–698.

LeDoux, J. E., Ruggiero, D. A., & Reis, D. J. (1985). Projections to the subcortical forebrain from anatomically defined regions of the medial geniculate body in the rat. *Journal of Comparative Neurology*, *242*, 182–213.

LeDoux, J. E., Sakaguchi, A., Iwata, J., & Reis, D. J. (1986). Interruption of projections from the medial geniculate body to an archi-neostriatal field disrupts the classical conditioning of emotional responses to acoustic stimuli in the rat. *Neuroscience*, *17*, 615–627.

LeDoux, J. E., Iwata, J., Cicchetti, P., & Reis, D. J. (1988). Different projections of the central amygdaloid nucleus mediate autonomic and behavioral correlates of conditioned fear. *Journal of Neuroscience*, *8*, 2517–2529.

MacLean, P. D. (1949). Psychosomatic disease and the visceral brain. Recent developments bearing on the Papez theory of emotion. *Psychosomatic Medicine*, *11*, 338–353.

MacLean, P. D. (1952). Some psychiatric implications of physiological studies on fronto-temporal portion of limbic system (visceral brain). *Electroencephalography and Clinical Neurophysiology*, *4*, 407–418.

McConnell, J. & Angevine J. B. (1983). Time of origin in the amygdaloid complex of the mouse. *Brain Research*, *272*, 150–156.

Mandler, G. (1975). *Mind and Emotion*, New York: Wiley.

Minsky, M. (1985). *The society of mind*. New York: Touchstone Books, Simonand Schuster.

Mishkin, M. & Aggleton, J. (1981). Multiple functional contributions of the amygdala in the monkey. In Y. Ben-Ari (Ed.) *The Amygdaloid Complex*. Amsterdam: Elsevier/North-Holland Biomedical Press, pp. 409–420.

Mishkin, M. (1982). A memory system in the monkey. *Transactions of the Royal Society, London, B, 298,* 85–95.

Murray, E. A. & Mishkin, M. (1985). Amygdalectomy impairs crossmodal association in monkeys. *Science, 228,* 604–606.

Nishijo, H., Ono, T., & Nishino, H. (1988). Single neuron responses in amygdala of alert monkey during complex sensory stimulation with affective significance. *Journal of Neuroscience, 8,* 3570–3583.

O'Keefe, J. & Nadel, L. (1978). The hippocampus as a cognitive map. Oxford: The Clarendon Press.

Olton, D., Becker, J. T., & Handleman, G. E. (1979). Hippocampus, space and memory. *Behavior and Brain Science, 2,* 313–365.

Ottersen, O. P. (1982). Connections of the amygdala of the rat. IV. Corticoamygdaloid and intraamygdaloid connections as studied with axonal transport of horseradish peroxidase. *205,* 30–48.

Pankseep, J. (1982). Toward a general psychobiological theory of emotions. *Behavioral and Brain Sciences, 5,* 407–468.

Papez, J. W. (1937). A proposed mechanism of emotion. *Archives of Neurology and Psychiatry, 79,* 217–224.

Radna, R. J. & MacLean, P. D. (1981). Vagal elicitation of respiratory-type and other unit responses in basal limbic structures of squirrel monkeys. *Brain Research, 213,* 45–61.

Rapaport, D. (1950). *Emotions and memory*. New York: International Universities Press, p. 282.

Ricardo, J. A. & Kho, E. T. (1978). Anatomical evidence of direct projections from the nucleus of the solitary tract to the hypothalamus, amygdala, and other forebrain structures in the rat. *Brain Research, 153,* 1–26.

Rickert, E. J., Bennett, T. L., Lane, P. L., & French, J. (1978). Hippocampectomy and the attenuation of blocking. *Behavioral Biology, 22,* 147–160.

Rolls, E. T. (1981). Responses of amygdala neurons in the primate. In Y. Ben-Ari (Ed.), *The amygdaloid complex*. Amsterdam: Elsevier, 383–393.

Sanghera, M. K., Rolls, E. T., & Roper-Hall, A. (1979). Visual responses of neurons in the dorsolateral amygdala of the alert monkey. *Experimental Neurology, 63,* 610–626.

Schachter, S. & Singer, J. E. (1962). Cognitive, social, and physiological determinants of emotional state. *Psychology Review, 69,* 379–399.

Shallice, T. (1982). Specific impairments of planning. Royal Society of London. *B. Biological Science, 298,* 199–209.

Shors, T. J., Levine, S., & Thompson, R. F. (1988). Effect of stress and adrenalectomy on long-term potentiation in rat hippocampus. *Neuroscience Abstracts, 14,* 443.

Solomon, P. R. (1977). The role of hippocampus in blocking and conditioned inhibition of the rabbit's nicitating membrane response. *Journal of Comparative Physiology and Psychology, 91,* 407–417.

Squire, L. R. & Zola-Morgan, S. (1983). The neurology of memory: the case for correspondence from findings for human and nonhuman primate. In J. A. Deutsch (Ed.), *The physiological basis of memory*. New York: Academic Press, pp. 200–269.

Swanson, L. W. (1983). The hippocampus and the concept of the limbic system. In W. Seifert (Ed.), *Neurobiology of the hippocampus*. London: Academic Press. pp. 3–19.

Ten Donkelaar, H. J., Lammers, G. J., & Gribnau, A. A. M. (1979). Neurogenesis in the amygdaloid nuclear complex in a rodent (the Chinese hamster). *Brain Research, 165,* 348–353.

Teyler, T. J. & DiScenna, P. (1987). Long-term potentiation. *Annual Review of Neuroscience*, *10*, 131–161.

Tomkins, S. S. (1962). *Affect, imagery, consciousness*. New York: Springer.

Turner, B. H., Mishkin, M., & Knapp, M. (1980). Organization of the amygdalopetal projections from modality-specific cortical association areas in the monkey. *Journal of Comparative Neurophysiology*, *191*, 515–543.

Ursin, H. & Kaada B. R. (1960). Function localization within the amygdaloid complex in the cat. *Electroencephalography and Clinical Neurophysiology*, *12*, 1–20.

Weiskrantz, L. (1956). Behavioral changes associated with ablation of the amygdaloid complex in monkeys. *Journal of Comparative Physiology and Psychology*, *49*, 381–391.

Zajonc, R. B. (1980). Feeling and thinking: preferences need no inferences. *American Psychologist*, *35*, 151–175.

COGNITION AND EMOTION, 1989, 3(4) 291–311

Infants' Expectations in Play: The Joy of Peek-a-boo

W. Gerrod Parrott

Georgetown University, U.S.A.

Henry Gleitman

University of Pennsylvania, U.S.A.

The role of expectations in infants' enjoyment of play was studied by observing their smiling, laughter, and eyebrow raises during a peek-a-boo game that contained occasional trick trials. In Experiments 1 and 2, 6-, 7-, and 8-month-olds ($n = 29$) participated in a peek-a-boo game in which, on occasional "person-switch" trials, one adult hid and a second adult "re-appeared" in his or her place. Infants in all age groups smiled less following person-switch reappearances than following normal ones, with the difference increasing with age. In Experiment 3, 7-month-old infants ($n = 10$) played a peek-a-boo game in which the adult occasionally reappeared in a different location. Smiling decreased for "location switches" just as it had for person switches. Infants in all age groups were more likely to exhibit eyebrow raises following trick reappearances than following normal ones. These findings suggest that infants as young as 6 months have expectations about the identity and location of a returning person, that conformity to these expectations contributes to infants' enjoyment of games such as peek-a-boo, and that infants of this age may not yet enjoy deviations from their expectations. Implications are discussed for theories of playful enjoyment, for the cognitive antecedents of positive affect, and for cognitive development.

Requests for reprints should be sent to W. Gerrod Parrott, Department of Psychology, Georgetown University, Washington, DC 20057, U.S.A. This research is based on a dissertation presented by the first author to the faculties of the University of Pennsylvania in partial fulfilment of the requirements for the degree of Doctor of Philosophy. Portions of this research were presented at the 1984 meeting of the Eastern Psychological Association.

We would like to thank Lila Gleitman, John Sabini, and Elizabeth Spelke for many helpful comments and suggestions. We gratefully acknowledge the assistance of Susan Bank, Amy Binder, Sharon Kessler, Deborah Kristeller, Lisa Sandler, Lisa Savarick, Lisa Weinstock, and Jane Weinzimmer in collecting and coding data. We also would like to thank Renee Baillargeon, Judy DeLoache, Elissa Newport, and two anonymous reviewers for their valuable comments and suggestions on earlier drafts of this manuscript.

© 1989 Lawrence Erlbaum Associates Limited

INTRODUCTION

In playful contexts, adults seem to enjoy deviations from their expectations. The violation of expectations has been found to contribute to adults' enjoyment of such things as jokes, suspense, drama, and music, and to account for smiling and laughter occurring during certain laboratory tasks (Berlyne, 1969; Gleitman, 1985; Meyer, 1956; Nerhardt, 1970; Suls, 1972). Older children, in playful contexts, also seem to enjoy deviations from their expectations (Lewis & Goldberg, 1969; McGhee, 1974; Shultz, 1976). Does the same hold for infants as well? Are precursors of later play, humour, and aesthetic enjoyment found in the first year of life? These are the questions that motivated the present research.

There are several theories of the relation between cognition and this type of emotion. Some theorists have argued that young infants possess the ability to enjoy the unexpected. For example, Pien and Rothbart (1980) assert that the enjoyment of incongruity humour presupposes only that incongruous events be perceived in a safe and playful context, and conclude that the capacity to enjoy such events may be present as early as 4 months of age (cf. Eastman, 1921, 1936; McGhee, 1979). Other theorists, however, maintain that incongruity alone will not suffice; instead, the incongruity must be resolved before enjoyment will result (Suls, 1972). Some theorists assert that infants are capable of such cognition (Shultz, 1976), while others assert that they are not (McGhee, 1974). There has been little research concerning any of these capacities in young infants. While there have been reports of infants enjoying such incongruities as the sight of the mother sucking on a baby bottle (Sroufe & Wunsch, 1972), we know of no studies investigating infants' enjoyment of violations of specific expectations.

There is, at least, evidence that young infants have the cognitive capacities necessary to form certain specific expectations, although in the case of younger infants some of this evidence is disputed or in need of replication. For example, infants seem able to form expectations about the identity of an object that reappears following a disappearance, a point that is of obvious relevance to discussions of object permanence (Bower, 1974; Piaget, 1954). This ability is well documented in 9-month-olds, although there is conflicting evidence about its existence in infants as young as 5 months of age (Gratch, 1982; Meicler & Gratch, 1980; Moore, Borton, & Darby, 1978). Infants may also have expectations about properties of objects while they are occluded, and thus may possess some capacities akin to object permanence at a younger age than formerly believed (Baillargeon, Spelke, & Wasserman, 1985). Furthermore, young infants seem able to acquire expectations about the location of events that occur in a regular spatial sequence (Canfield & Haith, 1986; Haith, Hazan, & Goodman, 1984).

Given that infants possess these abilities, and given the lack of empirical data concerning the relation between such cognition and emotion, we chose the peek-a-boo game as a context in which to test infants' responses to unexpected events. Peek-a-boo, of course, is a playful activity that is very popular with young infants (Parrott, 1985; Sroufe & Wunsch, 1972). The game has a simple, rule-governed structure which should facilitate infants' exercise of whatever capacities they possess for forming expectations about identity and location and for noting deviations from them (Bruner & Sherwood, 1976; Hodapp, Goldfield, & Boyatzis, 1984). The structure of the peek-a-boo game is similar to that of events enjoyed by adults and older children (Gleitman, 1985; Shultz, 1976), and a number of theorists have suggested that infants enjoy peek-a-boo because it presents them with deviations from their expectations in a playful context. Dewey (1894), for example, interpreted infants' enjoyment of peek-a-boo as resulting from a period of suspense or expectation, and Bruner and Sherwood (1976) were "struck by the skill of mothers in knowing how to keep the child in an anticipatory mood, neither too sure of outcome nor too upset by a wide range of possibilities" (p. 283). Pilot research in our laboratory suggests that infants playing peek-a-boo do seem to expect a reappearance. When infants were presented with an extremely long (20 seconds) disappearance following a series of normal peek-a-boo trials they continued to attend to the point of disappearance and they often stretched their necks as if to look for the vanished adult.

Thus, it seemed reasonable to use the peek-a-boo game to study the role of expectations in infants' enjoyment. In order to conduct our investigation we needed to address three questions. First, given that infants seem to expect something following the disappearance, what exactly do they expect? Secondly, do these expectations play a role in infants' enjoyment of playful activities? Thirdly, do infants, like older children and adults, smile and laugh more following deviations from their expectations than they do following the expected event? To answer these questions we studied 6- to 8-month-old infants playing peek-a-boo games that had several trick trials. On the trick trials of Experiments 1 and 2, the adult who appeared and said "peek-a-boo" was not the same person as the adult who had just disappeared. During both normal and trick trials we observed components of the infants' expressions of enjoyment (smiling and laughter) and surprise (eyebrow raises). While it is not possible to equate these facial expressions with these underlying emotional states, these expressions seem to be reliable and sensitive indicators of infants' emotional reactions (Izard & Dougherty, 1982), especially when observed in the context of a peek-a-boo game.

Our first question, of what infants expect to follow the disappearance, served to check our assumption that infants would find a trick reappearance to be less expected than a normal one. Common sense would suggest that infants expect the adult to reappear as he or she usually does and thus would be surprised on trick trials, but this intuition has not been confirmed empirically. Such confirmation is desirable given that some theories of infant cognition might predict that the infant who lacks object permanence would not expect a hidden player to return, and thus might be more surprised on normal trials than on trick trials. We addressed this issue by observing the occurrence of eyebrow raises following normal and trick reappearances. Evidence that brow raises are more likely to occur following trick reappearances than normal ones would support our assumption that normal trials are closer to infants' expectations.

If infants appear to expect one type of reappearance more than another, we can address our two primary questions. The question of whether infants' expectations *play a role* in their enjoyment was addressed by comparing the infants' smiling and laughter following the two types of reappearance. If infants smiled equally following each type of reappearance, it would suggest their enjoyment of the game was not based on expectations that included the identity of the adult, but rather was based just on enjoyment of a human face popping up and saying "peek-a-boo." Such a result would suggest that infants' expectations had no role in their enjoyment of the game, as may be the case in the "pre-peek-a-boo" game enjoyed by 3-month-olds that was reported by Stern (1974). On the other hand, if the infants enjoyed one type of reappearance more than the other, it would demonstrate that infants' expectations had a role in their emotional reaction to the game.

Our final question, whether infants *enjoy* deviations from their expectations, was addressed by noting the direction of any difference found between the infants' smiles following normal and person-switch reappearances. If infants enjoy deviations from their expectations in a playful context, then infants should smile more following trick trials than following normal ones. An additional test of this hypothesis was provided by Experiment 3, in which the reappearing adult's *location* was varied on trick trials, rather than his or her identity.

In all three experiments the magnitude of infants' smiling and laughter was measured at 1-second intervals both before, during, and after the adult's disappearance. These measurements permitted not only a comparison of infants' smiling during the two types of reappearance, but also allowed a check on whether the magnitude of smiling following the reappearance exceeded that preceeding the disappearance. This check, not conducted in previous research using the peek-a-boo game, helps determine whether the smiling following the reappearance exceeds that of a baseline level of social smiling.

EXPERIMENT 1

Method

Subjects. The subjects were 9 healthy, full-term infants, ranging in age from 7 months 3 days to 7 months 25 days (mean: 7 months 12 days). Two other infants participated in the experiment but did not complete it because they would not smile at the experimenters. Names of infants were obtained from birth announcements in Philadelphia area newspapers. Their parents were contacted by letter and telephone and were reimbursed for transportation expenses to the laboratory.

Apparatus. The experiment was conducted within a 3.2m by 2.4m carpeted area enclosed by a 1.2m tall surround which concealed equipment and minimised distractions. Two experimenters played peek-a-boo by hiding behind a wooden screen, 1.2m tall and 1.7m wide, which was placed 1m inside of the surround. The infant was positioned on the floor approximately 1m away from the screen, with the mother seated directly behind. The experimenters played with the infant on their hands and knees, peering at the infant around the left edge of the screen.

The experiment was videotaped by a camera located outside of the surround, behind and to the left of the experimenters. The camera lens protruded through a slit cut in the surround 79cm above the floor. The scene was framed to include the infant and the back of the experimenter's head when he or she peered out from behind the edge of the screen. Sound was recorded with a condenser microphone mounted on the camera.

The experimenters made sure that their disappearance interval was a constant 3 seconds by counting low-frequency, computer-generated pulses which sounded once every second through a loudspeaker located behind them at a volume barely audible to them.

Procedure. The experiment began with an initial getting-acquainted session of 5 to 10 minutes, during which the infant was placed onto the carpeted floor, was joined by the mother and the two experimenters, and was allowed to explore freely. During this period, the experimenters interacted with the infant while explaining the procedure to the mother and gathering information about the infant's prior experience with the peek-a-boo game. Previous research has shown that such a procedure effectively induces infants to accept strangers and to enjoy playing peek-a-boo with them (Rheingold & Eckerman, 1973). When the infant seemed at ease, he or she was positioned in front of the screen to begin the study. The infant was allowed to sit on the floor or on the mother's lap, or to stand, as he or she preferred. The mother was told not cue the infant's responses in any way, but, if necessary, to support him or her in sitting or standing and to dissuade him or her from crawling.

Two experimenters were chosen to be easily distinguishable in appearance. One was a male with short blond hair; the other was a female with long dark hair. One of the experimenters began to play peek-a-boo with the infant while the other hid behind the screen; which experimenter went first was counterbalanced across infants.

All peek-a-boo trials were run as follows. The experimenter established eye contact with the infant and said, "I'm gonna go away", and then ducked behind the barrier. After a disappearance of 3 seconds, the experimenter reappeared around the edge of the barrier, said "peek-a-boo!", smiled, and made eye contact with the infant. The next peek-a-boo trial began when (1) at least 4 seconds had elapsed, and (2) the infant was attending to the experimenter.

Before starting the experiment proper, the first experimenter completed at least three warm-up peek-a-boo trials, and continued until the infant smiled following a reappearance. Subsequent to this, the second experimenter joined the first, got the infant's attention (at which point the first experimenter hid behind the screen), and played at least one warm-up peek-a-boo trial, continuing until the infant smiled.

When warm-up trials with both experimenters had concluded, the experimental trials began. The second experimenter began by playing three *normal* peek-a-boo trials as described previously. The fourth trial was a *person-switch* trial. The second experimenter began by getting the infant's attention, said "I'm gonna go away", and then disappeared; 3 seconds later the first experimenter "reappeared" instead. Three normal trials followed by one person-switch trial constituted the first block of trials. The experiment consisted of four such blocks. The three normal trials of each block were conducted by the experimenter who had appeared on the previous person-switch trial so that the experiment continued without interruption.[1] Thus, the experiment was run as a two-factor, within-subject design, with type of reappearance (normal or person-switch) as one factor, and trial block (one through four) as another.

Coding of Facial Expressions.   The coding procedure was applied to all four person-switch trials and to the normal trial that preceded each person-

---

[1] If an infant became bored or fussy, the experiment was stopped for a few minutes and was then resumed at the beginning of a block of trials. Only two subjects required such a break in order to complete the experiment.

switch trial.[2] In order to ensure that coders were unaware of whether the trial being coded was a normal or a person-switch trial, a special coding videotape was prepared from the original. On this tape the order of the trials was scrambled and only the segment of the trial from immediately before the reappearance until the beginning of the next trial was recorded.

Eyebrow raises were coded for presence or absence during the first 4 seconds of the reappearance. A brow raise was defined as the result of the action of either or both of the two facial muscles that lift the eyebrows (AU-1 and AU-2 in the FACS system of Ekman & Friesen, 1978). Coders viewed the videotape both at normal speed and in slow motion in order to observe both gradual and quick brow movements. When a brow raise was observed, the coder would record the time that elapsed from the reappearance to the moment when the brow movement reached its maximum. This time was measured with a stopclock to the nearest tenth of a second. (Because analysis of the time of occurrence yielded no significant effects in the present studies, these data will not be reported below.) Eyebrow raises were rated on all trials by two independent coders. Reliability was assessed by counting the percentage of trials in which the two coders agreed within one-half second about the time of maximum intensity of any brow raise that was judged to have occurred. The mean percentage agreement between coders was 80%. Only eyebrow raises that were detected by both coders were counted in the data analysis.

Smiling and laughter were rated throughout each trial on a six-point scale. Similar scales have been used in previous research (e.g. MacDonald & Silverman, 1978; Pien & Rothbart, 1976; Shultz, 1972; Zigler, Levine & Gould, 1966). While such scales are not true interval scales, they are arguably appropriate for use with parametric analysis (Rothbart, 1976, 1977). Our own scale differed from those previously used in making finer

---

[2]Preliminary analysis of all three normal trials indicated that they were not significantly different. Procedures for coding eyebrow raises were identical to those reported below, including blind coding. The proportion of normal trials having eyebrow raises during the reappearance averaged 0.19 on the first, 0.11 on the second, and 0.17 on the third. The 3 (trials) × 4 (blocks) ANOVA showed no significant effect for trial, $F(2,16) = 0.61$, nor for blocks or the interaction. Procedures for coding smiles were less elaborate than those reported below, with coders, blind to condition, assigning a single rating (from 0 to 5) of infants' smiling during the first 4 seconds of the reappearance. Means for the three normal trials were virtually identical, being 1.92, 1.92, and 1.96 respectively, $F(2,16) = 0.02$. The ANOVA yielded no significant effects or interactions. Comparisons between normal and switch trials yielded the same pattern of results reported below for both eyebrow and smile data. Therefore, to save effort, second-by-second coding of smiles, described below, was applied only to switch trials and to the preceding normal trial in this and subsequent experiments, and data analysis is reported for these trials only.

distinctions in the magnitude of smiling (0 = no smile; 1 = small smile; 2 = medium smile; 3 = large smile; 4 = very large smile; 5 = laughter, or other "happy" vocalisations accompanied by a large smile). Coders were trained to use this scale by observing videotapes of pilot subjects and discussing coding criteria until they could agree on prototypical responses and on the reasons for the ambiguity of borderline responses.

Ten 1-second intervals were coded on each trial: three intervals prior to the disappearance, three during the disappearance, and four after the reappearance. The videotapes were divided into 1-second intervals by use of the timing pulse, and the magnitude of the infant's smile was rated at the end of each such interval. Coding reliability was assessed by recoding 25% of the trials (one normal and one person-switch trial randomly selected from each infant) as follows. Each of the 10 1-second intervals was copied onto a second videotape in random order. The resulting 180 intervals were then coded independently by the original coder and by a second one, both of whom were blind to the type of trial being coded. The Pearson correlations between the two coders was 0.80; the correlation between the first coder's ratings using this procedure and the same coder's original ratings was 0.88.[3]

Results

The eyebrow data were analysed by scoring a "1" if an eyebrow raise occurred within the first four seconds after a reappearance and scoring a "0" if no raise occurred within this period. These dichotomous data then were analysed with a two-way repeated measures analysis of variance with the two reappearance types forming one factor and the four blocks of trials forming the other. Eyebrow raises occurred following a significantly higher proportion of person-switch reappearances ($M = 0.44$) than following normal reappearances ($M = 0.17$), yielding a significant main effect for reappearance type, $F(1,8) = 10.00$, $P = 0.013$, supporting the assumption that infants were more surprised following the person-switch reappearances than following normal ones. Of the nine infants, six were more likely to raise their eyebrows after trick reappearances, two showed no difference, and one showed no brow raises at all. Neither the main effect for trial block nor the interaction was significant.

Figure 1 presents mean smile ratings on normal and person-switch trials plotted in one-second intervals before, during, and after the experimen-

---

[3]This type of second-by-second analysis was not applied to the eyebrow data because the extended duration and small size of many of these facial movements made such analysis both uninformative and unreliable.

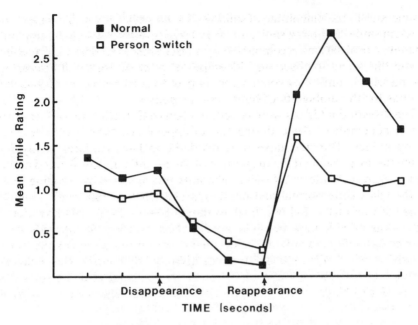

FIG. 1.   Smiling in 7-month-olds during normal and person-switch trials. (The first arrow indicates the moment of disappearance, the second that of reappearance.)

ter's disappearance. The ratings were averaged across trial blocks. As Fig. 1 shows, the infants typically smiled slightly before the experimenter's disappearance. These small smiles faded during the disappearance. On normal trials, smiles built rapidly when the experimenter reappeared, reaching a maximum after about 2 seconds, and then faded back to their pre-disappearance base level after 4 seconds. This pattern was evident in all nine infants, although the average point of maximum smiling occurred 2 seconds after the reappearance for six infants and 1 second after the reappearance for three. To demonstrate that smiling after reappearance exceeded the pre-disappearance base level on normal trials, the mean of the three smile ratings before disappearance ($M = 1.19$) was compared to the mean of the first three smile ratings after reappearance ($M = 2.28$) using a planned comparison repeated-measures analysis of variance, yielding $F(1,8) = 12.84$, $P = 0.0073$. There was no significant effect of trial block or of the interaction. This effect was present for seven of the nine infants. It therefore seems reasonable to conclude that the infants' smiling on normal trials was due to factors over and above mere face-to-face interaction and that the reappearance was genuinely enjoyable to most of the infants.

As Fig. 1 also shows, there was a considerable difference in the infants' smiling response following normal and person-switch trials: The reappearance smile was much more pronounced when there was a genuine *reappearance* than when there was not. This effect was present for eight of the nine infants. To demonstrate this difference, we compared smile ratings averaged for all four intervals following a reappearance on normal and person-switch trials using a planned comparison repeated-measures analysis of variance. There was more reappearance smiling on normal than on person-switch trials: The means were 2.13 and 1.18 respectively, $F(1,8) = 19.23$, $P = 0.0023$. There was no significant effect of trial block or of the interaction.

Because brow raises were more frequent on person-switch trials than on normal trials, it seemed possible that the observed difference in smiling could be an artefact caused by neuromuscular interference between these two facial actions. To address this possibility, we examined only those trials in which infants exhibited brow raises *neither* following the person-switch reappearance *nor* the preceding normal reappearance. By this criterion, 53% of all trials were deleted from analysis, including all those from one subject. The smile data for the remaining eight subjects were averaged across the four reappearance intervals and, because of the large percentage of missing blocks of trials, averaged across blocks as well. The resulting mean—2.13 for normal trials, 1.11 for person-switch trials—differed significantly, $F(1,7) = 11.13$, $P = 0.012$. Of the eight infants, seven showed the effect, one showed no difference. Thus, the decreased smiling following person-switch reappearances does not appear to be due to interference from eyebrow raises.

Discussion

The fact that infants were more likely to show brow raises following person-switch reappearances suggests that they were more surprised by this event than by a normal reappearance. Thus, the assumption that person-switch reappearances are more unexpected than normal ones seems warranted. The fact that there was no interaction between block number and the reappearance effect suggests that this effect was not due to learning during the experimental trials, and, thus, that the expectations involved were relatively local ones.

An interesting implication of this finding is that infants can maintain a representation of the experimenter's identity while he or she is out of view, a skill that some previous research, using paradigms similar to the disappearance and reappearance of peek-a-boo, has been unable to detect in infants younger than 9 months of age (Goldberg, 1976; Gratch, 1982; Meicler & Gratch, 1980; Muller & Aslin, 1978). The existence of this ability argues against certain theories of why infants enjoy the peek-a-boo game. Some authors have suggested that infants enjoy peek-a-boo precisely because of such presumed cognitive deficiencies (e.g. Shultz, 1976, 1979); as they see it, the tension—and eventual tension release—produced by the peek-a-boo game stems from the infant's effort to assimilate properties of a disappearing and reappearing object. Yet, the 7-month-old infants in this study showed by their eyebrow raises and their smiling that they were able to distinguish the reappearance of the same person from the "reappearance" of another.

Our main concern, however, was whether the infants' expectations affected their enjoyment of the game. The results suggested that enjoyment was affected, because the magnitude of infants' smiling and laughter differed significantly following normal and person-switch reappearances (although the usual cautions against equating smiling and laughter with enjoyment are, of course, in order). Given that expectations affected infants' enjoyment, did infants smile and laugh more following deviations from their expectations than they did following the expected event? The answer here was "no". The 7-month-old infants in this experiment not only failed to smile more following unexpected events as older children and adults typically do, they actually smiled less, a result that has implications for the development of the relation between cognition and emotion. This difference suggests either that the capacity to experience enhanced enjoyment from deviations from the expected develops at a later age, or that this capacity is not expressed in the peek-a-boo context.

In the light of the implications of this phenomenon, we wished to establish its reliability. We therefore performed a further experiment to replicate the results of Experiment 1 and to extend them to a wider age range.

EXPERIMENT 2

In this experiment, 6- and 8-month-old infants were studied in a variant of Experiment 1 which differed in only a few procedural details.

Method

Subjects. The subjects were 20 infants recruited in the same manner as those in Experiment 1. Ten were 6-month-olds (ranging from 6 months 3 days to 6 months 21 days, with a mean of 6 months 15 days) and 10 were 8-month-olds (ranging from 8 months 3 days to 8 months 28 days with a mean of 8 months 17 days). Five additional infants participated in the experiment but did not complete it: three would not smile at the experimenters, one was eliminated because of equipment failure, and one could not be stopped from crawling toward the screen.

Apparatus and Procedure. A new wooden screen was constructed which allowed peek-a-boo to be played over the top (rather than around the side, as in Experiment 1, which seemed to elicit more crawling). The screen was 1.0m tall and 1.5m wide and was placed 1m inside of the surround. The new screen allowed the camera to be positioned directly behind it in a port 64cm above floor level, providing a head-on view of the infant's face. The infant was positioned 1m in front of the screen and watched the experimenters disappear and reappear over the top of the screen. The procedure was otherwise identical to that of the previous experiment.

The videotapes were coded in the same manner as in the previous experiment. For the eyebrow raises of the 6-month-olds, the two coders agreed on 77% of the trials; for the 8-month-olds this proportion was 75%. As before, only eyebrow raises that were detected by both coders were counted in the data analysis. For the coding of smiling and laughter, the correlations between the original coder's initial second-by-second smile ratings and his later ratings of the scrambled-order segments were 0.85 for the 6-month-olds and 0.92 for the 8-month-olds. The corresponding correlations between the ratings of the first and the second coder were 0.78 for the 6-month-olds and 0.86 for the 8-month-olds.

Results

As with the 7-month-olds, the 6- and 8-month-olds in the present experiment raised their eyebrows following a greater proportion of person-switch reappearance ($M = 0.36$) than following normal reappearances ($M = 0.18$). The data were analysed using a three-way, mixed-model analysis of variance, with age as a between-subjects factor and reappearance type and trial block as within-subjects factors. The main effect for reappearance type reached significance, $F(1,18) = 7.42$, $P = 0.014$. There were no other significant main effects or interactions. Of the 20 infants, 13 more often showed eyebrow raises after person-switch reappearances than after normal ones; 4 showed the reverse tendency, while 3 never showed eyebrow raises following reappearances. Thus, trick trials again seem to have been less expected to most of the infants than were normal trials.

Figure 2 presents the second-by-second smile ratings, averaged across blocks, for the 6- and 8-month-olds, on normal and persons-switch trials.

Two planned comparison analyses of variance were performed to determine whether the findings of Experiment 1 on 7-month-olds held for the age groups in this experiment. The first examined normal trials only, and compared smiling in the two age groups, across trial blocks, for the three 1-second segments prior to disappearance and those just following normal reappearance. As in Experiment 1, smiling was more pronounced after

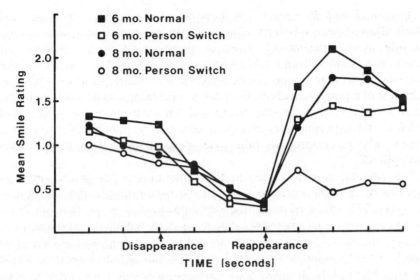

FIG. 2.   Smiling in 6- and 8-month-olds during normal and person-switch trials. (The first arrow indicates the moment of disappearance, the second that of reappearance.)

normal reappearance than prior to disappearance, with means of 1.71 and 1.15 respectively, $F(1,18) = 7.53$, $P = 0.013$. This tendency was evident for 15 of the 20 infants. There were no significant main effects for age or trial block, nor any significant interactions.

A second analysis of variance focused on the comparison between normal and person-switch trials. The analysis was performed on the mean of the four smile ratings after reappearance, with age group, trial block, and reappearance type as the three factors. As in Experiment 1, infants were found to smile more after a normal reappearance ($M = 1.66$) than after a person-switch reappearance ($M = 0.96$), $F(1,18) = 18.25$, $P = 0.0005$. The only other main effect to reach significance was that of trial block, caused by there being less smiling during the final block of trials (mean: 1.01) than on the first three (means, respectively: 1.22, 1.44, 1.57), $F(2.85, 51.37) = 3.15$, $P = 0.035$.[4] Presumably, this effect was due to fatigue.

The interaction of age and reappearance type approached significance, however, $F(1,18) = 3.47$, $P = 0.079$, suggesting that the difference in smiling following normal and person-switch reappearances tended to be even greater for the 8-month-olds than for the 6-month-olds. In order to

---

[4]Where appropriate, numerator and denominator degrees of freedom have been reduced using the Geisser–Greenhouse correction.

confirm that each age group smiled significantly less following trick reappearances, separate planned comparison analyses of variance were performed on each age group applying the Bonferroni correction recommended by Keppel (1982, pp. 146–150). The difference between normal and person-switch reappearance smiling was significant for both age groups. For the 6-month-olds the means were 1.76 and 1.36 respectively, $F(1,9) = 8.63$, $P = 0.016$; 9 of the 10 6-month-olds showed the effect. For the 8-month-olds the means were 1.56 and 0.56, $F(1,9) = 11.31$, $P = 0.0084$; 8 of the 10 8-month-olds showed the effect.

As in the previous experiment, the possibility that eyebrow raises interfered with smiling was addressed by an additional analysis, performed on only those trials in which there were no brow raises following either a normal or the following person-switch reappearance. Forty per cent of the trials were thereby excluded from the reanalysis, including all trials of two subjects (one in each age group). As before, smile ratings were averaged across the four reappearance intervals and collapsed across blocks. For 6-month-olds, the mean for normal reappearances was 1.62, for trick reappearances, 1.34; for 8-month-olds, 1.13 and 0.40, respectively. An Age × Reappearance Type ANOVA revealed that these differences in smiling following the two types of reappearance were significant even when no eyebrow raises were present, $F(1,16) = 7.01$, $P = 0.018$. Of the 18 infants, 12 showed the effect, 1 showed no difference. There were no significant differences between age groups, and there was no significant interaction.

Discussion

The results of this experiment replicate and extend those obtained with the 7-month-olds used in Experiment 1. The 6- and 8-month-old infants in Experiment 2 also raised their eyebrows less and smiled more after a normal reappearance than after a person-switch. In addition, there was the suggestion of a developmental trend. Older infants seemed to be more sensitive to a person-switch than were younger ones. The 6-month-olds were least sensitive, the 8-month-olds were most sensitive, and the 7-month-olds in Experiment 1 fell intermediate between them.

In the present experiments the infants' ability to remember the experimenters' identities and to develop an expectation about which would reappear affected their emotional response. Part of the infants' enjoyment of the peek-a-boo game seems to stem from their expectation that the appearance of the adult is a *re*appearance of the same adult who disappeared previously. When this expectation was violated, they enjoyed the game less. This result was present in the 6-month-old infants and was increasingly pronounced in the 7- and 8-month-olds. Thus our second question, of whether infants' expectations play a role in their enjoyment, may be answered in the affirmative.

With respect to our third question, infants did not enjoy deviations from their expectations as much as they enjoyed conformity to them, at least in these two experiments. In the light of the evidence, alluded to earlier, suggesting that tricks structurally similar to a person-switch are often enjoyable to older children and adults, it is interesting that infants smiled less following person-switch reappearances and puzzling that this effect *increased* in magnitude in the older age groups. There are a number of possible explanations for this finding, and the following experiment was conducted to begin investigating them.

EXPERIMENT 3

Why did the infants smile *less* at the unexpected reappearance? One possibility is that a participant's identity has a privileged status in the peek-a-boo game, perhaps in all social interactions, and is not the sort of thing that is supposed to get changed, even in fun. If so, could it be that infants enjoy unexpected changes in some other aspects of the game? As a first test of this hypothesis, infants were presented with trick trials in which the same adult reappeared in an unexpected location.

Method

Subjects. Ten healthy, full-term infants served as subjects in this experiment. Their ages ranged from 7 months 6 days to 7 months 24 days with a mean age of 7 months 16 days. Four additional infants participated in but did not complete the experiment: one never smiled, two became fussy, and data from the fourth were lost because of equipment failure. The method for procuring subjects was the same as in the previous experiments.

Procedure. The apparatus and most aspects of the procedure were identical to those employed in Experiment 2. Following the familiarisation period, the infant was positioned 1m in front of the centre of the screen. One experimenter (the one the infant seemed to be more responsive to) served as the adult player; the other operated the camera. The adult player disappeared and reappeared from either of two locations equidistant from the centre of the screen: one was 44cm to the right, the other 44cm to the left (which side was used first was counterbalanced across infants). On normal peek-a-boo trials, the player would reappear at the same location from which he or she disappeared; on location-switch trials, he or she would reappear at the other location. In analogy to the procedure used in the previous experiments, there were four blocks of trials, consisting of three normal trials followed by a location-switch trial.

The videotapes were coded as before. The two coders of the eyebrow data agreed on 75% of the trials. As before, only eyebrow raises observed by both coders were counted in the data analysis. Given the high reliability of the smile coding in the previous experiments, no additional reliability checks were performed.

Results

The data on eyebrow raises paralleled those of the previous experiments. Infants raised their eyebrows more after location-switch reappearances (M = 0.42) than after normal reappearances (M = 0.12). The results of the two-way, within-subject ANOVA resulted in a significant main effect for reappearance type, $F(1,9) = 13.50$, $P = 0.0051$. This difference was present for 8 of the 10 infants. The main effect for trial block approached significance due to a tendency for fewer raises to occur in all conditions on the fourth block of trials, presumably due to fatigue, $F(2.32, 20.88) = 3.00$, $P = 0.065$. The interaction was not significant.

Figure 3 presents the second-by-second smile ratings, averaged across trial blocks. Their pattern resembles those obtained in the person-switch experiments, with lesser smiles after a location-switch than after a normal reappearance. To demonstrate this difference, we compared smile ratings averaged for all four intervals following a reappearance on normal and location-switch trials; the means were 2.48 and 1.80 respectively. A repeated-measures analysis of variance yielded a significant main effect for reappearance type, $F(1,9) = 18.17$, $P = 0.0021$. All 10 of the infants showed this difference. There was no significant effect of trial block or of the interaction.

As in previous experiments, an additional analysis examined those trials in which no brow raise occurred following either a normal or the corresponding switch reappearance. A total of 50% of the trials were discarded, including all trials from one subject. Unlike the previous experiments, the resulting means—2.13 for normal reappearances, 2.01 for location-switch—did not differ significantly by an ANOVA, $F(1,8) < 1.0$. Inspection of the means of individual subjects revealed that the small difference between these means was due almost entirely to one subject who contributed data from only one trial. Overall, seven of nine subjects smiled more following normal trials than location-switch trials, $P = 0.09$ (sign test, one-tailed). In the light of this fact and the results of the previous two studies, it thus seems unlikely that the diminished smiling following location-switch reappearances resulted from the presence of brow raises, at least in most infants.

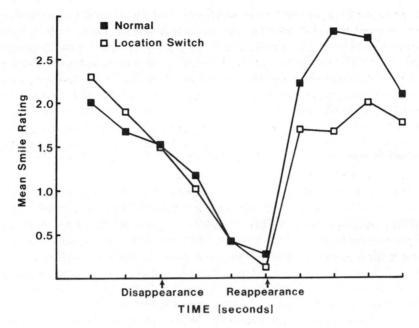

FIG. 3.   Smiling in 7-month-olds during normal and location-switch trials. (The first arrow indicates the moment of disappearance, the second that of reappearance.)

Discussion

The results of this experiment suggest that 7-month-olds in a peek-a-boo game are affected in much the same way by a switch in the location of the reappearing adult as they are by a switch in identity. This suggests that the failure to find *increased* smiling following a person-switch was not due to any property unique to identity, but rather, was most likely due to the effect of there having been a deviation from the infants' expectations. Why, then, does an expected reappearance lead to more smiling in infants than does an unexpected one, given prior findings that the unexpected often leads to more smiling and laughter in older children and adults (e.g. Nerhardt, 1970; Schultz, 1974).

One interpretation follows from "arousal-safety" theories of smiling, which hold that infants smile or laugh when physiological arousal or cognitive discrepancy ("tension") suddenly rises, or rises and then decreases, in a context they evaluate as safe (Rothbart, 1973; Sroufe & Waters, 1976; Stechler & Carpenter, 1967). Infants who play peek-a-boo with strange adults in a strange room, even after a familiarisation period, may not feel safe following a surprise; switches in person or location may eliminate whatever sense of security had existed. This account accords with previous research on the effects of perceived safety on responses to peek-a-boo (MacDonald & Silverman, 1978) and other playful activities (Sroufe, Waters, & Matas, 1974). Some of our findings conflict with this interpretation, however. For one, smiling rebounded quickly after switch trials, typically by the next normal trial, and it seems unlikely that evaluations of safety would return so quickly. Furthermore, infants did not display wariness or negative affect on switch trials, as arousal-safety theories might predict, but rather tended to smile weakly while seeming somewhat surprised. (See also Greenfield, 1972, and Pien & Rothbart, 1980, for similar findings in infants and 2-year-olds, respectively, who were playing games in "safer" contexts.)

Another possibility is that the violations of expectation used in these studies were two extreme. According to one hypothesis, infants will enjoy moderate discrepancies between expectation and actual experience (see McCall & McGhee, 1977). To test this suggestion, we conducted some pilot studies that employed smaller but readily distinguishable location-switches with 7-month-olds. The results showed that infants again failed to prefer the unexpected; infants smiled equally after normal and small location-switch reappearances (for details, see Parrott, 1985).

Perhaps a more likely interpretation follows from the theory that incongruities must be resolved before enjoyment can occur (Shultz, 1976; Suls, 1972). Observations by Greenfield (1972) suggest that young infants are capable of only highly specific expectations. If so, they may be unable to perceive the relation between a switch trial and a normal one (or be unable to perceive it quickly enough), and are thus unable to "get the point" of the switch—that is, to resolve the deviation from expectation by assimilating it to an overarching schema. Such a view is consistent with Sroufe and Wunsch's (1972) general finding that stimuli that involve incongruity and require some "cognitive sophistication" do not elicit laughter until the infants are nearly one year old. It implies that infants, like older children and adults, are not always amused by any deviation from their expectations, but prefer deviations that can be reinterpreted in a way that makes sense.

Although these experiments support incongruity-resolution theories of infants' enjoyment, this finding need not imply that unresolved incongruities *cannot* be enjoyed in infants. Some theorists have posited two types of humour, one based on incongruity that is resolved, and another based on unresolved incongruity (Eastman, 1921, 1936; Pien & Rothbart, 1976; Suls, 1983). While such theories cannot predict which of these two types of humour will apply in a given situation, they nonetheless suggest that if some aspect of the peek-a-boo game, say its structured format and the specific expectations it produces, prevented infants from enjoying sheer unexpectedness, it may be that infants might nevertheless enjoy the unexpected in a less structured context.

What cognitions lead to enjoyment in infants? The evidence of the present experiments suggests two types. One is the confirmation of an expectation. The infants were found to possess expectations about the location of an event and the identity of a reappearing person, and infants smiled most on trials in which these expectations were met. The pleasantness of confirmed expectations may result from infants experiencing a sense of mastery over a cognitive challenge. Confirmation of expectations has been found to produce smiling and laughter in infants and older childen if the expectations require cognitive effort (McGhee, 1974; Kagan, 1971). A second source of enjoyment is doubtless the arousing nature of the peek-a-boo reappearance itself. Even in younger infants, eye contact, sharp vocalisations, and looming are enjoyable in safe contexts (Rothbart, 1973; Stern, 1974). These variables continue to influence smiling in older infants (MacDonald & Silverman, 1978) and, indeed, throughout life. It is likely, therefore, that arousal enhanced infants' enjoyment. The picture that emerges is that, with development, the influence of arousal becomes increasingly modulated by cognitive factors.

The implication of the present research, then, is that there are indeed similarities in the causes of playful enjoyment in infancy and adulthood. In the case of a context like peek-a-boo, infants in the age range studied demonstrated a more complex cognition–emotion linkage than merely enjoying the arousing appearance of a human face; expectations about identity and location influenced the emotions of the infants in the present experiments. But, to enjoy deviations from these expectations, more cognitive capacity may be required than merely being able to have an expectation and recognise that it has been violated. It may also be necessary to recognise a relation between the expectation and the way it was violated, an ability that may not appear until the end of the first year.

Manuscript received 6 December 1988
Manuscript revised 15 February 1989

REFERENCES

Baillargeon, R., Spelke, E. S., & Wasserman, S. (1985). Object permanence in five-month-old infants. *Cognition*, *20*, 191–208.

Berlyne, D. E. (1969). Laughter, humor, and play. In G. Lindzey & E. Aronson (Eds), *The handbook of social psychology*, Vol. 3, 2nd edn. Reading, Mass.: Addison-Wesley, pp. 795–852.

Bower, T. G. R. (1974). *Development in infancy*. San Francisco: Freeman.

Bruner, J. S. & Sherwood, V. (1976). Peekaboo and the learning of rule structures. In J. S.

Bruner, A. Joly, & K. Sylva (Eds), *Play: Its role in development and evolution*. New York: Basic Books.

Canfield, R. L. & Haith, M. M. (1986, April). *Infant's visual anticipation of complex spatiotemporal patterns*. Paper presented at the International Conference on Infant Studies, Los Angeles.

Dewey, J. (1894). The theory of emotion. I. Emotional attitudes. *Psychological Review, 1*, 553–569.

Eastman, M. (1921). *The sense of humor*. New York: Scribner.

Eastman, M. (1936). *Enjoyment of laughter*. New York: Simon and Schuster.

Ekman, P. & Friesen, W. (1978). *Facial action coding system*. Palo Alto, CA: Consulting Psychologists Press.

Gleitman, H. (1985, August). *Some reflections on the psychology of the drama*. Presidential Address to the Division of the Psychology of Arts delivered at the meeting of the American Psychological Associaton, Los Angeles.

Goldberg, S. (1976). Visual tracking and existence constancy in 5-month-old infants. *Journal of Experimental Child Psychology, 22*, 478–491.

Gratch, G. (1982). Responses to hidden persons and things by 5-, 9-, and 16-month-old infants in a visual tracking situation. *Developmental Psychology, 18*, 232–237.

Greenfield, P. M. (1972). Playing peekaboo with a four-month-old: A study of the role of speech and nonspeech sounds in the formation of a visual schema. *The Journal of Psychology, 82*, 287–298.

Haith, M. M., Hazan, C., & Goodman, G. (1984, April). *Infants' expectation and anticipation of future visual events*. Paper presented at the International Conference on Infant Studies, New York.

Hodapp, R. M., Goldfield, E. C., & Boyatzis, C. (1984). The use and effectiveness of maternal scaffolding. *Child Development, 55*, 772–781.

Izard, C. E. & Dougherty, L. (1982). Two complementary systems for measuring facial expressions in infants and children. In C. E. Izard (Ed.), *Measuring emotions in infants and children*. Cambridge University Press.

Kagan, J. (1971). *Change and continuity in infancy*. New York: Wiley.

Keppel, G. (1982). *Design and analysis: A researcher's handbook*, 2nd edn. Englewood Cliffs, N.J.: Prentice-Hall.

Lewis, M. & Goldberg, S. (1969). The acquisition and violation of expectancy: An experimental paradigm. *Journal of Experimental Child Psychology, 7*, 70–80.

MacDonald, N. E. & Silverman, I. W. (1978). Smiling and laughter in infants as a function of level of arousal and cognitive evaluation. *Developmental Psychology, 14*, 235–241.

McCall, R. B. & McGhee, P. E. (1977). The discrepancy hypothesis of attention and affect in infants. In I. C. Uzhiris & F. Wiezman (Eds), *The structuring of experience*. New York: Plenum.

McGhee, P. E. (1974). Cognitive mastery and children's humor. *Psychological Bulletin, 81*, 721–730.

McGhee, P. E. (1979). *Humor: Its origin and development*. San Francisco: Freeman.

Meicler, M. & Gratch, G. (1980). Do 5-month-olds show object conception in Piaget's sense? *Infant Behavior and Development, 3*, 267–282.

Meyer, L. B. (1956). *Emotion and meaning in music*. University of Chicago Press.

Moore, M. K., Borton, R., & Darby, B. (1978). Visual tracking in young infants: Evidence for object identity or object permanence? *Journal of Experimental Child Psychology, 25*, 183–197.

Muller, A. A. & Aslin, R. N. (1978). Visual tracking as an index of the object concept. *Infant Behavior and Development, 1*, 309–319.

Nerhardt, G. (1970). Humor and inclination to laugh: Emotional reactions to stimuli of different divergence from a range of expectancy. *Scandinavian Journal of Psychology*, *11*, 185–195.

Parrott, W. G. (1985). Cognitive and social factors underlying infants' smiling and laughter during the peeka-boo game. (Doctoral dissertation, University of Pennsylvania, 1985). *Dissertation Abstracts International*, *46*, 1716B.

Piaget, J. (1954). *The construction of reality in the child*. New York: Basic Books.

Pien, D. & Rothbart, M. K. (1976). Incongruity and resolution in children's humor: A reexamination. *Child Development*, *47*, 966–971.

Pien, D., & Rothbart, M. K. (1980). Incongruity humor, play, and self-regulation of arousal in young children. In P. McGhee & A. Chapman (Eds), *Children's humour*. Chichester: Wiley, pp. 1–26.

Rheingold, H., & Eckerman, C. (1973). Fear of the stranger: A critical examination. In H. Reese (Ed.), *Advances in child development and behavior, Vol. 8*. New York: Academic Press.

Rothbart, M. K. (1973). Laughter in young children. *Psychological Bulletin*, *80*, 246–256.

Rothbart, M. K. (1976). Incongruity, problem-solving and laughter. In A. J. Chapman & H. C. Foot (Eds), *Humour and laughter: Theory, research, and applications*. London: Wiley.

Rothbart, M. K. (1977). Psychological approaches to the study of humour. In A. J. Chapman & C. Foot (Eds), *It's a funny thing, humour*. Oxford: Pergamon Press.

Shultz, T. R. (1972). The role of incongruity and resolution in children's appreciation of cartoon humor. *Journal of Experimental Child Psychology*, *13*, 456–477.

Shultz, T. R. (1974). Development of the appreciation of riddles. *Child Development*, *45*, 100–105.

Shultz, T. R. (1976). A cognitive-developmental analysis of humor. In A. J. Chapman & C. Foot (Eds), *Humour and laughter: Theory, research, and applications*. London: Wiley.

Shultz, T. R. (1979). Play as arousal modulation. In B. Sutton-Smith (Ed.), *Play and learning*. New York: Gardner Press.

Sroufe, L. A. & Wunsch, J. P. (1972). The development of laughter in the first year of life. *Child Development*, *43*, 1326–1344.

Sroufe, L. A. & Waters, E. (1976). The ontogenesis of smiling and laughter: A perspective on the organization of development in infancy. *Psychological Review*, *83*, 173–189.

Sroufe, L. A., Waters, E., & Matas, L. (1974). Contextual determinants of infant affective response. In M. Lewis & L. Rosenblum (Eds), *The origins of fear*. New York: Wiley.

Stechler, G. & Carpenter, G. (1967). A viewpoint on early affective development. In J. Hellmuth (Ed.), *The exceptional infant, Vol. 1*. New York: Brunner/Mazel.

Stern, D. N. (1974). Mother and infant at play: The dyadic interaction involving facial, vocal, and gaze behaviors. In M. Lewis & L. Rosenblum (Eds), *The effect of the infant on its caregiver*. New York: Wiley.

Suls, J. M. (1972). A two-stage model for the appreciation of jokes and cartoons. In J. H. Goldstein & P. E. McGhee (Eds), *The psychology of laughter*. New York; Academic Press.

Suls, J. (1983). Cognitive processes in humor appreciation. In P. E. McGhee & J. H. Goldstein (Eds), *Handbook of humor research*. Vol. 1. *Basic issues*. New York: Springer, pp. 39–57.

Zigler, E., Levine, J., & Gould, L. (1966). Cognitive processes in the development of children's appreciation of humor. *Child Development*, *37*, 507–518.

COGNITION AND EMOTION, 1989, 3(4), 313–342

Talking with Feeling: Integrating Affective and Linguistic Expression in Early Language Development

Lois Bloom

Teachers College, Columbia University, U.S.A.

Richard Beckwith

Princeton University, U.S.A.

The purpose of the longitudinal study reported here was to determine the developmental relation between the two systems of expression available to the young child in the period of early language learning: affect and speech. Two achievements in language were identified for a group of 12 infants: First Words, at the beginning of the single-word period (mean age about 13 months), and a Vocabulary Spurt, which occurred toward the end of the period (mean age about 19 months). Affect expression was coded continuously in the stream of the infants' activity as they and their mothers played with groups of toys and ate a snack. The occurrence of words was examined in relation to the expression of affect and the results of this study concern developments in the integration of these two forms expression. The children's words occurred closely in time with their expression of emotionally toned affect. We concluded, then, that they were learning words to express what their feelings were about even though none of the actual words they said were emotion terms. However, the cognitive requirements

---

Requests for reprints should be sent to Professor Lois Bloom, Box 5, Teachers College, Columbia University, New York, NY 10027, U.S.A. The research that is reported here was supported by research grants from The National Science Foundation and The Spencer Foundation to Lois Bloom, and the James S. McDonnell Foundation to Princeton University. We thank Joanne Bitetti Capatides, Mariette Newton-Danilo, Erin Tinker, Anne Spangler, and Roxanne DeMatteo for their help with the analyses reported here; Jeremie Hafitz, Matthew Rispoli, Joy Vaughn, Erin Tinker, Jennifer Saldano, and Scott Scheer for transcribing the children's speech; and Virginia Brennan, Suzanne Gottlieb, Mariette Newton-Danilo, Lisa Spiegel, and Pia Wikstrom for coding affect expression. We thank Robert Beckwith and Karen Clark for helping to develop the lag analyses. We have benefited from discussions of the results of this study with Catherine Best, Joseph Jaffe, Margaret Lahey, Karin Lifter, Dennis Molfese, Nancy Stein, Don Tucker, and Gerald Turkewitz, in addition to the members of our research group.

© 1989 Lawrence Erlbaum Associates Limited

for emotional expression and expression through speech resulted in several constraints on their integration. Words were said with neutral affect expression most often, with a peak in emotional expression in the moments immediately after words but a decrease in emotional expression before words. The peak in emotional expression with words was significantly greater, and the pre-word dip in emotional expression was significantly less, at the Vocabulary Spurt than at First Words. Thus, the two systems of expression converged in the period of single-word development as the children came to be able to say words with emotional affect. However, the words that were said together with emotional expression were said with positive rather than negative valence, with low rather than heightened intensity, and were among the most frequent and earliest learned words. These results are discussed in terms of the acquisition of language for expression and the different cognitive requirements for expression through affect and speech.

INTRODUCTION

The first forms of affect expression are already available to infants in the beginning months of life and are probably biologically determined (e.g. Emde, Gaensbauer, & Harmon, 1976; Izard, 1977). By the time language begins in the second year, the development of the system of emotional expression is well underway. The purpose of the study reported here was to determine how developments in emotional expression and language "fit" together in the course of early language development.

Developments in emotional expression consist of the infant gaining control over the mechanisms of expression, and modulating the forms of expression to conform to social and cultural expecations and practices (Izard & Malatesta, 1987). Language may be the most important context in which this learning occurs. First, language allows individuals to articulate something of the causes, the circumstances, and the objects of their emotional experience. The study reported here concerns the period of early word learning in the second year. This is the period when infants are learning words that can expess the objects of their emotions or what their feelings are *about*, while they continue to express *how* and *what* they feel through facial and vocal affect displays (Bloom, Beckwith, Capatides, & Hafitz, 1988b). Secondly, the linguistic resources that societies have evolved include words, structures, and discourse practices for expressing feelings and for modulating the facial and vocal expression of those feelings (Ochs & Schieffelin, 1989). However, the children in the present study had not yet begun to learn the words that name emotions or other forms of emotion language (which have been addressed in other studies with somewhat older children, e.g. Bretherton, & Beeghly, 1982; Ridgeway, Waters, & Kuczaj, 1985).

In reviewing studies of vocalisation in infants' prespeech emotional expressions, Malatesta (1981, p. 15) suggested that "the tendency to intonate speech affectively may have an early and innate origin". The nonspeech vocalisations of 8-month-old infants occur at times of obvious shifts in attention and changes in facial expression, particularly smiles (Hilke, 1988). We know that the words and sentences of school-aged children (e.g. Camras, 1985) and adults (e.g. Davitz 1964, 1969; Scherer, 1986) are often spoken with emotional expression. However, no studies, as far as we know, have examined relations between speech and affect expression in the period of language development in the second year, after the period of infant prespeech vocalisation and before the development of mature language.

COGNITION, LANGUAGE, AND EMOTION

Both speech and affect express something of the underlying contents of desires and beliefs, plans and goals. Expression, whether speech or affect, requires the allocation of cognitive resources for representing such contents in attention. However, the requirements for speech and affect expression also differ. Using language requires comparing the contents of attention with prior experience recalled from memory, recalling the linguistic forms to express these contents, and encoding (Bloom & Beckwith, 1988). The expression of emotion entails an evaluation (e.g. Frijda, 1986; Scherer, 1984; Wozniak, 1986) which includes, for example, considering the consequences of an aspect of the situation for some goal or plan (Oatley & Johnson-Laird, 1987; Stein & Levine, 1987), along with a subjective feeling and a display (e.g. Izard, 1977; Lewis & Michalson, 1985). For words to express something of what an emotional expression is about, cognitive resources need to be allocated for both speech and affect expression. Thus, the requirements for the two sorts of expression could compete with one another when the young child is expressing emotion and wants to say a word at the same time, and vice versa.

The competition for cognitive resources to meet the requirements for speech and affect expression may be most apparent in the early period of language learning, before the processes of lexical recall and speech become automatic. In previous research, we observed that 1-year-old infants who spent relatively more time in neutral affect expression achieved certain milestones in language learning earlier than infants who expressed emotionally toned affect more frequently (Bloom & Capatides, 1987a; Bloom, Beckwith, & Capatides, 1988a). We have interpreted this result to mean that neutral affect expression allows the deployment of cognitive resources for early language learning. Learning to say words and expressing emotion may compete with one another for the young child's attention and limited cognitive resources.

Such competition for cognitive resources may well have a neuropsychological basis related to what Kinsbourne has referred to as a "lateral gradient of attention". When cognitive processing requires skills that are specialised for the different cerebral hemispheres, the result is a competition for "relative degree of activation" of the two hemispheres (Kinsbourne, 1975, p. 81). Emotional expression and language involve different regions of the brain. While the emotions involve both subcortical as well as cortical regions in the brain, emotional expression and monitoring emotional arousal have predominantly right hemisphere specialisation (e.g. see Best & Queen, 1989; Kinsbourne & Bemporad, 1984; and Tucker & Frederick, 1989, for reviews of the relevant literature). Language, as is well known, is associated primarily with left-hemisphere activity. This is true for semantics and syntax (e.g. Berndt, Caramazza, & Zurif, 1983); phonological information (e.g. Molfese, Molfese, & Parsons, 1983); and for the motor implementation required for speech (e.g. Kent, 1984; Levy, 1969). However, sentence intonation and prosody have been attributed to right-hemisphere function (e.g. Blumstein & Cooper, 1974), as have the prosodic aspects of speech that are expressive of emotional feeling (e.g. Ross, 1985).

Evidence from infants suggests that cerebral asymmetries such as these are present in early infancy before the emergence of language, and may be predetermined rather than developmental (e.g. Best, 1988; Molfese, Freeman, & Palermo, 1975; Witelson, 1987). Integration of the processing activities in the two hemispheres and allocation of attentional capacities are mediated to a large degree by the corpus callosum (e.g. Levy, 1985). However, the corpus callosum is particularly slow to mature (Yakovlev & Lecours, 1967), and this fact has been cited to explain the relative lack of early hemispheric integration in other developmental domains, for example, graphomotor skill (Kirk, 1985) and face recognition (Levine, 1985).

In sum, different regions of the brain are specialised for language (the left hemisphere) and emotional expression (predominantly the right hemisphere). This separation of the neurological bases for the two kinds of expression, in different regions of the brain, could interfere with simultaneously saying a word and expressing emotion about the same content because of competition for activation between the two hemispheres. This constraint would limit the distribution of cognitive resources between the mental activities required for emotional expression and speech. In early language learning in particular, expression through speech could consume the young child's attention and interfere with the simultaneous expression of affect, and expression of emotion could pre-empt the attention required for speech. Although we expect children to learn language for expressing what their feelings are about, the two sorts of expression may be independent when language begins. However, with the automaticity that comes as language develops, we should see their integration.

Three hypotheses were offered in the present study in order to test the assumption that a limitation in resources constrains saying words and expressing emotionally toned affect at the same time. The distribution of cognitive resources should be reflected in the temporal relation between saying a word and expressing emotion, if the word pre-empts the cognitive activity required for expressing emotion, and vice versa. The result would be non-overlap between the two forms of expression. The first hypothesis, the Integration hypothesis, was that words and affect expression would be independent initially but would begin to overlap as words increase in number and frequency, reflecting increased automaticity of use.

Another set of hypothesis concerned the factors that might contribute to the integration of words and affect in the single-word period in the second year. One such factor could be emotional valence and the difference between positive and negative affect expression. More cognitive work occurs with expression of the negative emotions than with positive emotion. This is because the positive and negative emotions differ with respect to both the direction and the outcome of the evaluation of the situation relative to an individual's goals and behaviour (Oatley, 1988; Stein & Levine, 1989). With the positive emotions, a goal has been achieved and no new cognitive activity is required (Rothbart, 1973). In the case of the negative emotions, however, the result of evaluation includes cognitive activity for the construction of a new plan to remove an obstacle to the goal or the creation of a new goal (Stein & Jewett, 1987). Positive emotion is associated with the success of ongoing behaviour whereas negative emotion is associated with the interruption of behaviour (Kinsbourne, 1988). We might expect, then, that integrating affect expression and speech in the single word period would be more likely with positive than with negative affect expression.

Some evidence in the neuropsychological literature that has suggested differences in regions of brain activity for the positive and negative emotions would support this expectation. As already reported above, the neuropsychological evidence strongly supports a right-hemisphere special-isation for emotional expression in general (e.g. Borod & Koff, 1989; Tucker, 1986). However, there is research with brain-injured and normal populations to indicate that certain aspects of the expression of positive emotions may involve left-hemisphere activity as well (e.g. Kinsbourne & Bemporad, 1984; Sackheim & Gur, 1978; Schwartz, Ahern, & Brown, 1979). EEG studies with infants have also suggested a valence asymmetry in specialisation, with more left-hemisphere activity associated with posi-tive emotional expressions and more right-hemisphere activity with negative expressions (e.g. Davidson & Fox, 1982). The issue of differential hemisphere activation with positive and negative emotional expression is presently a controversial issue. However, if aspects of positive affect expression are attributable to left hemisphere activity, we might expect that speech would be more readily integrated with positive emotional expression than with negative emotional expression. The second hypothesis we tested was the Facilitating Affect hypothesis. Given the lesser cognitive load and the possibility of less interhemisphere competition with positive expression, the integration of speech and affect expression was expected to occur more often with positive than with negative expression.

Finally, saying words and simultaneously expressing emotion should not be independent of the words themselves. The words that children know best would presumably include their earlier learned and most frequent words. These should have greater automaticity and, as a result, be more likely to occur together with emotional expression than words that the child is just learning. Accordingly, the third hypothesis we tested was the Facilitating Words hypothesis. The integration of speech and emotional expression was expected to occur with the children's earlier learned and most frequent words since these are the words they presumably know best.

In sum, the hypotheses tested in this study were that the integration of words and affect expression would develop in the single word period, but with certain cognitive constraints. Namely, affect expressed with words would have positive more often than negative emotional tone, and the words that children said with emotional expression would be among their most frequent and earlier learned words.

METHODS

Our subjects were 12 infants, 6 girls and 6 boys, of different ethnic and economic backgrounds, from homes in the New York metropolitan area.[1] All were first-born and their mothers were not employed outside of the home at the time the study began. Each infant and mother visited our laboratory playroom once each month, from 8 or 9 months to about 30 months of age. Each session lasted one hour. The children were also visited at home every month until they were 15 months old, and then every 3 months thereafter. In addition, the mothers kept diaries of the words their children both said and understood at home, in the intervals between monthly playroom observations, and the diaries were reviewed during the home visits The research reported here was based on data from the video-

---

[1]These were the same subjects as in previous studies of the emergence of language in relation to developments in affect (Bloom et al., 1988; Bloom & Capatides, 1987a) and object play (Lifter & Bloom, 1989).

recorded playroom sessions, with the diaries used to determine the children's earliest words.

The observation playroom was furnished with a child-size table and chairs, a 3-foot plastic slide with a crawl-through tunnel between the steps and the incline, and a changing table. A set of toys was on the floor when the mother and infant entered the room. One of two investigators brought in additional groups of toys at 8-minute intervals according to a schedule, and a snack (cookies with juice for the baby and coffee or tea for the mother) after the first half hour. The toys were selected so as to balance possible girl or boy interest (e.g. doll, truck) and manipulative or enactment play (e.g. nesting blocks, miniature cutlery). We are aware of the possibility that the results of this study might have been influenced by the situation in which the data were collected. For example, the children might have expressed more negative affect if we had seen them in another context, such as bedtime at home, rather than the familiar playroom context in which they played with groups of toys with their mothers. Data were collected in the playroom so that we could control the situation, for example, the interactants and the groups of toys. The same groups of toys were brought into the playroom, in the same sequence, for all the children, and for each child over time.

The observations were video-recorded (SLO-383 Sony half-inch stereo Beta). The camera was mounted on a 3-foot high movable tripod in the playroom, and a second investigator manoeuvred the camera so that the infant was in view all the time. Each infant and mother interacted with one pair of investigators throughout the study, both in the playroom and the home visits, and the investigators and infant–mother pairs were matched for ethnicity. The infants and mothers were visited at home before the data collection began, and then saw the investigators twice a month; they gave every indication that they were relaxed and comfortable in these playroom sessions.

At the time of recording, a SMPTE time-code generator (FOR-A 3500) imposed an audio signal for each frame of the tape on the second sound track. This allowed the data to be manipulated to within one-thirtieth of a second (each second of video tape containing 30 frames) at the time of data processing. The videotape deck was interfaced at playback with a SMPTE time-code reader and an Apple II+ computer for data coding and transcription. Coders were naïve both to the hypothesis to be tested and the units of analysis in the study, and different persons were responsible for coding affect or transcribing speech. The time signal allowed the computer to merge the separate coding passes. This produced an integrated transcription that preserved the temporal relation between speech and affect expression as they occurred in real time. The processed data were transferred to an IBM-XT computer for analyses.

Children vary widely in onset and rate of language development, as is well known. For this reason, we equated the children in this study for language achievement rather than chronological age in order to study the integration of affect expression and developing language. Two language achievements in the single-word period were identified for each child. These were First Words (FW) and a Vocabulary Spurt (VS), both of which have been well-documented in the literature (e.g. Bloom, 1973; Corrigan, 1978; Fischer, Pipp, & Bullock, 1984; Gopnik & Meltzoff, 1987; Nelson, 1973; Stern & Stern, 1907). FW (mean age = 13 months 18 days) was the first observation in the playroom during which a child said one conventional word at least two times. The total number of words used by the 12 children in the 1-hour observation at FW was 63 types ($M = 6$) and 189 tokens ($M = 17$). VS (mean age = 19 months 18 days) was a sharp increase in the number of different words relative to the cumulative slope in the increase of vocabulary from month to month. This was operationalised as the observation in which 12 new words were said (an average of 3 per week since the preceding observation) after the child had already acquired at least 20 different words. The total number of words used by the 12 children in the 1-hour observation at VS was 479 types ($M = 40$) and 2224 tokens ($M = 188$). The data for this study consisted of the speech and affect expression in the first half hour of the two observations in which these developments in language occurred: First Words (FW) and a Vocabulary Spurt (VS).

Coding Affect Expression

The emotional signal carries both categorical and gradient information (Stern, Barnett, & Spieker, 1983). Categorical information is the particular emotion (such as anger, joy, or sadness) that is expressed. We are unaware of any explicit theoretical or empirical claims for the relation of categories of emotion to the emergence of language. For this reason, a coding scheme was devised to capture the gradient properties of affective expression, valence (hedonic tone) and intensity, and categories of emotions were not identified or labelled.[2]

Every change in expressed affect in the stream of an infant's activities was identified and entered into the computer with the time of onset. Affect coding was continuous, so that the onset time of any change in affect

---

[2]Neutral affect expression, which predicted early word learning in a previous study (Bloom & Capatides, 1987a), included expression of the emotions category of "interest" (C. Malatesta, pers. comm, 19 February 1987). Interest, as an emotion, has been considered important for processes of attention and cognition (Izard, 1986; Piaget, 1954/1981) and for this reason may be a fruitful topic for future research.

expression was also the offset time of the previous affect expression. This yielded a continuous record of (a) affect expressions, including neutral expression, and (b) the duration of affect expressions from one change in expression to another. An affect expression was any change in affective vocalisations (whining, laughing, and the like), or observable change in the infant's facial expression, body tension, or posture. Affective vocalisation and facial expression were each considered sufficient by themselves for coding decisions, but body tension or posture required behaviour cues from one other channel.

These affect expressions were coded for their *valence*, whether neutral, negative, positive, mixed, or equivocal tone. A neutral expression was defined by the face being in a resting or baseline position as described by Ekman and Friesen (1975), and without body tension or affective vocalisation. Mixed affect expressions included elements of both positive and negative valence; equivocal expressions were neither positive, negative, nor neutral, as happened with surprise or excitement. Non-neutral affect expressions were also coded for *intensity* with three levels of intensity indicating the fullness of a display. Thus, the coding scheme for describing the quality of expressed affect included three levels of intensity: 1, 2, 3, and five qualities of valence: neutral, negative, positive, mixed, and equivocal. Affective vocalisations such as cries and whines were entered into the coding descriptively.[3]

Ambiguous episodes (the occurrence of a momentary vocalisation or facial movement that could not be assigned to one of the above categories) were also coded with time of onset. In addition, the child was sometimes moving away from the camera, or the face was not visible for affect coding, with no cues from body tension or affective vocalisation. These intervals of "backturn" were also coded for onset so that coding affect expression in the stream of the infant's activity was not interrupted. Ambiguous affect expression and episodes of backturn were not included in the data analyses. The average amount of coded time, excluding backturn and ambiguous cases, was 24.5 minutes at FW and 24.03 minutes at VS.

---

[3]Photographs of examples of these categories of coded affect expressions are presented in Bloom et al. (1988b). The coding scheme, with description of the coding categories and decision rules, is available from the authors. See Schlosberg (1954) and Young (1959), for accounts of the "pleasantness-unpleasantness" and intensity dimensions of emotion; Stern et al. (1983), for discussion of gradient and categorical information in the emotional signal; and Adamson & Bakeman (1982); Ricciuti & Poresky (1972); and Stechler & Carpenter (1967), for other studies that have used gradient information in the study of affect expression.

Reliability

Three coders initially worked in rotating pairs during training, in order to increase the accuracy of coding and to ensure initial confidence in their judgements. Training continued until the paired coders (the three coders each rotated with one another) achieved a predetermined level of at least 85% agreement with a segment of data that had been coded by the investigators responsible for training and considered as a standard. Segments were selected randomly from different children for this post-training test of reliability and each segment lasted from 2 to 5.5 minutes. Percentage agreement was computed separately for the categories of valence (positive, negative, neutral, mixed, and equivocal) and intensity (one, two, and three degrees) of the categories of nonneutral valence. This level of reliability for the coder pairs, after training and before the actual coding for the study was begun, was high: for valence, Pair 1 = 92%, Pair 2 = 90%, Pair 3 = 100%; and for intensity, Pair 1 = 89%, Pair 2 = 89%, and Pair 3 = 85%.

After continuing to code in pairs for several weeks, reliability was assessed for the individual coders working independently in the following way. Each individually coded a 3.5-minute segment that included at least 25 coding entries. The percentage agreement between each member of a pair coding independently was high: Pair 1 = 100%; Pair 2 = 94% and Pair 3 = 94% for both valence and intensity. At that point the coding was begun for the data used in this study with the coders working independently. The Kappa coefficients of agreement (Cohen, 1960) for valence and intensity ranged from 0.67 to 0.85, for inter-individual reliability and from 0.72 to 1.0 for intra-individual reliability. Cohen's Kappa corrects for chance agreement and is a more conservative measure than the per cent agreement. These Kappa scores are comparable to those reported in the literature for similar measures and considered evidence of high reliability (e.g. Adamson & Bakeman, 1985). The mean discrepancy in recording affect onset time was an average of 16 video frames, or approximately 0.5 second, for the three coder pairs. (As noted above, the offset of an affect expression was the onset of the next expression.)

Speech Transcription

The initial speech transcription was a paper and pencil one. A second transcriber reviewed this transcription in the context of entering it into the computer. Disagreements between the two were resolved by having both review the video recording and transcription together. Lexical items were entered orthographically; nonlexical vocalisations were entered phonetically. All vocalisations were entered with the times of onset and offset.

Accuracy in determining onset and offset times, after training, was high. The mean discrepancy between pairs of independent coders was 2 video frames (1/15 second) for speech onset time, and 5 video frames (1/6 second) for speech offset. (The somewhat lesser accuracy in finding onset time of an affect expression was due to the fact that several kinds of cues were used to code affect, e.g. facial expression and body tension).

Data Analyses

Two different measures were used to determine the overlap of speech (discrete events) and affect expression (coded as a continuous variable). The first was a *frequency* measure: The number of times a word was said with affect expression, coded according to each of the categories of valence (positive, negative, neutral, mixed, and equivocal) and intensity (1, 2, 3). Every speech event (a single word most often) was located in the computerised transcript. The affect expressed at the same time that a word was spoken was identified as follows. With each occurrence of a word, the computer searched backward from the speech onset time until the first onset time of an affect expression was encountered, and forward to the end of a 10-frame window (1/3 second) after speech offset. Within this interval between onset of affect expression and 10 frames after speech offset, affect expression coded with any nonneutral valence took precedence over neutral valence, and higher levels of intensity took precedence over lower levels, for assigning the affect value at the time of speech. For example, if a neutral expression was encountered before speech onset but then an instance of +1 affect expression was encountered either (a) during speech (between speech onset and speech offset), or (b) within the 10-frame window after speech offset, that word was considered to have occurred with +1 affect (emotional expression with positive valence and a low intensity level). The use of the 10-frame window after speech offset was the control for the margin of error in coding times of speech offset and affect onset.

The second analysis was a measure of the *time* spent in overlap or the number of video frames with overlapping word and affect expression at FW and VS. The number of frames (with 30 video frames per second) was counted for time spent saying words while expressing neutral affect and expressing non-neutral affect.

The temporal relation between saying words and expressing emotion in real time was determined through a form of lag sequential analysis (Sackett, 1974, 1979; Bakeman, 1978). The mean duration of speech (primarily single words but occasionally phrases) was 0.88 seconds (26.3 frames) at FW and 0.85 seconds (25.6 frames) at VS. With the occurrence of a word considered as the anchor lag, 15 1-second lags before and 15 1-second lags after each word were scanned for the occurrence of emotionally toned affect expression. The baseline rate of emotional expression was determined by dividing the amount of time each child spent in emotional expression overall (Bloom et al., 1988a) by the total amount of coded time. This was then considered the expected frequency of expression per 1-second lag.

To determine whether emotion was expressed during a lag, the onset and offset of every emotional expression was examined and any overlap with a lag was noted. The lag was considered to have included emotional expression if any overlap occurred. A running count was kept for each instance of emotional expression that occurred in each of the 15 1-second lags before and after a child's words. The running count was then divided by the number of words to determine the number of times that emotion was expressed in the lag relative to the opportunity for expression. This number, the proportion of lags with emotional expression, was compared to the baseline rate of affect expression overall. The baseline rate of emotional expression was then subtracted from each lag's proportion of affect to obtain a difference score from baseline. This yielded an emotion expression profile for each child which consisted of the percentages of the difference from baseline in each lag. The differences from baseline were then divided by the standard deviation of the differences for each child (Z-scores) and the means for the Z-scores were used to generate a composite profile for the group of children. This profile was then plotted as the mean difference in standard deviation units from the baseline expression of emotion in each lag.

The remaining analyses concerned those factors that might be expected to contribute to the integration of emotionally toned affect expression and speech at VS. First, in order to determine the possible differential effects of positive and negative valence, the analysis of overlapping *time* (number of frames) was performed for positive and negative expression separately. Secondly, analyses were performed in order to determine the possible differential effect from the words themselves that the children were learning. The two factors that were examined were (a) earlier word learning, whether words at VS had occurred at FW, had occurred in the interval between FW and VS, or were reported in the mothers' diaries, and (b) word frequency.

RESULTS

The results of this study consist of (a) the *frequency* of overlapping word and affect expressions and the *time* spent in overlapping word and affect expression at the two language achievements, FW and VS; (b) the temporal, *lag sequential* relation between word and affect expression at FW and

VS; (c) the relative time spent in saying words with *positive and negative* affect expression; and (d) the effects of early learning and word frequency on emotional expression with speech, and the words the children said with overlapping emotional valence.

Overlapping Word and Affect Expression

The frequency of overlapping word and affect expression at FW and VS is presented in Fig. 1. Here we have the percentage of the number of words spoken by all the children with positive, negative, and neutral valence and the different values of intensity. The children said most of their words when they were also expressing neutral affect. When they did speak and express emotion at the same time, that emotion was more likely to be level one (+1 or −1) intensity. At VS, more words were said with level 1 intensity and fewer words with levels 2 and 3 than was expected, given the frequency of emotional expression at the different intensity levels, chi-square = 13.26, $P < 0.001$. The same comparison was not significant at FW, $P > 0.50$. Thus, the children were not inclined to be speaking at VS when they were expressing emotion with heightened intensity (+2,3, or −2,3).

However, while the children said most of their words with neutral valence, they were also expressing neutral affect most of the time (84% of the time, on average) (Bloom et al., 1988a). Thus, one could argue that speech with neutral valence was predicted by the amount of time spent in neutral affect. The second analysis, then, concerned overlapping speech time and emotion time. The number of video frames (with 30 frames per second) was counted for time spent speaking and expressing affect. Times

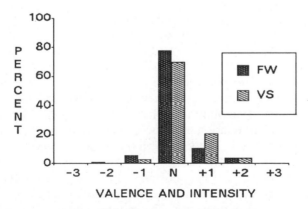

FIG. 1.   Word and affect expression overlap.

TABLE 1
Total Time (No. of Frames) in Expressing Affect and Speaking at First Words
(FW) and Vocabulary Spurt (VS), (n = 12 children)

Affect	Speaking		Not Speaking	
	Neutral	Emotion	Neutral	Emotion
FW	3263	608	444 174	78 006[a]
VS	12 850	5133[c]	415 328	85 628[b]

[a]Chi-square (1 d.f.) = 1.78, P = 0.182 ns. [b]Chi-square (1 d.f.) = 1578.48, $P < 0.001$. [c]Chi-square (1 d.f.) = 271.63, $P < 0.001$.

(number of coded frames) spent speaking, not speaking, expressing neutral affect, and expressing emotionally toned affect are presented in Table 1 for FW and VS. At FW, the amount of speech time/emotion time overlap was independent of the amount of emotion time at FW, chi-square = 1.78, P = 0.182. In contrast, at VS, speech was expressed with emotion more than expected, given the time spent in expressing emotion, chi-square = 1578.48, $P < 0.001$. Comparing FW and VS, speech time/emotion time overlap increased between the two language achievements, chi-square = 271.63, $P < 0.001$, confirming the Integration hypothesis. These results mean that at the moment of speech, the two systems of expression, speech and emotion, were independent when these infants began to say words. However, by the time they reached the vocabulary spurt, they had integrated the two systems of expression.

Temporal Relation between saying Words and Expressing Emotion

The results of the lag sequential analyses at FW and VS are presented in Figs 2 and 3 respectively. The horizontal line in the figures represents the baseline rate or expected frequency of emotional expression per 1-second lag, based upon the amount of time the children spent in emotional expression overall. The observed frequency of emotional expression is presented as the difference in mean standard deviation units from the baseline expression of emotion in each of the 15 pre- and 15 post-word 1-second lags, plotted in relation to the word lag. Each graph represents the collapsed data from the 12 children, with the resulting curves smoothed by a least squares best fit of the data.

If the two sorts of expression, emotion and words, were unrelated to one another, then we would expect an essentially random interaction between expressing affect and saying words. The result would be a lagged function

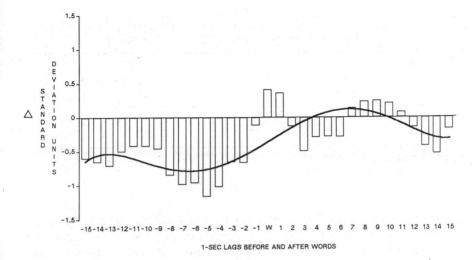

FIG. 2.   First words: Profile of emotional expression and saying words. (Difference in mean s.d. units from the baseline rate of emotional expression in 1-second lags.)

similar to baseline. However, if the content of a child's words and the feelings underlying the child's emotional expressions were about the same thing, as we might expect, then we should find words and emotionally toned affect expression tending to occur together, which is what we found. The expression of emotionally toned affect clustered around the words, but the resulting function had the shape of a sine wave. The critical features of the function were a dip in the frequency of affect expression at about 5 seconds before the word lag, with a steep rise through the word lag and a peak just after the word.

When the lagged functions are compared at FW and VS, the shape of the curves is essentially the same with two differences. The pre-word dip below baseline is steeper at FW, and the post-word peak above baseline is sharper at VS. The occurrence of emotional expression was below baseline in all 15 pre-word lags at FW, but in only 8 of the pre-word lags at VS. The means of the standard deviation units was used as a heuristic to statistically test the differences in relative area at FW and VS. The area beneath the curve *below* baseline before the word lag was significantly greater at FW ($M = 0.681$) than at VS ($M = 0.177$) ($t(28) = 5.286$, $P < 0.001$). Looking at the 5 lags in the centre of each graph, i.e. the word lag with the 2 pre-word and the 2 post-word lags, the area beneath the curve *above* baseline is significantly greater at VS ($M = 0.889$) than at FW ($M = 0.156$) ($t(8) = -2.306$, $P < 0.05$). These differences are consistent with the results of the analysis of the overlap of time spent in speech and emotional expression

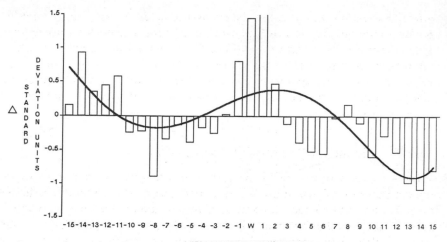

FIG. 3.   Vocabulary spurt: Profile of emotional expression and saying words. (Difference in mean s.d. units from the baseline rate of emotional expression in 1-second lags.)

which revealed the development that occurred between FW and VS in the integration of affect and word expression. The remaining analyses considered the factors at VS that contributed to this development: the effects of (a) affect valence and (b) the words the children were learning.

The Valence of Words said with Emotional Affect

The words that these infants said with emotional expression at VS were said with positive valence primarily. Time (number of coded frames) spent speaking, not speaking, expressing positive affect, and expressing negative affect at VS is presented in Table 2. Time spent in speech with positive

TABLE 2
Time (No. of Frames) Speaking and Not Speaking with Positive and Negative Affect Expression at VS, (n = 12 children)

	Affect	
	Positive	Negative
Speaking	4277	545
Not speaking	70 347	13,579[a]

[a]Chi-square (1 d.f.) = 81.06, $P < 0.001$

affect expression was greater than was predicted by the time spent in positive affect expression overall, and time spent in speech with negative affect expression was less than was predicted by the time spent in negative affect expression overall, chi-square $= 81.06$, $P < 0.001$. Thus, the Facilitating Affect hypothesis was confirmed; if these infants expressed emotion and speech together, the emotion they expressed was more likely to be positive than negative.

The Words said with Emotion Expression

What were the words that these infants said when they were also expressing emotion? The Facilitating Words hypothesis was based on the assumption that the words the children said at the same time they expressed emotionally toned affect would be the words they knew best. To test the first hypothesis, that these words would be their most frequent words, each child's words were rank ordered according to their overall frequency (number of tokens) at VS. This rank order of overall frequency was compared with the rank order of frequency of words occurring with emotionally toned affect. The rank orders were counted as matching for an individual child when at least two of the three most frequent words overall were included among the four most frequent words said with emotional expression. The second hypothesis was that the words said with emotionally toned affect would have been among the children's earliest learned words. For this analysis, the words reported in the mothers' diaries, the children's words at FW, and words that were said in the interval between FW and VS were examined for the occurrence of those words said with emotionally toned affect at VS. The effects of frequency and previous occurrence for the individual children are presented in Table 3.

For the 12 children, 8 of the frequency rank orders matched; 1 (Robert) nearly matched (1 word, "Mommy"/"Mama" was ranked highest in both orders); and 3 rank orders did not match. For 8 of the children, 50% or more of the different words they said with emotionally toned affect at VS had occurred in their previous lexicons. Either frequency, previous occurrence, or both predicted which words were said together with emotional expression at VS for all the children except one, Vivian. These results mean that the words these children said with emotional expression tended to be the words they presumably knew well: Words that they said most frequently and/or words they had learned to say at an earlier time.

Included as words in the speech transcription were those words that have traditionally been considered most likely to carry emotional tone, e.g. the interjections such as "Oh" and "Uhoh" (Sapir, 1921). However, these interjections were not more likely than other words to occur with emotional expression. A total of 69 different words were said with emotional

TABLE 3
Frequency and Previous Occurrence of Words with Emotionally Toned Affect at VS
(m = months)

FREQUENCY[a]
Matching:
  8/12 children: Alvin, Charlie, Cory, Diana, Greta, Harry, Reggie, Shirley
Nearly matching:
  1 child: Robert
Not matching
  3/12 children: Clark, Jessica, Vivian

PREVIOUS OCCURRENCE[b]
More than 75%, 3/12 children:
  83%, Cory (6 m);[c] 82%, Clark (3 m); 80%, Robert (6 m)
50–75%, 5/12 children:
  64%, Jessica (11 m); 60%, Charlie; 57%, Shirley (3 m); 50%, Greta (7 m); 50%, Harry (5 m)
Less than 50%, 4/12 children:
  40%, Diana (5 m); 38%, Reggie (9 m); 29%, Alvin (9 m); 27%, Vivian (3 m)

[a]Matching rank orders of word frequency (tokens) overall and emotionally toned words at VS.
[b]Proportion of emotionally toned words (types) at VS which also occurred in previous lexicons.
[c]Interval between FW and VS in parentheses.

valence at VS by the group of 12 children as a whole. None of these words were names for emotional feelings. Most of the words (47, or 68%) were said by only one child and often only once (22 of the 47 words, or 47%). A small group of words were said with emotion by at least three of the children and these are listed in Table 4. Several of the words in Table 4 are among those that one might have expected would have inherent emotional connotation in addition to their referential meaning for young children. These were (a) the relational words frequently reported in infant vocabularies ("no" and "more"); (b) words typically associated with well-known routines ("Hi," and "Whee" when rolling the ball, using the slide, and the like); and (c) person words ("Mama" and its variants, and "Baby"). Both "Mama" and "Baby" were also said of the small rubber family figures. Of the words used by four or more children, only the highly routinised words "Hi" and "Whee" were said with emotionally toned affect primarily (90% and 79% of the total speech frames respectively).

Finally, in order to test the conclusion that words said with emotional expression tended to be among the children's earliest learned and most frequent words, lag sequential analyses were performed with these words excluded from the word lists at FW and VS. For this *post hoc* analysis, the deviation of each lag from baseline was divided by the maximum deviation

TABLE 4
The words said with Emotional Expression by 3 or more Children at VS
(n = 12 children)

Word	No. of Children	Word Frequency (Total Tokens)	Proportion of Total Speech Time (Frames)
baby	8	44	0.41
Mama	6	37	0.43
Hi	5	10	0.90
Whee	5	19	0.79
more	4	53	0.19
no	3	16	0.50
cow	3	45[a]	0.16
spoon	3	8	0.60
three	3	6	0.70
eye	3	4	0.67

[a]33 of these tokens spoken by one child, Charlie.

in the 31 1-second lags (before, during, and after the words) and the resulting profiles were averaged across children. At FW, the words excluded were (a) words reported earlier in the mothers' diaries (before the children said their first words in the playroom), and (b) the single most frequent word in each child's FW lexicon. The observed frequency of emotional expression at FW was below baseline in all but 2 of the 31 lags and, most importantly, neither of the 2 occurred before the word. At VS, words were excluded for the individual children (a) if they had occurred at FW or in mothers' diaries, and/or (b) their frequency at VS was 2 standard deviations or more above the mean for the frequency of words overall. At VS, when the most frequent and earliest learned words were excluded, the profiles for 10 of the 12 children had the same shape as the original VS profile in Fig. 3, but differed in amplitude for both the pre-word dip, which was steeper, and the post-word peak, which was not as high. Thus, the expression of emotion was particularly inhibited when these children said words that were not among their most frequent and earliest learned words and were, presumably, words that they knew less well.

DISCUSSION

We have asked, in this study, how the two systems of expression available to the 1-year-old child, affect and speech, relate to one another in the period of transition from infancy to language. The results we reported will be discussed in terms of (a) the allocation of cognitive resources for speech and emotional expression; (b) the language of emotion; and (c) the acquisition of language for expression.

Allocation of Cognitive Resources for Emotional Expression and Language

The major results of this study were as follows. At First Words, most of the children's words were said while they were expressing neutral affect, and the time spent in saying words with emotionally toned valence did not differ from what was expected, given the time spent in emotional expression overall. However, by the time they reached a Vocabularly Spurt, toward the end of the period of single-word speech, the children had integrated the two systems of expression. At VS, the time they spent saying words with overlapping emotional expression was greater than was predicted by the amount of time they spent in emotional expression overall.

The integration of the two systems of expression was influenced by several factors. One of these was emotional valence: Words at VS were more likely to be said with positive expression than with negative expression. Another was intensity: Words were more likely to be said with low intensity of emotional expression than with heightened intensity levels. Other factors having to do with the words the children were learning also contributed to the integration of affect expression and speech at VS. The words said at the same time that the children expressed emotion tended to be words that the children learned earliest, used most frequently, and/or they were person words (i.e. "Mama" and "baby") and parts of well-known play and other routines. These constraints on saying words together with the expression of emotion can be attributed to the different cognitive requirements that the two systems of expression entail. Positive emotion requires less cognitive work than the negative emotions. Earlier learned, more frequent words are presumably the words that children know best, with the result that they have greatest automaticity and relative ease of expression.

The suggestion has been made that words emerge as the socialised forms of infants' feeling states, particularly "anxiety" and "affective conflict" (Dore, 1983, p. 168). However, most of the words of the children whom we studied were said with neutral affect expression. When they did express emotion and words at the same time, it was with positive affect far more often than negative affect. Others have suggested that words emerge as the socialised forms of infants' affective vocalisations (e.g. Hilke, 1988). However, the fact that infants are able to integrate smiles with non-speech vocalisations by the time they are 8 months old, as Hilke has demonstrated, does not predict that words will just naturally follow. Expression through nonlexical vocalising before speech, and saying words once language begins, are not the same. They cannot be equated in terms of their relative cognitive cost to the young language learning child. Words are not effortless. At the minimum, infants need to adapt their own sounds to conform to those in the words they hear; identify sound–meaning correspondences in the language; and recall these correspondences to say a word. Thus, the ability to produce speech with emotional intonation is not innate. While the forms of emotional expression may themselves be innately determined, the ability to integrate these forms with speech is learned.

If the cognitive activity needed for saying words competes with the cognition required for the experience and expression of emotion, one result would be suppression of emotional expression at times of word learning and/or use. At a micro level, the results of the lag analyses showed such a suppression of emotionally toned affect approximately 5 seconds before the occurrence of a word. We are interpreting the pre-word dip below the baseline level of emotional expession (in Figs 2 and 3) as the time during which the mental activity associated with the expression of emotion is, essentially, suspended. This is the time the child uses for the cognitive work that recalling and saying a word involves. This effect was heightened for words that were relatively infrequent, learned most recently, and so, presumably, less well known. The lag analyses in Figs 2 and 3 also show that after the post-word peak in emotional expression, the expression of emotion once again dipped below baseline. Although we have not looked as yet at other events surrounding the children's words, we know that their mothers invariably responded to what they said. We speculate that this dip below baseline level of emotional expression in the post-word lags reflects an inhibition in emotional expression that can be attributed to the children's *listening* to their mothers' responses to what they themselves had just said.

The peak in affect expression comes after having said the word. At this time the child's cognitive resources are freed for the cognitive work that the experience and expression of emotion involves. Given that most of the children's emotional expression was positive, this burst of emotional expression just after a word is reminiscent of the smile of recognition observed with younger infants by McCall (1972) and Zelazo (1972), and smiles following mastery (Sroufe & Waters, 1976) or assimilation after "concentrated attention" (Kagan, Lapidus, & Moore, 1978). Thus, words and emotional expression were closely associated in time, but emotion was more likely to be expressed in the seconds immediately *after* a word.

The cognition required for the experience and expression of emotion could be expected to pre-empt the cognitive activity required for *learning* words as well. At a more macro level, we have reported elsewhere that more frequent expression of emotion did not enhance *early* language acquisition for the children in this study (Bloom & Capatides, 1987a).

Those children who expressed emotionally toned affect less often and, correspondingly, spent more time in neutral affect expression, reached achievements in language (first words, a vocabulary spurt, and the use of multi-word speech) earlier than the children who expressed emotion more frequently. A similar result for language acquisition has been reported as well by Epport (1987) and Nachman (1986). A related finding is that higher ratings by mothers of smiling and laughter at 8 and 12 months of age was correlated with lower developmental test scores (the mental development index of the Bayley Scales of Infant Development, which includes a number of measures relevant to language) in a study by Fagen, Singer, Ohr, & Fleckenstein (1987).

In addition, learning language appeared to have a stabilising effect on emotionality, which is a dimension of temperament. The early word learners in our study were more stable over time in their profiles of emotionality than were the later word learners (Bloom & Wikstrom, 1987). For example, all of the correlations (Pearson r) for time spent in positive affect expression at 9, 13, 17, and 21 months were significant ($P = 0.05$ or less) for the early word learners, and the ages 13, 17, and 21 months coincided fairly closely with their ages of language achievements. Stability was observed for the later word learners only between 17 and 21 months which was the time of their greatest language change in this period. Thus, in addition to the more local effects in the mutual influence between expression of affect and speech revealed in the present study, language development in the second year may, itself, have had a stabilising influence on emotional expression (Bloom et al., 1988a; Bloom & Wikstrom, 1987). Further research is needed to explore such covariation of developments in different domains in the second year (Connell & Furman, 1984; Dunn, 1986; Fogel & Thelen, 1987).

In sum, we propose that the different cognitive requirements for emotional expression and language compete for the young language-learning child's attentional resources. Competition for the resources required for (a) the experience and expression of emotion, and (b) expressing a word at the same time that articulates what the emotion is about, was reflected in the temporal relation between saying words and expressing emotional affect. While the expression of emotion is generally considered to be automatic and effortless, the children in this study did not, in fact, express emotion just before saying words.

The findings reported here are consistent with accounts in the neuropsychological literature concerning different hemispheric specialisation in the brain for language and emotion. Separation of functions in the different hemispheres of the brain results in a competition for attention and activation when tasks require both functions (Kinsbourne, 1975). We have proposed that saying words with emotionally toned valence is such a task that is particularly difficult for the young language-learning child, especially given the relatively immature status of the late-maturing corpus callosum. The question of integrating the results of separate processing by the two hemispheres of the brain was raised by Tucker (1986) who suggested that "lateralized contributions to communication . . . may develop before the child has the capacity to coordinate them" (p. 273). However, we expect that the effects we observed are not limited to the earliest stages of language learning. Older children and even adults may well experience the same competition between the two systems of expression for cognitive resources, at times when the experience of emotion is particularly heightened and/or the content of speech is particularly abstract, complex, or obscure.

The Language of Emotion

The children in this study learned words that could express what their feelings were about in this period of time before they learned the actual names for the emotions themselves. Acquisition of words for naming emotions and feeling states is a relatively late development (Beckwith, 1989), even in cultures, such as Samoa, where talk between children and their mothers is "intensely emotional" (Ochs, 1986, p. 252). Reports in the literature of the "early" use of emotion words by English-speaking children have not been observational but have relied instead on mothers' reports of whether such words occur at all, through the use of checklists The youngest children in these studies have generally not been less than 20 months old (e.g. Bretherton, Fritz, Zahn-Wexler, & Ridgeway, 1986).

Similarly, the mothers of the children whom we studied used emotion words very infrequently when talking in the moments that surrounded their children's emotional expression. Instead, they talked about the situations that were the causes, consequences, and circumstances of their children's emotional expressions (Capatides, 1989). When the mothers' speech before and after each affect expression by the child was examined, the names for the emotions (e.g. "happy", "mad",) were rare and actually decreased in frequency in the period from 9 to 21 months. The mean number of emotion word tokens for the 12 mothers, in 30-minute observations, was 2.5, 1.17, 0.83, 0.5 at 9, 13, 17, and 21 months respectively. In fact, these frequencies include the most frequent affect word the mothers used, "like", which may have marginal status as an emotion term. Mothers' conversations about "feeling states" have been described by Dunn, Bretherton, & Munn (1987) for children in the same age range. In the list of "feeling-state labels" that the mothers in their study used, "emotional states" was one of three categories (along with "quality of consciousness" and "sensations and physiological states"). Similarly, the number of names of emotions in the category of "emotional states" was extremely small and most of the words the mothers used in this category (e.g. "enjoy", "mind", "temper", "laugh", and the like) were *not* emotion terms, for example, in the sense described by Clore and Ortony (1987). In any event, the mean number of mother utterances referring to *any* of the three categories of feeling states in their study, pro-rated for 30 minutes for the sake of comparison, was 1.75 and 2.75 at 18 months and 24 months respectively.

In sum, children's early words in the second year of life do not name their emotions and so they cannot *tell* us what they are feeling. Rather, they continue to rely on expression of emotion through facial and postural displays of affect while the words they are learning express what their feelings are about. Moreover, the language that 1-year-old children hear instructs them in the sorts of experiences that are associated with different feeling states, more often than it provides labels for the emotions themselves (Capatides, 1989; Dunn et al., 1987).

The Acquisition of Language for Expression

In the present study, the two forms of expression, affect and speech, occurred closely in time. We can assume, then, that the words these children were learning in this period were words for expressing something of the objects and circumstances of their emotional experience. This result supports the proposal that words are learned to express what the young child has in mind: The contents of attention and feeling states. Children learn language for expression rather than as an instrument for getting things done in the world (Bloom & Beckwith, 1988). To be sure, young children's words influence what other persons do, but that effect is subordinate to the expressive power that the infant achieves through language. The power of expression comes with the ability to take something that is hidden within the individual and make it manifest, to put it in a public place (Taylor, 1979). Hidden within the individual are the contents of feelings, beliefs, and desires. Affect and language are two modes of expression that allow us to attribute such internal properties to the expressor. Affect can express how the infant feels about such mental contents. By learning language, the infant comes to express and articulate *what these contents are* and to attribute such contents to others.

Cognitive theories of emotion stress the importance of goals and plans, and changes in the environment that influence success or interfere with an individual's goals or plans. If these are the facts that produce emotional experience (e.g. Oatley, 1988) and underlie knowledge about what emotions are (e.g. Stein & Levine, 1989), then learning to talk about such items of experience is at least as important as learning the emotion terms themselves. In fact, to the extent that the infant's facial expression and postural displays of emotion are available to others, emotion terms would be more redundant than informative. We have already shown in other research that expression having to do with subjective, emotion-eliciting events contributes to how children learn the language of causality (Bloom & Capatides, 1987b; Hood & Bloom, 1979). Children begin to talk about the causal connections entailed in emotional experience even before they learn such linguistic terms for causality as "because", "so", and "why". Similarly, the children in the present study learned the language for expressing the causes and objects of their emotion, which had to do, no doubt, with the success or failure of their goals and plans, before they even began to acquire a lexicon of emotion terms.

While the feeling state itself is not expressed with words, at least part of the contents attributable to the expression of affect in the first year is now made manifest with words in the second year. But, in addition, as children approach the second year of life, all that they have learned about objects, persons, and the self inform their beliefs and desires, and these cannot be expressed by affect alone. Other modes of expression are required. Waiting in the wings, so to speak, is language. Language is the pre-eminent mode of expression and is provided by society and culture for making manifest and public that which is internal to the individual. The infant's cognitive, social, and biological resources are soon bent to the task of its acquisition.

Language does not replace affect expression and children continue to express their feelings through affect as they learn language (Bloom et al., 1988b). Indeed, with further development, they will also become aware of new and different feeling states that require increasingly more subtle and controlled forms of expression. These include the more socially and personally complex emotions (for example, jealousy, guilt, and shame). Language can express many aspects of the objects, circumstances, and feelings associated with the more complex emotions, but by no means all their aspects. For this reason, the integration of affect and language will continue to develop for expression in the increasingly wider contexts of the child's development.

Manuscript received 7 February 1989
Manuscript revised 24 March 1989

REFERENCES

Adamson, L. & Bakeman, R. (1982). Affectivity and reference: Concepts, methods, and techniques in the study of 6- to 18-month old infants. In T. Field, & A. Fogel (Eds), *Emotion and early interaction*. Hillsdale, N.J.: Lawrence Erlbaum Associates Inc.

Adamson, L. & Bakeman, R. (1985). Affect and attention: Infants observed with mothers and peers. *Child Development*, *56*, 582–593.

Bakeman, R. (1978). Untangling streams of behavior: Sequential analyses of observational data. In G. Sackett (Ed.), *Observing behavior*, Vol. II. *Data collection and analysis methods*. Baltimore, MD: University Park, pp. 63–78.

Beckwith, R. (1989). The language of emotion, the emotions, and nominalist bootstrapping. In C. Moore & D. Frye (Eds), *Children's theories of minds*. Hillsdale, N.J.: Lawrence Erlbaum Associates Inc.

Berndt, R., Caramazza, A., & Zurif, E. (1983). Language functions: Syntax and semantics. In S. Segalowitz (Ed.), *Language functions and brain organisation*. New York: Academic Press, pp. 5–28.

Best, C. (1988). The emergence of cerebral asymmetries in early human development: A literature review and a neuroembryological model. In S. Segalowitz & D. Molfese (Eds), *Brain lateralization in children: Developmental implications*. New York: Guilford Press, pp. 5–34.

Best, C. & Queen, H. (1989). Baby, it's in your smile: Right hemisphere bias in infant emotional expressions. *Developmental Psychology*, *25*, 264–276.

Bloom, L. (1973). *One word at a time*. The Hague: Mouton.

Bloom, L. & Capatides, J. (1987a). Expression of affect and the emergence of language. *Child Development*, *58*, 1513–1522.

Bloom, L. & Capatides, J. (1987b). Sources of meaning in complex syntax: The sample case of causality. *Journal of Experimental Child Psychology*, *43*, 112–128.

Bloom, L. & Wikstrom, P. (1987, July). *The role of temperament in language development*. Paper presented at the meeting of the International Congress for the Study of Child Language, Lund, Sweden.

Bloom, L. & Beckwith, R. (1988). Intentionality and language development. Unpublished manuscript.

Bloom, L., Beckwith, R., Capatides, J., & Hafitz, J. (1988b). Expression through affect and words in the transition from infancy to language. In P. Baltes, D. Featherman, & R. Lerner (Eds), *Life span development and behavior, Vol. 8*. Hillsdale, N.J.: Lawrence Erlbaum Associates Inc., pp. 99–127.

Bloom, L., Beckwith, R. & Capatides, J. (1988b). Developments in the expression of affect. *Infant Behavior and Development*, *11*, 169–186.

Blumstein, S. & Cooper, W. (1974). Hemispheric processing of intonation contours. *Cortex*, *10*, 146–158.

Borod, J. & Koff, E. (1989). The neuropsychology of emotion: Evidence from normal, neurological, and psychiatric populations. In E. Perecman (Ed.), *Integrating theory and practice in clinical neuropsychology*. New York: The IRBN Press and Lawrence Erlbaum Associates Inc.

Bretherton, I. & Beeghly, M. (1982). Talking about internal states: The acquisition of an explicit theory of mind. *Developmental Psychology*, *18*, 906–921.

Bretherton, I., Fritz, J., Zahn-Wexler, C., & Ridgeway, C. (1986). Learning to talk about emotions: A functionalist perspective. *Child Development*, *57*, 529–548.

Camras, L. (1985). Socialization of affect communication. In M. Lewis & C. Saarni (Eds), *The socialization of the emotions*. New York: Plenum, pp. 141–160.

Capatides, J. (1989). *Mothers' socialization of their children's affect expression*. Ph.D. dissertation, Columbia University.

Clore, G. & Ortony, A. (1987). The semantics of the affective lexicon. In V. Hamilton, G. Bower, & N. Frijda (Eds), *Cognitive perspectives on emotion and motivation* Dordrecht: Kluwer, pp. 367–397.

Cohen, J. (1960). A coefficient of agreement for nominal scales. *Educational and Psychological Measurement*, *20*, 37–46.

Connell, J. & Furman, W. (1984). The study of transitions: Conceptual and methodological issues. In R. Emde & R. Harmon (Eds), *Continuities and discontinuities in development*. New York: Plenum, pp. 153–173.

Corrigan, R. (1978). Language development as related to stage 6 object permanence development. *Journal of Child Language*, 5, 173–189.

Davidson, R. & Fox, N. (1982). Asymmetrical brain activity discriminates between positive and negative affective stimuli in human infants. *Science*, *218*, 1235–1237.

Davitz, J. (1964). *The communication of emotional meaning*. New York: McGraw-Hill.

Davitz, J. (1969). *The language of emotion*. New York: Academic Press.

Dore, J. (1983). Feeling, form, and intention in the baby's transition to language. In R. Golinkoff (Ed.), *The transition from prelinguistic to linguistic communication*. Hillsdale, N.J.: Lawrence Erlbaum Associates Inc, pp. 167–190.

Dunn, J. (1986). Commentary: Issues for future research. In R. Plomin & J. Dunn (Eds), *The study of temperament: Changes, continuities and challenges*. Hillsdale, N.J.: Lawrence Erlbaum Associates Inc, pp. 163–171.

Dunn, J., Bretherton, I., & Munn, P. (1987). Conversations about feeling states between mothers and their young children. *Developmental Psychology*, *23*, 132–139.

Ekman, P. & Friesen, W. (1975). *Unmasking the face: A guide to recognizing emotions from facial cues*. Palo Alto, CA: Consulting Psychologists Press.

Emde, R., Gaensbauer, T., & Harmon, R. (1976). *Emotional expression in infancy*. New York: International Universities Press.

Epport, K. (1987). *The relationship between facial affect expressiveness and language ability in children born preterm and "at-risk"*. Ph.D. Dissertation, University of California, Los Angeles.

Fagen, J., Singer, J., Ohr, P., & Fleckenstein, L. (1987). Infant temperament and performance on the Bayley Scales of Infant Development at 4, 8, and 12 months of age. *Infant Behavior and Development*, *10*, 505–512.

Fischer, K., Pipp, S., & Bullock, D. (1984). Detecting discontinuities in development: Method and measurement. In R. Emde & R. Harmon (Eds), *Continuities and discontinuities in development*. New York: Plenum, pp. 95–121.

Fogel, A. & Thelen, E. (1987). Development of early expressive and communicative action: Reinterpreting the evidence from a dynamic systems perspective. *Developmental Psychology*, *23*, 747–761.

Frijda, N. (1986). *The emotions*. Cambridge University Press.

Gopnik, A. & Meltzoff, A. (1987). The development of categorization in the second year and its relation to other cognitive and linguistic developments. *Child Development*, *58*, 1523–1531.

Hilke, D. (1988). Infant vocalizations and changes in experience. *Journal of Child Language*, *15*, 1–15.

Hood, L. & Bloom, L. (1979). What, when, and how about why: A longitudinal study of early expressions of causality. *Monographs of the Society for Research in Child Development*, *44*, No. 6.

Izard, C. (1977). *Human emotions*. New York: Plenum.

Izard, C. (1986). Approaches to developmental research on emotion-cognitive relationships. In D. Bearison & H. Zimiles (Eds), *Thought and emotion: Developmental perspectives*. Hillsdale, N.J.: Lawrence Erlbaum Associates Inc, pp. 21–37.

Izard, C. & Malatesta, C. (1987). Perspectives on emotional development I: Differential emotions theory of early emotional development. In J. Osofsky (Ed.), *Handbook of infant development* (2nd edn). New York: John Wiley, pp. 494–554.

Kagan, J., Lapidus, D., & Moore, M. (1978). Infant antecedents of cognitive functioning. *Child Development*, *49*, 1005–1023.

Kent, R. (1984). Brain mechanisms of speech and language with special reference to emotional interactions. In R. Naremore (Ed.), *Language science. Recent advances.* San Diego: College-Hill Press, pp. 281–383.

Kinsbourne, M. (1975). The mechanism of hemispheric control of the lateral gradient of attention. In P. Rabbitt & S. Dornic (Eds), *Attention and performance, Vol. 5.* New York: Academic Press, pp. 81–97.

Kinsbourne, M. (1988). A model of adaptive behavior related to cerebral participation in emotional control. In G. Gainotti (Ed.), *Emotions and the dual brain.* New York: Springer.

Kinsbourne, M. & Bemporad, E. (1984). Lateralization of emotion: A model and the evidence. In Fox, N. & Davidson, R. (Eds), *The psychobiology of affective development.* Hillsdale, N.J.: Lawrence Erlbaum Associates Inc, pp. 259–281.

Kirk, U. (1985). Hemispheric contributions to the development of graphic skill. In C. Best (Ed.), *Hemispheric function and collaboration in the child.* New York: Academic Press, pp. 193–228.

Lewis, M. & Michalson, L. (1985). Faces as signs and symbols. In Zivin, G. (Ed.), *The development of expressive behavior: Biology–environment interactions.* New York: Academic Press, pp. 153–180.

Levine, S. (1985). Developmental changes in right-hemisphere involvement in face recognition. In C. Best (Ed.), *Hemispheric function and collaboration in the child.* New York: Academic Press, pp. 157–191.

Levy, J. (1969). Possible basis for the evolution of lateral specialization of the human brain. *Nature, 224,* 614–615.

Levy, J. (1985). Interhemispheric collaboration: Single-mindedness in the asymmetric brain. In C. Best (Ed.), *Hemispheric function and collaboration in the child.* New York: Academic Press, pp. 11–31.

Lifter, K. & Bloom, L. (1989). Object knowledge and the emergence of language. *Infant Behavior and Development, 12.*

Malatesta, C. (1981). Infant emotion and the vocal affect lexicon. *Motivation and Emotion, 5,* 1–23.

McCall, R. (1972). Smiling and vocalization in infants as indices of perceptual-cognitive processes. *Merrill-Palmer Quarterly, 18,* 341–347.

Molfese, D., Freeman, R., & Palermo, D. (1975). The ontogeny of brain lateralization for speech and nonspeech stimuli. *Brain and Language, 2,* 356–368.

Molfese, V., Molfese, D., & Parsons, C. (1983). Hemisphere processing of phonological information. In S. Segalowitz (Ed.), *Language functions and brain organization.* New York: Academic Press, pp. 29–49.

Nachman, P. (1986). *A comparison of toddlers cared for by mothers and substitute caregivers at the Margaret S. Mahler Research Nursery.* Paper presented at the Meetings of the San Francisco Psychoanalytic Institute, San Francisco, September.

Nelson, K. (1973). Structure and strategy in learning to talk. *Monographs of the Society for Research in Child Development, 38,* No. 149.

Oatley, K. (1988). Plans and the communicative function of emotion. In V. Hamilton, G. Bower, & N. Frijda (Eds), *Cognitive perspectives on emotion and motivation.* Dordrecht: Kluwer, pp. 345–364.

Oatley, K. & Johnson-Laird, P. (1987). Towards a cognitive theory of emotions. *Cognition and Emotion, 1,* 29–50.

Ochs, E. (1986). From feelings to grammar: A Samoan case study. In B. Schieffelin, & E. Ochs (Eds), *Language socialization across cultures.* Cambridge University Press, pp. 251–272.

Ochs, E. & Schieffelin, B. (1989). Language has a heart. *Text, 9,* 7–25.

Piaget, J. (1954/1981). *Intelligence and affectivity: Their relationship during child development* (T. Brown & C. Kaegi, Trans.). Palo Alto, CA: Annual Reviews Inc.

Ricciuti, H. & Poresky, R. (1972). Emotional behavior and development in the first year of life: An analysis of arousal, approach-withdrawal, and affective responses. In A. Pick (Ed.), *Minnesota symposium on child psychology, Vol. 6.* University of Minnesota Press, pp. 69–96.

Ridgeway, D., Waters, E., & Kuczaj, S. (1985). Acquisition of emotion-descriptive language: Receptive and productive vocabulary norms for ages 18 months to 6 years. *Developmental Psychology, 21,* 901–908.

Rothbart, M. (1973). Laughter in young children. *Psychological Bulletin, 80,* 247–256.

Ross, E. (1985). Modulation of affect and nonverbal communication by the right hemisphere. In M-M. Mesulam (Ed.), *Principles of behavioral neurology.* Philadelphia: F. A. Davis, pp. 239–257.

Sackett, G. (1974). *A nonparametric lag sequential analysis for studying dependency among responses in behavioral observation scoring systems.* Unpublished paper presented to the Western Psychological Association, San Francisco.

Sackett, G. (1979). The lag sequential analysis of contingency and cyclicity in behavioral interaction research. In Osofsky, J. (Ed.), *Handbook of infant development.* New York: John Wiley, pp. 623–649.

Sackheim, H. & Gur, R. (1978). Lateral asymmetry in intensity of emotional expression. *Neuropsychologia, 16,* 473–481.

Sapir, E. (1921). *Language.* New York: Harcourt, Brace.

Scherer, K. (1984). On the nature and function of emotion: A component process approach. In K. Scherer & P. Ekman (Eds), *Approaches to emotion.* Hillsdale, N.J.: Lawrence Erlbaum Associates Inc, 293–318.

Scherer, K. (1986). Vocal affect expression: A review and a model for future research. *Psychological Bulletin, 99,* 143–165.

Schlosberg, H. (1954). Three dimensions of emotion. *Psychological Review, 61,* 81–88.

Schwartz, G., Ahern, G., & Brown, S. (1979). Lateralized facial muscle response to positive and negative emotional stimuli. *Psychophysiology, 16,* 561–571.

Sroufe, A. & Waters, E. (1976). The ontogenesis of smiling and laughter: A perspective on the organization of development in infancy. *Psychological Review, 83,* 173–189.

Stechler, G. & Carpenter, G. (1967). A viewpoint on early affective development. In J. Hellmuth (Ed.), *Exceptional infant: The normal infant, Vol. 1.* Seattle: Special Child Publications, pp 164–189.

Stein, N. & Jewett, J. (1987). A conceptual analysis of the meaning of basic negative emotions: Implications for a theory of development. In C. Izard & P. Read (Eds), *Measurement of emotion in infants and children, Vol. 2.* Cambridge University Press, pp. 238–267.

Stein, N. & Levine, L. (1987). Thinking about feelings: The development and origins of emotional knowledge. In R. Snow & M. Farr (Eds.), *Aptitude, learning, and instruction.* Vol. 3, *Cognition, conation, and affect.* Hillsdale, N.J.: Lawrence Erlbaum Associates Inc, pp. 165–197.

Stein, N. & Levine, L. (1989). The development of the knowledge of emotions. *Cognition and Emotion, 3*(4), 343–378.

Stern, D. (1977). *The first relationship.* Cambridge Mass.: Harvard University Press.

Stern, D., Barnett, R., & Spieker, S. (1983). Early transmission of affect: Some research issues. In J. Call, E. Galenson, & R. Tyson (Eds), *Frontiers of infant psychiatry.* New York: Basic Books, pp. 74–84.

Stern, C. & Stern, W. (1907). *Die Kindersprache.* Leipzig: Barth.

Taylor, C. (1979). Action as expression. In C. Diamond & J. Teichman (Eds), *Intention and intentionality, Essays in honor of G.E.M. Anscombe.* Ithaca, NY: Cornell University Press, pp. 73–89.

Tucker, D. (1986). Neural control of emotional communication. In P. Blanck, R. Buck, &

R. Rosenthal (Eds), *Nonverbal communication in the clinical context*. University Park, PA: Pennsylvania State University Press, pp. 258–307.

Tucker, D. & Frederick, S. (1989). Emotion and brain lateralization. In H. Wagner, & T. Manstead (Eds), *Handbook of psychophysiology: Emotion and social behavior*. New York: John Wiley.

Witelson, S. (1987). Neurobiological aspects of language in children. *Child Development*, *58*, 653–688.

Wozniak, R. (1986). Notes toward a co-constructive theory of the emotion-cognition relationship. In D. Bearison & H. Zimiles (Eds), *Thought and emotion: Developmental perspectives*. Hillsdale, N.J.: Lawrence Erlbaum Associates Inc, pp. 39–64.

Young, P. (1959). The role of affective processes in learning and motivation. *Psychological Review*, *66*, 104–125.

Yakovlev, P. & Lecours, A. (1967). The myelogenetic cycles of regional maturation of the brain. In A. Minkowski (Ed.), *Regional development of the brain in early life*. Oxford: Blackwell, pp. 3–70.

Zelazo, P. (1972). Smiling and vocalizing: A cognitive emphasis. *Merrill-Palmer Quarterly*, *18*, 349–365.

COGNITION AND EMOTION, 1989, 3(4), 343–378

The Causal Organisation of Emotional Knowledge: A Developmental Study

Nancy L. Stein and Linda J. Levine

Department of Behavioral Sciences, University of Chicago, U.S.A.

Using a theory of emotional understanding, the basis for distinguishing among happiness, anger, and sadness was investigated. Three- and six-year-old children and adults predicted and explained people's emotional responses to different types of events. The events varied as to whether a person's goal was to attain or to avoid a state, whether the goal was achieved or not, who or what was responsible for success or failure, and whether the outcome was intentional or accidental. For all groups, the attainment and maintenance of goals was the primary focus of explanations for emotions and for the plans that followed emotions. A distinct set of features was used to infer and explain happiness as opposed to anger and sadness. Happiness was elicited by goal success and was followed by plans to maintain or enjoy current goal states. Anger and sadness were elicited by goal failure and were followed by plans to reinstate, replace, or forfeit goals. Anger occurred more frequently than sadness when an aversive rather than a loss state occurred, when an animate agent rather than a natural event caused a negative outcome, and when attention was focused on the cause rather than the consequence of goal failure. Two dimensions associated with anger changed as a function of age. First grade children, and adults were more likely than preschool children to predict anger in response to intentional

---

Requests for reprints should be sent to Nancy L. Stein, Department of Psychology, University of Chicago, 5848 University Avenue, Chicago, Illinois 60637, U.S.A.

This research was supported in part by a Spencer Seed Grant and a Biomedical Research Grant to the first author and in part by a fellowship from the Center for Developmental Studies at the University of Chicago and by a National Institute of Child Health and Human Development Predoctoral Trainee award to the second author. The writing of the paper was also supported by a grant from the National Science Foundation, BSN-8206304, to the Center for Advanced Study in the Behavioral Sciences.

We would like to thank Linda Camras, Hillel Einhorn, Susan Goldin-Meadow, Janellen Huttenlocher, Cal Izard, James Stigler, and Thomas Trabasso for their comments on an earlier draft of this paper. A special thanks also to Lois Bloom, Susan Folkman, and Jim Russell for insightful discussions and supportive commentaries. We would also like to thank Craig Berresford, Mitchell Dunieir, Michelle Parker, and Michael Gorman for assisting in data collection and analysis.

© 1989 Lawrence Erlbaum Associates Limited

harm, and their explanations for anger were more likely to refer to the agent or cause of goal failure. For all age groups, however, the majority of subjects responded to aversive situations with anger responses, independent of the causal conditions that produced the aversive state. The results therefore indicate that anger can be produced without intentional harm, but that intentional harm becomes an important dimension in attributing anger, especially as a function of development.

INTRODUCTION

The present study was designed to assess the development of knowledge about emotion. We had three distinct goals in carrying out this research. First, we wanted to examine the similarities and differences in the ways in which young children and adults understand happiness, anger, and sadness. Secondly, we wanted to determine the degree to which knowledge about emotion corresponds to our theoretical analysis of emotional experience (Stein & Jewett, 1986; Stein & Levine, 1987; 1990). Thirdly, we wanted to compare our analyses of happiness, anger, and sadness to those of other researchers (Averill, 1979; Dahl, 1979; Oatley & Johnson-Laird, 1987; Roseman, 1979; 1984; Scherer, 1984; Shaver, Schwartz, O'Connor, & Kirson, 1987; Weiner, 1985).

Over the past 10 years, a consistent set of findings has emerged regarding the development of children's knowledge about emotion. In the second and third years of life, children begin to refer to many aspects of internal states (Bretherton & Beeghley, 1982; Bretherton, Fritz, Zahn-Waxler, & Ridgeway, 1986; Dunn, Bretherton, & Munn, 1987), especially changing states of consciousness (e.g. sleepy, tired, bored) and changing physiological and sensory states (e.g. states of pleasure-displeasure, pain, distress, and temperature change). Studies by Huttenlocher and Smiley (1990; Huttenlocher, Smiley, & Charney, 1983; Smiley & Huttenlocher, 1989) corroborate these findings, further indicating that at about $2\frac{1}{2}$ years, children begin to describe other people as subjects of experience, and they begin to understand that other people have internal states similar to their own (Huttenlocher & Smiley, 1990; Huttenlocher et al., 1983).

Given that children are rapidly developing concepts of self and person during the third and fourth years of life, an understanding of emotion concepts should develop along with this social knowledge. Specifically, the beginning of the fourth year appears to be a time when children learn to distinguish among various emotion terms and express their knowledge about different emotion states. Recent studies by Russell and Bullock (1986; Bullock & Russell, 1985) have shown that 3-year-olds can differentiate happy, mad, and scared faces from one another. Trabasso, Stein, and Johnson (1981) have also shown that 3-year-olds can differentiate the causes and consequences of happiness from those of negative emotions and that they can distinguish the causes of fear from those of anger and sadness. The only emotion terms having any causal overlap were anger and sadness, with children generating similar causes and outcomes for both emotions (also see Borke, 1971).

These findings set the stage for further examination of children's understanding of emotion. Although we know that 3- and 4-year-old children make distinctions between a small set of emotion terms, we have yet to describe the bases upon which these distinctions are made. To provide a more detailed analysis, a theory is needed that would explain how knowledge about emotion is organised, how emotions are differentiated from one another, and how people use knowledge about emotion to understand and predict behaviour in social and personal situations.

Several researchers have formulated cognitive models of emotional experience that can be used to guide the study of emotional understanding (Averill, 1979; Frijda, 1987; Mandler, 1975, 1984; Lazarus & Folkman, 1984; Oatley & Johnson-Laird, 1987; Roseman, 1979, 1984; Scherer, 1984; Shaver et al., 1987; Stein & Jewett, 1986; Stein & Levine, 1987, 1990; Stein & Trabasso, 1989; Weiner, 1985). Although differences are bound to exist between understanding and experiencing an emotion (Russell, 1987), a high degree of similarity should also characterise the two processes. When attempting to understand others' emotions, people often draw on their own experience as well as their knowledge of others (Karniol, 1982; Kahneman & Tversky, 1982; Thompson, 1987a&b; Trope, 1982). Moreover, the understanding and experience of emotion both involve an assessment of the conditions that produce emotion and the plans and behaviour that follow emotion (Lazarus & Smith, 1988; Stein & Trabasso, 1982; 1989; Trabasso et al., 1981). Therefore, the general structure and content of knowledge about emotion should be similar when experiencing and/or understanding an emotion episode.

The present study uses theoretical analyses of emotional experience to generate specific hypotheses about the development of emotional understanding. Although most models use an adult standard for describing emotional experience, several analyses (Oatley & Johnson-Laird, 1987; Roseman, 1979, 1984; Scherer, 1984; Shaver et al., 1987; Stein & Jewett, 1986; Stein & Levine, 1987, 1990) describe the specific knowledge that is used to appraise and respond to an emotion-eliciting event. By using these analyses to identify the dimensions necessary to evoke an emotion, children's understanding of different emotions can be compared and contrasted to that of adults.

Almost all current cognitive models of emotional experience hold that emotions are intimately related to a person's goals and values. Emotional responses are thought to occur when a person detects a change in his or her ability to attain or maintain a valued state (Arnold, 1960; Frijda, 1987;

Mandler, 1975, 1984; Lazarus & Folkman, 1984; Roseman, 1979, 1984; Scherer, 1984; Shaver et al., 1987; Stein & Jewett, 1986; Stein & Levine, 1987, 1990; Stein & Trabasso, 1989; Weiner, 1985). An emotion is evidence that attention has focused on the change, that an evaluation has been made about how the change has affected, or will affect, the status of a valued state, and that some plan will be constructed to cope with the change (Frijda, 1987; Oatley & Johnson-Laird, 1987; Roseman, 1984; Stein & Jewett, 1986; Stein & Levine, 1987, 1990; Stein & Trabasso, 1989).

If understanding of emotional experience corresponds to the process of experiencing an emotion, then knowledge of an emotion-eliciting event should reflect an awareness of: (1) the valued state that has undergone, or may undergo, a change; (2) the conditions that caused the change; (3) the consequences of the change for goal maintenance or attainment; (4) the wishes to maintain or change the new status of a goal; and (4) the plans available for maintaining, reinstating, or abandoning a goal. To illustrate how these dimensions might underlie emotional understanding and allow for differentiation among emotions, we refer primarily to the model developed by Stein and Levine (1987, 1990). However, we point out the similarities and differences between Stein and Levine's model and those of other researchers, focusing on the analyses of happiness, anger, and sadness.

According to Stein and Levine (1987), as well as other investigators (Frijda, 1987; Oatley & Johnson-Laird, 1987; Roseman, 1979, 1984; Shaver et al., 1987), happiness can be distinguished from anger and sadness by the combination of goals and outcomes that result when changes are detected in the ability to maintain or attain valued states. Happiness is experienced when either of the following sets of conditions result: (1) a person attains or maintains a desired state; or (2) a person leaves or avoids an undesirable state. In other words, happiness occurs when people are able to attain what they want or avoid what they do not want. In contrast, anger and/or sadness occur when either of the following sets of conditions result: (1) a person fails to attain or maintain a desired state; or (2) a person fails to leave or avoid an undesirable state. These two types of goal failure will be referred to as "loss states" and "aversive states" respectively. Goal failure versus achievement, then, are the predominant features that distinguish happiness from anger and sadness in most cognitive models of emotional experience.

Because anger and sadness both result from goal failure, two dimensions are necessary to distinguish between them: (1) the focus of attention once goal failure has occurred; and (2) inferences made about the possibility of goal reinstatement. Stein and Levine (1987, 1990) point out that when people experience either anger or sadness, they are typically aware of both the changes that have occurred with respect to their goals and the event that produced these changes. The expression of anger, however, indicates that a person has focused on the conditions that caused failure, whereas sadness indicates that a person has focused on the consequences or implications of failure. Evidence for this assertion was provided in a study by Stein and Jewett (1986). Six-year-old children, explaining why they would feel angry as opposed to sad, focused more on the agent who caused failure. They also generated more plans to remove the agent as a source of harm. Children explaining why they would feel sad focused more on the consequences of failure, and generated more plans to abandon the original goal.

Specific properties of the event that cause goal failure are expected to influence whether people focus on the causes or the consequences of goal failure (Heider, 1958; Stein & Jewett, 1986; Stein & Levine, 1987; Weiner, 1985). When a person's goal has been thwarted, an immediate concern is to assess the possibility of reinstating the original goal state. If a human agent obstructed a person's goal, then attention is likely to focus on the agent in order to evaluate, stop, or change the obstructive behaviour and reinstate the goal (Hart & Honere, 1959; Heider, 1958; Stein & Jewett, 1986; Stein & Levine, 1987; Weiner, 1985). When attention is directed toward an agent or the conditions responsible for goal failure, then anger is predicted.

The intent of the agent carrying out a harmful act is also expected to influence the focus of attention once goal failure occurs. Agents who intend harm have control over their actions and may continue them or obstruct other goals. If the possibility exists of changing the agent's behaviour, thereby reinstating the goal, then anger should be evoked. Even if permanent harm has occurred, anger may still be evoked if attention shifts to a new goal that the injured party may be able to reinstate. For example, once the agent becomes the target of concern, attention may be directed towards assessing whether standards for interpersonal conduct have been violated (Roseman, 1984; Scherer, 1984; Shaver et al., 1987; Stein & Levine, 1987, 1990). If an agent has violated these standards, then anger may be expressed in the service of changing the agent's behaviour in future social interactions.

A critical question regarding the causes of anger, however, concerns the necessity of having an agent intentionally harm a victim. Several investigators (e.g. Averill, 1979; Ortony, Clore, & Collins, 1988; Roseman, 1979; Weiner, 1985) contend that people get angry only when they infer that someone intended to harm them or when they anthropomorphise an object and attribute harmful intentions to it. According to this view, when harm is caused accidentally, or by a natural event, sadness should predominate.

Stein and Levine (1987, 1990), as well as others (Oatley & Johnson-Laird, 1987; Shaver et al., 1987), however, do not consider intentional harm to be a prerequisite for anger. The essential component regulating anger is a belief that an obstructed goal can somehow be reinstated (Oatley & Johnson-Laird, 1987; Stein & Levine, 1987, 1990). Moreover, the emotional reaction to accidental harm or harm brought about by a natural event is thought to be governed by inferences made about the availability of a plan. Anger should be expressed in those situations where subjects believe that they can reinstate the original goal, even when a natural event obstructed goal attainment. Sadness should be evoked if the person infers that goal reinstatement is not possible, and if the person's attention does not shift to a related goal that can be reinstated.

By manipulating the presence or absence of intentional harm, as well as the presence or absence of an animate agent, we should be able to test the conditions necessary for evoking anger. Moreover, by varying the type of goal failure (loss vs. aversive state), we should be able to describe more accurately the type of outcomes that lead to anger and sadness. Although the loss of a valued state can evoke either anger or sadness (Stein & Jewett, 1986), it is unclear how an event resulting in an aversive state will be perceived. According to Berkowitz and Heimer (1989), putting someone into an aversive state almost always results in irritation or anger. However, the cause of an aversive state has not been systematically varied. Thus, including aversive and loss states, and manipulating the cause of such states, should lead to a fuller understanding of the conditions that evoke anger and sadness.

Stein and Levine (1987) also hold that emotions are distinguished by the wishes and plans that accompany them. The wishes and plans associated with happiness should be distinct from those associated with anger and sadness. Happiness results from goal attainment, so the primary wishes and plans associated with happiness should be either to maintain and enjoy the goal state or to enjoy other goals made possible as a result of achieving the original goal. Anger and sadness result from goal failure, so both emotions should be associated with wishes to reinstate the goal and with plans to either reinstate the goal, abandon it, or substitute a new goal.

Because anger and sadness involve processing different aspects of the precipitating event, the plans associated with these emotions should differ. Anger involves a detailed processing of the cause of obstruction and implies a belief that some plan may be available to reinstate the goal. Thus, the primary plan associated with anger should be to reinstate the goal. In contrast to anger, sadness involves a detailed processing of the impact that the current failure may have on other important goals. Sadness also implies a belief that attainment of the goal under consideration may be permanently blocked. Thus, the plans associated with sadness should involve abandoning the goal and/or substituting a new goal.

The present study represents an attempt to test these hypothesis with 3- and 6-year-old children and college students. Currently, an active tension

exists in the developmental literature regarding young children's understanding of the causes of emotions. On the one hand, several researchers
(e.g. Donaldson & Westerman, 1986; Harris, Olthof, & Meerum Terwogt,
1981; Harris & Olthof, 1982; Harter, 1979) have concluded that young
children believe emotions to be directly linked to external events and do
not understand that emotions are contingent on people's goals, values, and
beliefs. Not until the ages of 9 to 11 are children thought to understand that
internal states play a mediating role in emotional reactions. The primary
evidence used to support this position is that young children rarely refer to
the goals, beliefs, and internal feeling states when answering questions
such as "How do you know that you are happy, afraid, etc?" or "What
makes feelings come and go away?"

On the other hand, another group of researchers has shown that by the
age of $3\frac{1}{2}$ to 4 years, children have a good understanding of internal states
and their role in regulating actions (Bloom & Capatides, 1987; Shultz,
1980; Trabasso et al., 1981; Wellman, 1988; Wimmer, Hogrefe, & Sodian,
1988), and children also understand the basic concepts of animacy and
intentionality (Dubois & Shultz, 1988; Gelman, Spelke, & Meck, 1983;
Shultz, 1980; Wolf, 1982; Wolf, Rygh, & Altshuler, 1984). Moreover,
when young children are asked direct questions about the causes of
actions, they almost always give motivational answers (Trabasso et al.
1981). When they talk about causality, they almost always refer to psychological rather than physical states (Bloom & Capatides, 1987).

The present study was designed to examine whether young children
understand that emotions are evoked by situations that concern people's
goals and values. It was also designed to assess whether they make
distinctions among specific emotions similar to those of adults. With these
issues in mind, three dimensions were varied across a set of episodes with
the purpose of eliciting happiness, anger, or sadness. The dimensions were
whether a protagonist wanted to attain or avoid a state, whether or not the
goal was achieved, and properties of the agent who caused the outcome.
Following the presentation of each episode, an interview was carried out.
It was designed to examine subjects' explanations for emotions as well as
their understanding of the thoughts, wishes, and plans that follow emotional reactions.

METHOD

Subjects

Forty-eight preschool children (ages 3:1–4:7, M = 3:9, 48 first grade
children (ages 6:2–7:6, M = 6.9), and 48 college students from the
University of Chicago participated in the study. The preschool and elemen-

tary school children were recruited from schools in the Hyde Park area of Chicago, including the University Laboratory School and two privately owned nursery cooperatives. All children came from middle- to upper-middle-class families. To gain admission to each school, children and their parents were required to undergo an interview with the teachers. Although no formal admission requirements were provided by the schools used in this study, the interviews served the function of alerting teachers to potential academic or emotional problems. From both the schools' observations and our own, none of the participating children had severe language or learning disabilities. Approximately half of the subjects were male and half were female in all age groups.

Stimulus Materials

The stimuli consisted of four sets of narrative episodes. The episodes illustrated four combinations of goals (wanting something vs. not wanting something) and outcomes (having something vs. not having something). In the first set of episodes, a protagonist got something to play with that was wanted (e.g. got a toy or a puppy that was wanted). In the second set, the protagonist lost something that he or she played with and valued (e.g. lost a favourite toy or puppy). In the third set, the protagonist did not have to do something that he or she did not want to do (e.g. was able to avoid eating spinach or was able to avoid walking to school on a cold snowy day). In the fourth set, the protagonist had to do something that he or she did not want to do (e.g. had to eat spinach or had to walk to school on a cold snowy day). Two episodes were constructed for each goal-outcome combination to determine whether our findings would be replicated for each of the goal-outcome combinations.

To construct episodes that included each of these four combinations of goals and outcomes, each narrative began with a protagonist in the state opposite to the end state. For example, episodes that ended with the protagonist getting something he wanted to play with began with the statement that the protagonist wanted a particular object but did not yet have it. Thus, each of the eight episodes began with a protagonist expressing a particular desire. However, the ability to attain or maintain a desired state, or the ability to avoid an undesirable state, changed from the beginning to the end of the episode.

The change of state in each episode was brought about by one of three types of causal agents. The agent was either a human being acting intentionally, a human being acting unintentionally, or an inanimate agent (such as the wind or a wave). To illustrate the differences in the narratives that were constructed for the three types of causal agents, consider the beginning of one of the episodes:

"Jimmy's favourite toy car is broken and he would really like another one."

In the first causal condition, a human agent intentionally caused Jimmy to get something he wanted:

Onc day, Jimmy's friend comes over and brings Jimmy a present. Jimmy opens the present and finds a new toy car in the box. Now Jimmy has a toy car to play with.

In the second condition, a human agent accidentally caused the protagonist to get something that he wanted:

One day, Jimmy's friend comes over to play and brings a box of his old toy cars with him. When Jimmy's friend goes home, Jimmy sees that his friend lcft onc of the toy cars in his bedroom. Jimmy calls his friend on the telephone, and says he will bring back the toy car tomorrow. But, now Jimmy has a toy car to play with.

In the third condition, a natural event caused the protagonist to get something he wanted:

One day, when Jimmy is playing in the sand by the lake, a big wave splashes up on the beach and gets everything all wet. When the water goes back down, Jimmy sees a shiny toy car that was left on the sand by the wave. Now Jimmy has a toy car to play with.

Thus a total of 24 different episodes were constructed by varying three causal agents and constructing two episodes corresponding to each of the four goal-outcomes combinations.

The content of the episodes was selected as a result of pilot tests with children who were not included in this study. When asked to generate events that they liked very much or disliked very much, children most frequently described getting or losing a special toy or a pet. They also talked about aversive stimuli such as disliked foods and being cold, hot, or in pain. These topics are similar to those that 24-month-old children spontaneously talk about with their mothers (Dunn et al., 1987). Thus, the cpisodes were based on events that are very familiar to young children, not only in our sample but in other populations as well.

Design

The experiment had a repeated measures design with two between-subject factors, Age and Causal Condition, and two within-subject factors, Type of Outcome and Story Replication. Causal Condition refers to the type of agent that brought about the outcome, (i.e. a human being acting intentionally, a human being acting unintentionally, or natural event). The Type of Outcome refers to the goal-outcome combination that resulted at the end of an episode (e.g. getting to play with something that was wanted, avoiding an undesired state). Story Replication refers to the inclusion of two stories for each type of goal-outcome combination.

Subjects at each age level were randomly assigned to one of the three Causal Conditions, with the restriction that the numbers of males and females in each condition were approximately equal. Subjects in each condition heard eight episodes, two episodes corresponding to each of the four possible goal-outcome combinations. The order in which the four goal-outcome combinations were presented was counterbalanced.

Procedure

For the two groups of children, the following procedures were used. Subjects were interviewed individually. Each interview was tape recorded and written notes were also taken. At the beginning of each session, children were asked to label drawings of a happy, sad, and angry face. These drawings were displayed during the interview to remind children of the three emotion choices. When the drawings were first presented, children were asked how the person in each of the three pictures felt. Ninety-one per cent of the preschool children and 98% of the first grade children labelled the facial expressions correctly. For those children who gave an incorrect label, the experimenter supplied the correct one. The child was then asked to re-label the three faces until all the correct emotion terms were given twice in a row. The few children who made errors initially had no difficulty with the re-labelling task.

The experimenter then read the eight episodes. After each episode, children were asked nine questions. The first question was asked while pointing to the drawings of happy, sad, and angry faces. The experimenter asked "How do you think (the protagonist) would feel if that happened to (him/her)? Would (s/he) feel happy, sad, or angry? You can pick more than one feeling if you think (the protagonist) would feel more than one way". The order in which the emotion drawings were presented was counterbalanced across the episodes.

Children were given the three emotions, "happy", "sad", and "mad", from which to choose based on the consistent finding in the literature that these are among the first emotion words that children understand and use (Bretherton & Beeghley, 1982; Bretherton, Fritz, Zahn-Waxler, & Ridgeway, 1986; Dunn et al., 1987; Ridgeway, Waters, & Kuczaj, 1985). In addition, in pilot tests of our materials, when children were given a free choice of emotional responses, they almost always used the terms happy, good, mad, sad, or bad. Moreover, they rated their feelings as fairly intense, (M = 4.3 on a 5-point scale of intensity). Upon questioning children who used the words mad and bad, all children knew that mad meant angry. The use of bad most often signified sadness, and the few times it did not, being angry or mad was mentioned.

In the second question, children were asked to explain why the protagonist would feel each emotion they chose. A series of four probe questions was used to elicit explanations for each emotion. Children were first asked for their reasons for choosing a particular emotion. The content of the child's first explanation was then used to elicit a second explanation for the emotion. For example, if a child said "Jimmy's happy because he got a toy car", the next probe would be "Why did getting a toy car make Jimmy happy?" Multiple probe questions were asked because many different conditions can be used to explain an emotional response. Allowing children to give more than one explanation provides a more detailed account of their knowledge about the causes of emotions.

The third and fourth questions asked children to recall the protagonist's goal and the outcome of the episode (e.g. Did Jimmy want a toy car? Does Jimmy have one now?). The fifth question asked children to identify the agent or event responsible for the change in the protagonist's state (e.g. Who gave Jimmy the toy car?). The sixth question asked whether the agent acted intentionally or not (e.g. Did Jimmy's brother mean to give him a toy car?).

Finally, questions seven, eight, and nine were asked to assess children's inferences about the thoughts, wishes, and plans associated with the protagonist's change in state. Question seven asked children to describe the protagonist's first thought after the occurrence of the emotion-eliciting event (e.g. "What was Jimmy's first thought when his friend gave him a toy car?"). This question was asked to determine whether the type of emotional response would predict whether the first thought was directed toward the outcome that had already occurred or towards plans that had yet to be enacted. Question eight asked subjects to describe the protagonist's wishes (e.g. "What did Jimmy wish he could do?"). Question nine asked subjects to describe the protagonist's actual plans (e.g. "What did he really do?"). These two questions were included to determine if children distinguish between plans that they would like to enact if conditions permitted them to carry out their desires, and plans constrained by knowledge of the situation and the possible negative consequences of acting on their wishes.

The adults were given the same interview with the following changes: The adults were tested in small groups and wrote their responses to each question after reading each episode. Adults were not asked to label different facial expressions, nor did they have access to the pictures during their interviews. In addition, adult subjects were given the following instructions about how to interpret the episodes: "You'll find that the stories are quite simple. This is because they were written to be understood by 3-year-old children. Please answer the questions in a straightforward manner. That is, don't try to figure out how a child of a particular age would answer the questions. Instead, just answer the questions by imagining that the events in the story mattered to you as an adult." Following these instructions, the sequence in which the episodes were presented and the procedures used to collect the data were identical to those used with the children. The one exception pertained to question two, the emotion explanation question. Adults were asked to provide two explanations for their emotion choices, instead of four. This was done because the written presentation made it difficult to ensure that subjects would generate the additional explanations correctly by inserting the content of their previous explanations into each new explanation request.

Coding of Explanations, First Thoughts, Wishes, and Plans

All open-ended responses were coded by raters who were blind to information about the subject and the emotional response being described. First, a list of all explanations was made and then coded with respect to whether subjects included the following five dimensions: (1) the outcome of the episode (e.g. she had to eat spinach, he got to play with a puppy, his toy car broke); (2) the goal or value of the protagonist (e.g. she really wanted a puppy, she loved puppies, he hated spinach, he didn't like the cold); (3) the cause of the outcome (e.g. the toy car *fell* on the floor); (4) the agent or event that brought about the outcome (e.g. *his friend* dropped the toy car on the floor; *her mom* dropped the hot dog on the floor); and (5) the consequences of the loss or aversive state (e.g. now he can't play with the puppy anymore). The verbs that subjects used (e.g. had, got, lost, broke, had to vs. wanted, loved, hated, didn't like) were used to distinguish statements of outcomes from statements of goals. Two raters working independently coded the explanation data for 80 stories and agreed exactly for 84% of the responses. After making independent judgements, the raters resolved any disagreements by discussing the response until they reached a consensus.

First thoughts were coded with respect to two dimensions: whether the response included reference to the outcome of the situation (e.g. he got the puppy; his toy car was broken) and whether the response included reference to a plan of action (i.e. he really wanted to fix his toy car; he wanted to get the puppy back; he wanted to play with the puppy). Two raters working independently coded the first thought data for 80 stories and agreed on exactly 92% of the responses. Again, disagreements were resolved by discussing the response until a consensus was reached. The categories for coding the wishes and plans are described in the results section. The inter-rater reliability of two coders working independently on the wish and plan data from 80 stories was 89%.

RESULTS: THE CAUSES OF EMOTION

The Causes of Positive vs. Negative Emotions

Because Stein and Levine (1987) contend that goal success and failure are used to distinguish happiness from anger or sadness, the data were first analysed to determine whether goal achievement or goal failure predicted emotion choices. Answers were counted as correct if a positive emotion was inferred in response to outcomes where a desired state was attained or where an undesirable state was avoided. Similarly, credit was given if a negative emotion was inferred in response to outcomes where a desired state was not maintained or where an undesirable state was not avoided.

A four-factor, repeated measures ANOVA was carried out on the emotion choice data with two between-subject factors, Age and Causal Condition, and two within-subject factors, Type of Outcome and Story Replication. The results indicated that Age, $F(2,135) = 27.03$, $P < 0.01$, and Type of Outcome, $F(3,135) = 12.70$, $P < 0.01$, were significant, as was their interaction, $F(6,135) = 6.69$, $P < 0.01$. The data, which are presented in Table 1, are interpreted in the light of this interaction.

The interaction indicated that all age groups achieved nearly perfect accuracy in choosing negative emotions in response to episodes ending in negative outcomes. Preschool children, however, were less accurate than the other two age groups in choosing a positive emotion in response to episodes ending in positive outcomes (Tukey's HSD, m.s.d. = 0.12, $P < 0.01$). Even so, a substantial majority of 3-year-olds (82%) did choose the correct emotion for positive outcome episodes. Thus, the presence of a

TABLE 1
Proportion of Correct Emotion Choices in Response to Positive and Negative Outcomes

Age Group	Positive Outcome and Positive Emotion	Negative Outcome and Negative Emotion
Preschool	0.82	0.97
First grade	0.98	1.00
Adult	1.00	1.00

significant age effect should not be interpreted as a lack of understanding on the young child's part.

Children's responses to probe questions substantiate the conclusion that preschool children had little difficulty associating positive and negative outcomes with the appropriate emotion choice. When asked explicitly to identify the goal of the protagonist and to say whether or not the goal was achieved, 91% of the preschoolers and 98% of the first graders gave correct responses. Of those children who gave correct responses, 94% of the preschoolers and 99% of the first graders chose the predicted emotion.

Explanations for positive and negative emotions were then analysed. According to Stein and Levine (1987), two primary dimensions serve as causes for emotional responses: desiring or wanting to be in a particular state (i.e. a goal) and then detecting a change in the ability to maintain or attain the state (i.e. an outcome). People must want to attain (maintain) a particular state first and then detect a change in the ability to attain (maintain) the state. Otherwise an emotional response will not occur. Thus, all responses were scored to determine how frequently references were made to: (1) goals (i.e. wants, likes, loves her puppy; does not like, does not want, hates spinach); and (2) outcomes that reflected a change with respect to goal attainment, maintenance, or failure (i.e. she has a puppy, she got a puppy, she got one, she only has spinach to eat, she has to eat spinach, she lost her doggy). Figure 1 shows the cumulative proportion of responses, from the first why probe to the fourth, that included goal and outcome information.

A two factor (Age and Type of Explanation), repeated measures ANOVA was carried out on data from the first why probe question. The results showed significant main effects for Type of Explanation, $F(1,141) = 79.45$, $P < 0.01$, and Age, $F(2,141) = 23.78$, $P < 0.01$, with a significant interaction between the two, $F(2,141) = 9.60$, $P < 0.01$. All subjects mentioned outcomes more frequently than goals, and adults included more of both types of information than preschool children. The interaction indicated that first graders mentioned goals more frequently than adults (Tukey's HSD, m.s.d. $= 0.21$, $P < 0.05$). No significant differences were found between first grade and preschool responses or between preschool and adult responses.

The pattern of citing outcomes more frequently than goals as explanations for emotions remained constant over the four probe questions. First grade children consistently produced more of both types of explanations than preschool children did. By the fourth probe, however, all subjects included goals over 60% of the time. Thus, even the youngest children have access to goal information and use it to explain emotional responses. In fact, the majority of explanations given for the four probe questions

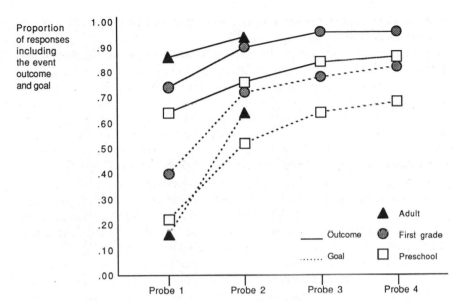

FIG. 1. Cumulative probabilities for each age group of citing the outcome and goal as explanations for emotional responses.

included both outcome and goal information (60% for adults, 75% for first graders, 59% for preschoolers).

For those explanations that included both goal and outcome information, the content of the explanations was clearly differentiated for positive and negative emotions. Stating that the protagonist got what he wanted or avoided something that he didn't like was included 95% of the time as reasons for happiness. Stating that the protagonist did not get what he wanted or could not avoid a state that he disliked was given 99% of the time for sadness or anger. There were no developmental differences in matching specific explanations to the appropriate emotions. Three-year-old children were just as accurate as adults in specifying the correct goal and outcome information to match their emotion choices.

The Causes of Anger vs. Sadness

The next set of analyses were carried out to determine whether the kinds of causal agents responsible for negative otucomes would predict whether anger or sadness was chosen. A four-factor, repeated measures ANOVA was carried out on the proportion of anger responses given for each type of negative outcome. The results showed three significant main effects: Age, $F(2,135) = 25.03$, $P < 0.01$; Causal Condition, $F(2,135) = 11.75$, $P < 0.01$;

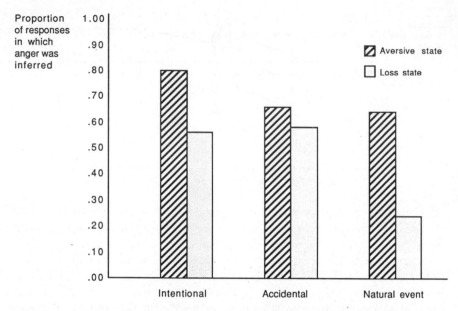

FIG. 2.   Proportion of anger responses as a function of responding to aversive or loss states.

and Type of Negative Outcome, $F(1,135) = 39.45$, $P < 0.01$. An interaction between Causal Condition and Type of Negative Outcome, $F(2,135) = 6.15$, $P < 0.01$, was also found. Adults chose anger more frequently than children did (adults, $M = 0.78$; first graders, $M = 0.55$; preschoolers, $M = 0.43$; Tukey's HSD, m.s.d. = 0.15, $P < 0.01$). No significant differences were found between the two groups of children. The proportion of anger responses for each Causal Condition and Type of Negative Outcome is presented in Fig. 2.

Anger was chosen more frequently in all Causal Conditions when episodes ended in an aversive state rather than a loss state. The type of causal agent did, however, affect the proportion of anger responses. When an animate agent intentionally or accidentally caused a protagonist to suffer a loss, anger responses were more frequent than when a natural event caused the loss. Thus, the mere presence of an animate agent was enough to increase the amount of anger inferred in loss states; the agent's motive did not need to be perceived as intentional. On the other hand, when an animate agent intentionally put a protagonist in an aversive state, anger responses were more frequent than when an accidental or natural caused the aversive state (Tukey's HSD, m.s.d. = 0.20, $P < 0.01$).

To explore more fully the relationship between anger and intentional harm, two sets of conditional probabilities were calculated and appear in Table 2. The first set, presented in Table 2A, shows the mean probability

TABLE 2
Relationship Between Anger and Intentionality for Each Age
Group

A.	Proportion of Anger Responses When Intent To Harm is Inferred		
	Preschool	First grade	Adult
	0.49	0.72^a	0.91^b

B.	Proportion of Intent to Harm Responses When Anger is Inferred		
	Preschool	First grade	Adult
	0.53	0.53	0.45

$^aP < 0.01, n = 18; ^bP < 0.01, n = 16.$

of inferring anger, given that the subject said the agent intended to harm the protagonist. Because the Natural Event condition did not have an animate agent causing harm, the probabilities were tabulated for only those conditions where a human agent caused the loss or aversive state.

For first graders and adults, the probability of choosing anger given that intentional harm was inferred was significantly above chance (first grade: $t= 3.79$, d.f. $= 18$, $P < 0.01$; adult: $t = 10.23$, d.f. $= 16$, $P < 0.01$). This probability was not significantly different from chance for preschool children. These young children were just as likely to infer sadness or anger, given that intentional harm was inferred. The differences between the preschool children and the older subjects cannot be attributed to a failure to understand the fact that harm was intended. Preschooler's answers to the question about whether or not the agent intended harm were accurate 81% of the time.

Table 2B shows the probability of inferring intentional harm, given that anger was expressed. The probabilities in all three age groups are not above chance level responding. Thus, the perception of intentional harm is not necessary for anger to be evoked. The presence of intentional harm raises the probability that anger will be expressed under aversive conditions. However, many situations involving both loss and aversion elicit anger without the presence of intentional harm and without the presence of an animate agent.

The data on the relationship between the presence of intentional harm and the expression of sadness are, for the most part, the inverse of those reported for anger. Sadness was expressed more in states of loss than in states of aversion. Moreover, the presence of intentional versus accidental harm did not affect the amount of sadness expressed for either loss or aversive states. In states of loss, however, the absence of a human agent and the presence of a natural cause did affect the amount of sadness expressed. Losses caused by a natural event generated the most sadness when compared with the other two types of loss.

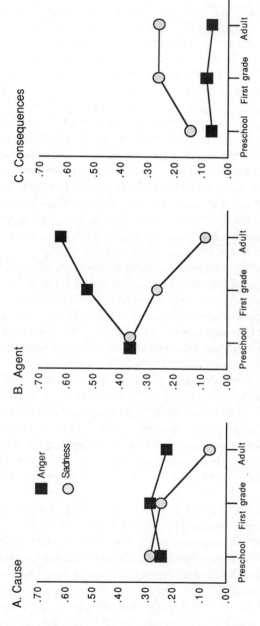

FIG. 3. Proportion of answers for each age group that referred to (A) the causes, (B) the agent, and (C) the consequences of goal failure in explanations for anger and sadness.

The final analysis for anger and sadness focused on the differences between the explanations given for the two emotions. Explanations for anger and sadness should reflect a difference in the focus of attention, once goal failure occurs and the negative outcome is certain. Explanations for anger should indicate a greater focus of attention on the agent or the cause of goal failure (i.e. the event that caused the change in state, for example, "the toy car fell on the floor"). Explanations for sadness, on the other hand, should show that attention has focused on the consequences of goal failure. Subjects' answers to the first two why probe questions were analysed with respect to whether they included mention of the cause, the agent, and the consequences of emotion-eliciting events. An ANOVA was carried out on each of these three dimensions, and the results are presented in Fig. 3.

For explanations referring to the *cause* of goal failure, a main effect of Age, $F(2,141) = 8.00$, $P < 0.01$, and an Age × Emotion interaction, $F(2,127) = 3.77$, $P < 0.02$, were found. Adults referred to the cause of goal failure significantly more in explanations of anger than sadness (Tukey's HSD, m.s.d. $= 0.37$, $P < 0.01$). Preschool and first grade children, however, were equally likely to mention the cause of goal failure in explanations of anger and sadness.

For explanations that included references to the *agent*, a main effect of Emotion, $F(1,127) = 29.84$, $P < 0.01$, and an interaction between Age and Emotion, $F(2,127) = 23.26$, $P < 0.01$, were found. First grade children and adults mentioned the agent more frequently in explanations of anger than sadness (Tukey's HSD, m.s.d. $= 0.24$, $P < 0.05$). Preschool children, however, included references to the agent equally often in explantions of anger and sadness. Analysis of the explanations that referred to the *consequences* of goal failure showed a main effect of Emotion, $F(1,127) = 50.77$, $P < 0.01$. Although references to the consequences of goal failure were not frequent, all subjects included more consequences in explanations for sadness than anger.

In sum, the explanations of anger and sadness generated by adults and first grade children showed clear differentiations. Both age groups were more likely to include a reference to the agent in explanations of anger than sadness, and adults were more likely to refer to the cause of goal failure in anger explanations than in sad ones. Sad explanations were oriented more toward the consequences of goal failure than were angry ones. Although preschool children also focused more frequently on the consequences of goal failure when sadness rather than anger was inferred, they focused on the causes and the agent equally often when explaining anger and sadness.

RESULTS: THE CONSEQUENCES OF EMOTION

First Thoughts following Positive and Negative Outcomes

According to Stein and her colleagues (Stein & Jewett, 1986; Stein & Levine, 1987, 1990) the first thoughts subsequent to a change in the ability to maintain or attain a goal depends upon the nature of the outcome. If a valued goal has been attained and happiness is experienced, no further planning is necessary to attain a goal, so the first thoughts should reflect the completion of a goal. Thus, attention should be focused on the outcome of an episode (e.g. Jimmy got a new toy car). When people fail to attain a goal, however, and anger or sadness is experienced, their first thoughts should reflect the necessity to resolve the failure. Thus, attention should be focused on a wish or plan to reinstate the original goal or a plan to forfeit or replace a goal.

To test this hypothesis, responses to the first thought question (e.g. What was the first thing that Jimmy thought about when his brother broke his toy?) were scored for reference to either an outcome (e.g. she got a puppy, his car was broken) or to a wish or plan of action (e.g. he wanted to fix his car, he didn't want to eat the spinach). The results indicated that a clear majority of subjects (at least 66% over all groups) referred to either outcomes or plans of action in response to the first thought question. No differences were found due to age or emotion. Those subjects not focusing on either plans or outcomes mentioned one of two other dimensions: the cause or agent responsible for goal failure or attainment and the degree to which the blocked or attained goal was valued.

An ANOVA was carried out with Age as the between-subject variable and Emotion (Happy vs. Angry/Sad) and Focus of First Thought (Outcome vs. Plan) as the within-subject variables. The results indicated that when goals were attained and happiness was expressed, subjects focused more on outcomes (0.46) than plans (0.27). When goals were blocked and anger or sadness was expressed, subjects focused more on plans (0.42) than on outcomes (0.29), $F(1,134) = 13.70$, $P < 0.01$, Tukey's HSD, m.s.d. = 0.11, $P < 0.01$. No other significant effects were found.

Wishes and Plans

Positive vs. Negative Emotions.   Responses to the wish question (e.g. What did Jimmy wish he could do?) and the plan question (e.g. What did Jimmy really do?) were expected to be clearly differentiated as a function of the outcome of an episode and the emotion expressed. Wishes and plans following positive outcomes, where happiness is expressed, should focus on maintaining or enjoying the current goal state. In contrast, wishes and plans following negative outcomes, where anger and sadness are expressed, should focus on goal reinstatement, substitution, forfeiture, or revenge.

In order to test this hypothesis, responses were scored for the inclusion of one of two sets of wishes or plans: (1) goal maintenance or participation in activities made possibly by goal success; or (2) goal reinstatement, forfeiture, substitution, or revenge. An ANOVA, with Age as the between-subject variable and Emotion (Happy vs. Angry/Sad) and Wish or Plan as within-subject variables showed a main effect for Emotion $F(1,141) = 2180.87$, $P < 0.01$, reflecting an almost complete lack of overlap between wishes and plans generated for happiness as opposed to anger and sadness. In response to goal attainment and the expression of happiness, 91% of subjects' wishes and 85% of their plans focused on goal maintenance or goal-related activities. In response to goal failure and anger/sadness, 94% of subjects' wishes and 93% of their plans referred to desires to reinstate, substitute, forfeit a goal, or seek revenge.

Wishes and Plans for Positive Emotions.   Given the lack of overlap between wishes/plans generated for happiness versus anger/sadness, the data for each class of emotion were separated for further analysis. Table 3A contains the kinds of wishes and plans associated with happiness. These were: (1) goal maintenance; (2) engaging in goal-related activities made possibly by the achievement of the original goal; (3) attending to a new goal unrelated to the original one; and (4) showing gratitude to the person who caused goal achievement. A separate ANOVA was carried out on each kind of strategy, with Age as the between-subject variable and Wish or Plan as the within-subject variable. The top left part of the table refers to the frequency of mentioning a particular strategy in response to the wish versus plan question. These data are collapsed over age. The top right part of the table shows the frequency of mentioning each strategy as a function of age, collapsing over wish and plan. No interactions between Wish/Plan and Age were found in any of the analyses.

Differences between wishing and planning were found for two of the four strategies: Goal Maintenance and Engaging in Goal-Related Activities. All subjects stated the desire to maintain the current goal more frequently in their wishes than in their plans, $F(1,141) = 33.47$, $P < 0.01$. On the other hand, the desire to participate in goal-related activities occurred more frequently in plans than in wishes, $F(1,141) = 7.27$, $P < 0.01$. These data suggest that people initially think about how they can maintain and prolong a pleasant state of affairs. They then plan, however, to take advantage of the activities and rewards that go along with having

TABLE 3
Proportion of Subjects Giving Different Kinds of Wishes and Plans for Positive and
Negative Emotions

A. *Kinds of Wishes and Plans for Positive Emotions*

Strategy	Wish	Plan	Preschool	First grade	Adult
Maintain goal	0.38	0.24	0.24	0.32	0.37
Goal-related activities	0.35	0.40	0.43	0.33	0.34
Attend to new goal	0.10	0.07	0.16	0.07	0.04
Gratitude	0.07	0.13	0.03	0.12	0.16

B. *Kinds of Wishes and Plans for Negative Emotions*

Strategy	Wish	Plan	Preschool	First grade	Adult
Goal reinstatement	0.70	0.19	0.45	0.47	0.47
Goal substitution	0.16	0.16	0.25	0.18	0.05
Goal forfeiture	0.01	0.45	0.12	0.27	0.30
Revenge	0.08	0.05	0.07	0.05	0.08
Cry or grieve	0	0.07	0.02	0.03	0.06

achieved a desired state. For example, if protagonists got a puppy, they were expected to wish to be able to keep the puppy. However, what subjects expected them to actually plan to do was play with the puppy.

Developmental differences are illustrated in the top right half of Table 3. Adults and older children were more likely than preschool children to want to maintain the current goal state, $F(2,141) = 4.50$, $P < 0.02$; Tukey's HSD, m.s.d. = 0.11, $P < 0.05$, and to express gratitude toward the person responsible for their success, $F(2,141) = 6.35$, $P < 0.01$; Tukey's HSD, m.s.d. = 0.08, $P < 0.05$. Preschool children, however, were more likely than first graders and adults to generate wishes and plans to accomplish a new goal unrelated to the original one, $F(2,141) = 11.69$, $P < 0.01$; Tukey's HSD, m.s.d. = 0.07, $P < 0.01$.

These data suggest that adults and first graders are more aware than the youngest children that the act of achieving a goal state does not necessarily guarantee that the state persists. In many situations, efforts to maintain a positive state must be made in order to continue enjoying the state. Moreover, both first graders and adults focused more on the agent responsible for success. The expressions of gratitude by these subjects indicated that they made causal inferences with regard to agency following goal success and positive emotions. The youngest children, on the other hand, were more likely to consider the episode finished, turning their attention to the accomplishment of other goals.

Wishes and Plans for Negative Emotions.   Table 3B incudes the wishes and plans generated in response to expressing a negative emotion. Irrespective of the particular negative emotion expressed, significant differences were found when the wishing and planning strategies were compared. Goal reinstatement was primarily stated as a wish, $F(1,141) = 346.93, P < 0.01$. Goal forfeiture was almost exclusively stated as an actual plan, $F(1,141) = 423.63, P < 0.01$. Finally, crying or grieving, although rare, was almost exclusively stated as a plan. These findings held across all age groups.

Developmental differences occurred primarily in the use of goal substitution, $F(2,141) = 13.43, P < 0.01$, and goal forfeiture, $F(2,141) = 21.21$, $P < 0.01$. Both preschool and first grade children were more likely to consider goal substitution as a viable strategy than were adults (Tukey's HSD, m.s.d. $= 0.10, P < 0.05$). First grade children and adults, however, were more likely to forfeit their goals than were the youngest children (Tukey's HSD, m.s.d. $= 0.12, P < 0.01$). Interactions between Age and Wish or Plan did occur, but these were more a function of the negative emotion expressed. Thus, our final set of analyses focused on the type of wish and plan generated as a function of expressing anger or sadness. Table 4 contains these data, with the wishes and plans analysed separately. The wish data are presented at the top of the table and the plans are presented at the bottom.

Two types of analyses are presented. The first is the rank order of the different wishes generated. The second is the differences between the three age groups in the frequency of generating specific wishes. As Stein and Levine (1987, in press) predicted, the primary wish for all subjects following both anger and sadness was to reinstate the goal. For children, goal substitution was the next most frequent wish, with revenge being ranked third. Goal forfeiture was never given as a wish for either anger or sadness. The ranking of adult wishes was identical to those for children, with one exception. Adults never wanted to substitute a goal when expressing their desires about anger. They focused on only two wishes: goal reinstatement and revenge.

Developmental differences occurred when comparing the frequencies for generating specific wishes. Adults were more likely than both groups of children to wish to reinstate the original goal, $F(2,135) = 5.13, P < 0.02$; Tukey's HSD, m.s.d. $= 0.12, P < 0.01$. Both groups of children, however, were more likely than adults to substitute a new goal, $F(2,135) = 12.00, P < 0.01$; Tukey's HSD, m.s.d. $= 0.10, P < 0.01$. Wishes also differed as a function of the emotion expressed. All subjects wished to reinstate the original goal more frequently when anger was expressed than when sadness was expressed, $F(1,135) = 5.13, P < 0.03$. They were more likely to substitute a new goal following sadness than they were following anger,

TABLE 4
Proportion of Subjects Giving Different Kinds of Wishes and Plans for Anger and Sadness

A. *Proportion of Different Kinds of Wishes for Anger and Sadness*

	Preschool		First grade		Adult	
Strategy	Anger	Sadness	Anger	Sadness	Anger	Sadness
Goal reinstatement	0.66	0.63	0.76	0.61	0.89	0.78
Goal substitution	0.15	0.21	0.12	0.36	0	0.09
Goal forfeiture	0.03	0.01	0	0	0	0.02
Revenge	0.10	0.05	0.10	0.01	0.11	0.02

B. *Proportion of Different Kinds of Plants for Anger and Sadness*

	Preschool		First grade		Adult	
Strategy	Anger	Sadness	Anger	Sadness	Anger	Sadness
Goal reinstatement	0.44	0.24	0.15	0.18	0.04	0.15
Goal substitution	0.16	0.32	0.07	0.15	0	0.12
Goal forfeiture	0.23	0.27	0.64	0.45	0.89	0.46
Revenge	0.05	0.08	0.06	0.02	0.02	0
Cry or grieve	0	0.05	0.02	0.12	0.04	0.20

$F(1,135) = 10.53, P < 0.01$. Wishes to forfeit the goal or seek revenge were quite rare and did not vary as a function of age or choice of emotion.

Basically these results imply two things. For the type of aversive or loss states created in our emotion episodes, goal reinstatement was the most frequent wish, independent of whether anger or sadness was expressed. When differences were found, however, they were always in the direction proposed by Stein and Levine. Reinstatement occurred more frequently with anger than sadness, and substitution occurred more frequently with sadness than with anger. Wishes for revenge, when they occurred at all, were almost always associated with anger. An important finding was that subjects never wished to forfeit the goal, implying that the goal is still valued, even though, in reality, hopes of attaining it might have to be abandoned.

Analyses of the actual plans tell a different story than the wish data. As we previously showed, goal reinstatement was more frequently a wish than a plan for all age groups. The frequency of plans to reinstate the goal, however, varied as a function of age, $F(2,135) = 12.01, P < 0.01$, as did the frequency of plans to substitute a new goal, $F(2,135) = 8.39, P < 0.01$. Preschool children generated more plans to reinstate goals (Tukey's HSD, m.s.d. $= 0.12, P < 0.01$) and to substitute a new goal (Tukey's HSD, m.s.d. $= 0.11, P < 0.01$) than older children and adults. All subjects planned to substitute new goals more frequently in response to sadness than to anger, $F(1,135) = 8.59, P < 0.01$. Here, the preschool data conformed more closely to the predictions offered by Stein and Levine than did the data from the first grade children and adults.

For goal forfeiture, significant main effects were found for Age, $F(2,135) = 17.88, P < 0.01$, Emotion, $F(1,135) = 10.45, P < 0.01$, and their interaction, $F(2,135) = 6.95, P < 0.01$. First grade children and adults planned to forfeit goals more often than preschool children, and forfeiture was more likely to follow anger than sadness. The youngest children planned to forfeit goals equally often in response to sadness and anger.

Because forfeiture was *not* the predicted response to anger, *post hoc* analyses were completed to yield some understanding of why forfeiture was such an important anger plan. Although forfeiting the original goal was given in response to both loss and aversive states, it more frequently followed aversive rather than loss states ($M = 0.67$ for aversive states, $M = 0.20$ for loss states), $F(2,141) = 193.47, P < 0.01$. When spinach was the only food available and when one was hungry enough, the most logical plan was to eat the spinach, despite one's dislike for it. Thus, even though most subjects expressed anger in response to aversive situations, and even though they wanted to reinstate the original goal, the specific conditions of the situation seriously constrained the plans that they could actually propose.

An informal analysis of reasons given for choosing a plan showed that subjects were actively reasoning about the effects of carrying out their wishes on their ability to attain other important goals. For example, when they considered the consequences of not having any dinner versus those of eating something they did not like, they seemed to decide that eating a disliked food and not being hungry was more important than avoiding a disliked food. Thus, the focus on goal forfeiture during planning and the differences between wishes and plans reflect the fact that subjects consider and weigh the possibility of acting on their wishes. A theory about the connection between an expressed emotion and an enacted plan must take into account reasoning about the effects that different plans might have on the attainment of other valued goals.

DISCUSSION AND CONCLUSIONS

The Use of Goal-Outcome Information in Understanding Emotions

Several conclusions can be drawn from the study. The results supported the view that both children and adults use goal-outcome combinations (e.g. wanting something but failing to attain it) to predict positive versus negative emotions and to explain why a particular emotional response occurred. Explanations included references to outcomes (e.g. she got the puppy) 90% of the time and to goals (e.g. she really wanted a puppy) 65% of the time. Thus, emotion explanations for all subjects, including adults, referred primarily to the outcome of an event and secondarily to the goal or value associated with the outcome. In addition, predictions about the first thoughts that a protagonist would have upon experiencing an emotional reaction also referred primarily to goals and outcomes.

These findings clearly indicate that 3-year-old children are aware of both aspects of emotion-eliciting situations: the outcome or the external situation and the goal associated with the outcome. Our findings thus contrast with the claims that young children attend only to a person's external situation when predicting and explaining people's emotions (Donaldson & Westerman, 1986; Harris, 1985; Harris et al., 1981; Harris & Olthof, 1982; but see Harris & Saarni, 1989, for evidence supporting the view that young children may have a more sophisticated understanding of emotion).

Two reasons may account for the salience of outcome information across age groups. First, in any emotion-eliciting situation, either the outcome or the value of the goal can be cited as a cause of an emotional response. Given that goals were the second most frequent cause cited by all subjects, we would not claim that young children lack an understanding of their role in emotional reactions. Rather, we would argue for the psychological and communicative salience of outcomes relative to goals. When people answer questions about causes, they typically pick out aspects of a situation that have recently changed or that are unusual rather than aspects that have remained constant (Hart & Honere, 1959; Hilton & Slugowski, 1986; Mackie, 1980). Citing the outcome focuses on the changes that occurred with respect to the maintenance of a valued state. Citing the value of the goal state focuses on the factor that remained constant throughout the episode. In providing explanations for emotions, then, emphasis should typically be placed on the changing conditions rather than the constant ones.

Secondly, outcomes may be more salient because of their importance in the discourse of emotion. If outcomes, rather than goals, were deleted from explanations, it would be difficult to infer the exact change that occurred in the status of a goal. However, the value of a goal or a desire is relatively easy to infer, given outcome information. For example, if Jimmy says he is angry because his brother broke his toy car, it is easy to infer that Jimmy liked his toy car. However, if Jimmy says he's angry because he liked his toy car, uncertainty exists about the state of the toy car and even about the role that the car played in producing anger. The relative ease of inferring the correct value of the goal and the relative difficulty of inferring the correct outcome have been shown in both children's and adults' understanding of stories (Stein, 1979; Stein & Policastro, 1984; Stein & Trabasso, 1982). Moreover, Gnepp (Gnepp, 1989; Gnepp & Gould, 1985) has arrived at similar conclusions in studies of emotion situations. Thus, it is not surprising that both children and adults explain emotional responses by referring to outcomes more often than goals.

The Causes and Consequences of Positive vs. Negative Emotions

As predicted by Stein and Levine (1987), the reasons given for happiness did not overlap with those given for negative emotions. Many investigators have cited the distinctiveness of positive versus negative emotions (Dahl, 1979; Frijda, 1987; Oatley & Johnson-Laird, 1987; Roseman, 1979, 1984; Russell, 1989; Scherer, 1984; Weiner, 1985). Our data corroborate earlier findings and extend them to the language and thinking about the causes and consequences of emotions. Positive and negative emotions are associated with thoughts, explanations, wishes, and plans of action that are mutually exclusive of one another.

The non-overlapping nature of the two classes of emotions may be one reason that children as young as three can discriminate between the positive/negative continuum so accurately. As Clark (1985) and many others have shown, distinctiveness of two related sets of concepts leads to rapid learning. Moreover, positive emotions may have very different effects on subsequent thinking than negative emotions. As our results showed, the first thoughts following the attribution of a positive emotion were more likely to focus on the outcome of the situation. The plans following happiness most often focused on goal enjoyment or just maintaining the positive state. As Schwarz (1988) has shown, this type of thinking often leads to a less evaluative mode with respect to subsequent thinking. People who are happy tend to be less critical of the types of evidence presented in an argument and more willing to be lenient in their judgements of others.

Negative emotions, on the other hand, almost always led to a desire to reinstate the obstructed goal. Thus, subsequent thinking should be focused on efforts to actualise this wish. As a result, negative emotions should involve more attention to achieving the original goal and less attention to new tasks unrelated to the original goal. Indeed, Schwarz (1988) argues that the experience of negative emotion is more oriented toward analytical and causal thinking, especially in regard to the conditions that preclude goal attainment. The question arises as to whether the experience of negative emotion leads to more analytical thinking in general or whether the analysis is focused primarily on resolving goal failure. Our results show that attributions made about negative states indicate a clear involvement in reinstatement activities. However, our data also suggest that many times the goal cannot simply be reinstated, and so attention gets focused on those goals that can be attained. Thus, a basic dimension in predicting how thinking will be affected by negative emotion states may be related to whether or not the current problem can be solved. In any case, however, the long-range effects of positive and negative emotion states is clearly an important issue for future research.

The Causes of Anger and Sadness

As predicted, both anger and sadness were attributed in response to goal failure, and the same event could elicit attributions of either anger or sadness. However, several dimensions emerged to distinguish the two emotions. Aversive states evoked more anger than loss states, and aversive states evoked more anger than sadness, even when the cause of the aversive state was a natural event. In fact, 60% of all subjects attributed anger to the victim in these situations. Furthermore, in both aversive and loss states, anger was still expressed about 60% of the time in conditions where an agent accidentally caused harm to the victim. These data are consistent with Berkowitz and Heimer's (1989) finding that university students reported feeling angry when put into physically aversive states, even when they did not think that they had been mistreated. Thus, the conditions that evoke anger are more general than has been claimed by theories that require attributions of intentional harm (e.g. Averill, 1979; Ellsworth & Smith, 1988; Ortony et al.; Pfeifer, 1982; Smith & Ellsworth, 1985; Weiner, 1985). Neither intentional harm nor the presence of an animate agent is necesary for attributions of anger to occur.

The belief that an agent intended harm, however, significantly increased the frequency of attributing anger. This finding, however, was the primary source of developmental differences in the present study. The belief that an agent intended harm significantly increased the probability of choosing anger for first grade children and adults. These subjects also included more references to the agent or the cause of harm when explaining attributions of anger rather than sadness. In contrast to these data, preschool children's expressions of anger were *not* associated with the perception that another person intended to cause harm. Even though they understood the agent's intent, preschool children were as likely to express sadness as anger when intentional harm was perceived. They were also equally likely to include reference to the agent and cause of harm in explanations for anger and sadness.

The finding that anger is associated with intentional harm for older children and adults may speak more to the cultural and social significance of this emotion than to the dimensions necessary for evoking anger. In our society, anger is not generally condoned, except in circumstances where one individual purposefully harms another. Focusing on an agent's intent to cause harm is one way of making anger socially acceptable or of validating an angry response. In fact, Lutz (1985a,b) reports that the Ifaluk, a people living in the Mieronesian islands, have two different words for anger: one that occurs without a justifiable cause and one that occurs under socially acceptable circumstances. The former type of anger is tolerated more frequently in children under the age of six, but not in older children and adults. The older members of this society are expected to know the conditions that are appropriate for the expression of anger. Intentional harm, then, may be cited as the prototypical cause of anger because it involves a socially justifiable way of communicating about anger (Averill, 1979). Thus, learning about the appropriate conditions for the expression of an emotion becomes a critical factor for study, especially with respect to emerging concepts of different emotions (Saarni, 1989).

It should be stressed, however, that the prototypical concept of anger does not necessarily correspond to the conditions that are actually necessary to evoke anger. From the results of this study, we can say that anger may be the response to any event, with inanimate or animate causes, that blocks the attainment or maintenance of a valued state. These data suggest that the core dimensions that define anger, even for adults, are goal obstruction and an unwillingness to accept goal failure as a long-term solution. In other words, anger results from a belief that some plan of action may eventually be found to reinstate the goal, especially in conditions where aversive states result.

Sadness was chosen more frequently in response to loss situations than in aversive situations, especially when an inanimate event caused the loss (see Ellsworth & Smith, 1988; Roseman, 1984; and Shaver et al., 1986, who report similar findings). As predicted, in explanations for sadness, all age groups described the consequences of goal failure more frequently than in explanations for anger. When sadness was expressed, subjects may have attended to the consequences or implications of goal failure because they believed that it was not possible to reinstate the loss. Therefore, mentioning the agent, which was characteristic of older subjects' explanations of anger, would be irrelevant to the plans that would have to be formulated to cope with failure. Other investigators (Dahl, 1979; Izard, 1977; Roseman, 1984; Scherer, 1984) have characterised anger as associated with feelings of power and sadness as associated with feelings of powerlessness. If power is defined as the belief that some plan of action can be undertaken to reinstate valued goals, then our results lend support to this distinction between anger and sadness.

The Consequences of Anger and Sadness

As predicted, the desire to reinstate the failed goal was the most frequent wish given by all subjects, independent of the negative emotion expressed. Wishes to reinstate the goal were somewhat less frequent following sadness because the wish associated with sadness sometimes focused on substituting a new goal. However, 62% of the children and 78% of the adults still expressed the wish to reinstate the goal under conditions of sadness. This finding supports the notion that even though goals may be permanently blocked, the desire for a particular goal state does not necessarily decrease in intensity or value.

When subjects generated plans, however, goal reinstatement became a much less frequent strategy. Plans to forfeit the original goal and substitute new goals were adopted instead. This shift was particularly true of first grade children and adults. These older subjects were less optimistic (or more realistic) than preschool children about the possibility of attaining blocked goals. The focus on goal forfeiture and substitution may result from older subjects' greater knowledge about the real-world constraints placed on goal achievement. However, a clear majority of preschool children also showed awareness of the constraints on goal achievement. Their actual plans also differed significantly from their wishes: To a lesser extent, they showed the same shift, from wishes to reinstate the original goal to plans to forfeit the goal or substitute a new goal.

In contrast to Stein and Levine's predictions, subjects were particularly likely to forfeit goals following anger and aversive states. When asked why they selected this plan, most indicated that it was impossible to reinstate the goal given current conditions. Enduring the state was the only available option. These findings suggest that initial feelings of anger, with the associated wishes of reinstating goals, are evaluated in conjunction with the constraints on actually carrying through such actions. This analysis involves assessing how a plan of action will affect other important goals. If enacting a plan would lead to the obstruction of other important goals, (e.g. if choosing not to eat spinach would lead to real hunger) then a decision to forfeit the original goal would be made, despite the existence of an aversive state and an angry feeling.

These results speak to the necessity of exploring two issues regarding anger. First, in our stories, even though an aversive state could not be avoided, these conditions were temporary. That is, eating spinach or walking to school in the cold had to be tolerated only once. We did not ask our subjects to predict how people would respond if the unpleasant situations persisted or occurred repeatedly. If aversive states continued, then the initial emotional response of anger might lead to a different plan of action. We would then expect subjects to take a more active role in attempting to change the continuing aversive state. We would also expect their attention to be directed toward understanding and attempting to change those conditions that led to the presence of the aversive state.

The second issue is whether anger may still be expressed even when aversive or loss states are believed to be permanent. According to our analysis, anger can still be expressed under these conditions. However, the cause of anger should be that certain personal expectations and interpersonal codes have been violated, *in addition to* suffering from an aversive or loss state. For example, if a favourite toy has been permanently broken by one's brother, the destruction of personal property may be perceived as both a social and moral violation. In these cases, some restitution or punishment may be seen as necessary (Roseman, 1979, 1984; Scherer, 1984; Shaver et al., 1987) before a person can cope with a loss. The belief here is that people who engage in destructive behaviour have violated the appropriate standards for interpersonal conduct. Thus, the victim often feels that some direct plan must be enacted to ensure that these violations never again occur.

Developmental Differences in Understanding Emotion Concepts

The fact that preschool children did not use intentional harm in their judgements of anger may indicate that they have yet to fully understand the conditions that constitute a moral or social violation. Although young children often operate with aggression toward others when they are angry (Goodenough, 1931), the nature of their thinking in these situations has not been fully examined. Aggression may occur strictly in the service of removing another person from the path of goal attainment. Future research should address the issue of whether preschool children make inferences about moral or social violations when displaying aggression in response to intentional harm. Clearly, more attention should be focused on examining children's knowledge about the conditions that elicit emotion.

Although some current studies (see Saarni & Harris, 1989, for a compendium of recent developmental studies on emotional understanding) focus on children's developing knowledge of goal-directed action, many (Harter & Whitesell, 1989; Ridgeway et al., 1985) have focused on the developmental changes in children's understanding of emotion state words and language. For example, Harter and Whitesell (1989) are interested in children's developing knowledge of the emotion lexicon and the age at which children begin to use and express knowledge of more complex emotion terms.

Although this is a valuable enterprise, it is different from studying children's knowledge about the causes and consequences of attaining or failing to attain goals. The results of the present study show that young children rapidly acquire a complex working knowledge of the conditions that preclude or facilitate goal attainment. Moreover, recent studies by Capatides (1989), Dunn (1988), and Miller and Sperry (1987) attest to the richness of the language and interchanges between mothers and children when discussing emotional reactions and failure or success at attaining goals. However, Capatides (1989) has illustrated that mothers rarely label or use emotion state words in discussing children's emotional responses to failure or success. Instead, mothers focus on the outcomes of success when children experience positive emotions, and they focus on ways to reinstate a failed goal when children express negative emotions, much like our subjects' first thought responses. Because of the infrequent use of emotion terms (see also Huttenlocher & Smiley, 1990, for convergent findings), children may acquire a rich understanding of the causes and consequences of emotional experience but use only a small set of emotion state terms to refer to their feelings. Thus, in future studies, it will be critical to distinguish between children's knowledge of the emotion lexicon versus their knowledge of the causal constraints for experiencing a specific emotion.

Our study showed that many similarities exist when very young children's knowledge of emotion is compared with adults, supporting the view that children rapidly acquire a basic working knowledge of the conditions that motivate people and control action. The developmental differences in conceptions of anger, however, support the working hypothesis that through exposure to many different situations, children acquire further knowledge about the conditions that regulate both the understanding and experience of emotion. Specifically, knowledge about the conditions that are socially acceptable in feeling and expressing particular emotions appears critical as does the knowledge about the consequences of pursuing different courses of action.

Manuscript received 28 November 1988
Manuscript revised 7 March 1989

REFERENCES

Arnold, M. B. (1960). *Emotion and personality: Psychological aspects, Vol. 1.* New York: Columbia University Press.

Averill, J. R. (1979). Anger. In H. E. Howe and R. A. Dienstbier (Eds), *Nebraska symposium on motivation: Human emotions, Vol. 26.* Lincoln, Nebraska: University of Nebraska Press, pp. 1–80.

Berkowitz, L. & Heimer, K. (1989). Aversive events and negative priming in the formation of feelings. In L. Berkowitz (Ed.), *Advances in experimental social psychology.* New York: Academic Press.

Bloom, L. & Capatides, J. (1987). Sources of meaning in the question of complex syntax: The sample case of causality. *Journal of Experimental Child Psychology, 43,* 112–128.

Borke, H. (1971). Interpersonal perception of young children: Egocentrism or empathy. *Developmental Psychology, 5,* 263–269.

Bretherton, I. & Beeghley, M. (1982). Talking about internal states: The acquisition of an explicit theory of mind. *Developmental Psychology, 18,* 906–921.

Bretherton, I., Fritz, J., Zahn-Waxler, C., & Ridgeway, D. (1986). Learning to talk about emotions: A functionalist perspective. *Child Development, 57,* 529–548.

Bullock, M. & Russell, J. A. (1985). Further evidence in preschooler's interpretations of facial expressions. *International Journal of Behavioral Development, 8,* 15–38.

Capatides, J. (1989). *Mother's socialization of children's affect expression.* Unpublished doctoral dissertation. Teachers College, Columbia University.

Clark, E. V. (1985). The principle of contrast: A constraint in language acquisition. In B. MacWinney (Ed.), *Mechanisms in language acquisition. 20th Annual Carnegie Symposium on Cognition.* Hillsdale, N.J.: Lawrence Erlbaum Associates Inc.

Dahl, H. (1979). The appetite hypothesis of emotion: A new psychoanalytical model of motivation. In C. E. Izard (Ed.), *Emotions in personality and psychopathology.* New York: Plenum, pp. 201–233.

Donaldson, S. K. & Westerman, M. A. (1986). Development of children's understanding of ambivalence and causal theories of emotion. *Developmental Psychology, 22,* 655–662.

Dubois, P. & Shultz, T. R. (1988). The development of the understanding of human behavior: From agency to intentionality. In Astington, J. A., Harris, P. L., & Olson, D. R. (Eds), *Developing theories of mind.* Cambridge University Press.

Dunn, J. (1988). *The beginnings of social understanding.* Cambridge, Mass.: Harvard University Press.

Dunn, J., Bretherton, I., & Munn, N. (1987). Conversations about feeling states between mothers and their young children. *Developmental Psychology, 23,* 132–139.

Ellsworth, P. C. & Smith, C. A. (1988). From appraisal to emotion: Differences among unpleasant feelings. *Motivation and Emotion, 12,* 271–302.

Frijda, N. H. (1987). Emotion, cognitive structure, and action tendency. *Cognition and Emotion, 1,* 115–143.

Gelman, R., Spelke, E. S., & Meck, E. (1983). What preschoolers know about animate and inanimate objects. In D. Rogers and J. A. Sloboda, (Eds.), *The acquisition of symbolic skills*. New York: Plenum, pp. 297–326.

Gnepp, J. (1989). Children's use of personal information to understand other people's feelings. In C. Saarni & P. L. Harris (Eds), *Children's understanding of emotion*. Cambridge University Press.

Gnepp, J. & Gould, M. E. (1985). The development of personalized inferences: Understanding other people's emotional reactions in light of their experiences. *Child Development*, 56, 1455–1464.

Goodenough, F. L. (1931). *Anger in young children*. Minneapolis, Mn.: University of Minnesota Press.

Harris, P. L. (1985). What children know about the situations that provoke emotions. In M. Lewis & C. Saarni (Eds), *The socialization of affect*. New York: Plenum, pp. 161–186.

Harris, P. L. & Olthof, T. (1982). The child's concept of emotion. In G. Butterworth and P. Light (Eds), *Social cognition: Studies of the development of understanding*. Chicago: University of Chicago Press, pp. 188–209.

Harris, P. L. & Saarni, C. (1989). Children's understanding of emotion: An introduction. In C. Saarni & P. L. Harris (Eds), *Children's understanding of emotion*. Cambridge University Press.

Harris, P. L., Olthof, T., & Meerum Terwogt, M. (1981). Children's knowledge of emotion. *Journal of Child Psychology and Psychiatry*, 22(3), 247–261.

Hart, H. L. A. & Honore, A. M. (1959). *Causation and the law*. Oxford University Press.

Harter, S. (1979). *Children's understanding of multiple emotions: a cognitive-developmental approach*. Address given at the Ninth Annual Piaget Society Meeting, Philadelphia.

Harter, S. & Whitesell, N. R. (1989). Developmental changes in children's understanding of single, multiple and blended emotion concepts. In C. Saarni & P. L. Harris (Eds), *Children's understanding of emotion*. Cambridge University Press.

Heider, F. (1958). *The psychology of interpersonal relations*. New York: Wiley.

Hilton, D. & Slugowski, B. R. (1986). Knowledge-based causal attribution: The abnormal condition focus model. *Psychological Review*, 93, 75–88.

Huttenlocher, J. & Smiley, P. (1990). The development of the concept of person. In N. L. Stein, B. Leventhal, & T. Trabasso (Eds), *Psychological and biological approaches to emotion*, Hillsdale, N.J.: Lawrence Erlbaum Associates Inc.

Huttenlocher, J., Smiley, P., & Charney, R. (1983). The emergence of action categories in the child. *Psychological Review*, 90(1), 72–93.

Izard, C. E. (1977). *Human emotions*. New York: Plenum.

Kahneman, D. & Tversky, A. (1982). The simulation heuristic. In D. Kahneman, P. Slovic, & A. Tversky (Eds), *Judgement under uncertainty: Heuristics and biases*. Cambridge University Press.

Karniol, R. (1982). Settings, scripts, and self schemata: A cognitive analysis of the development of prosocial behavior. In N. Eisenberg (Ed.), *The development of prosocial behavior*. New York: Academic Press, pp. 251–278.

Lazarus, R. S. & Folkman, S. (1984). *Stress, appraisal, and coping*. New York: Springer.

Lazarus, R. S. & Smith, C. A. (1988). *Knowledge and appraisal in the cognition–emotion relationship*. Unpublished manuscript, University of California, Berkeley.

Lutz, C. (1985a). Ethnopsychology compared to what? Explaining behavior and consciousness among the Ifaluk. In G. M. White and J. Kirkpatrick (Eds), *Person, self, and experience: Exploring pacific ethnopsychologies*. Berkeley, Ca.: University of California Press.

Lutz, C. (1985b). Cultural patterns and individual differences in the child's emotion meaning sytem. In M. Lewis & C. Saarni (Eds), *The socialization of affect*. New York: Plenum, pp. 161–186.

Mackie, J. L. (1980). *The cement of the universe: A study of causation*. Oxford: The Clarendon Press.

Mandler, G. (1975). *Mind and emotion*. New York: Wiley.

Mandler, G. (1984). *Mind and body: Psychology of emotion and stress*. New York: Norton.

Miller, P. & Sperry, L. (1987). The socialization of anger and aggression. *Merrill-Palmer Quarterly, 33*, 1–31.

Oatley, K. & Johnson-Laird, P. (1987). Toward a cognitive theory of emotion. *Cognition and Emotion, 1*(1), 29–50.

Ortony, A., Clore, G., & Collins, A. (1988). *The cognitive structure of emotion*. Cambridge Univeristy Press.

Pfeifer, R. (1982). *A computer simulation approach to the study of emotional behavior*. Proceedings of the Fourth Annual Conference of the Cognitive Science Society. Ann Arbor, Michigan, pp. 188–190.

Ridgeway, D., Waters, E., & Kuczaj, S. A. (1985). A question of emotion-descriptive language: Receptive and productive vocabulary norms for ages 18 months to 6 years. *Developmental Psychology, 21*(5), 901–908.

Roseman, I. J. (1979). *Cognitive aspects of emotion and emotional behavior*. Paper presented at the American Psychological Association Meetings, New York.

Roseman, I. J. (1984). Cognitive determinants of emotions: A structural theory. In P. Shaver (Ed.), *Review of personality and social psychology: Emotions, relationships, and health, Vol. 5*. Beverly Hills: Sage, pp. 11–36.

Russell, J. A. (1987). Comments on articles by Frijda and by Conway and Bekerian. *Cognition and Emotion, 1*(2), 193–197.

Russell, J. A. (1989). Culture, scripts, and children's understanding of emotion. In C. Saarni & P. L. Harris (Eds), *Children's understanding of emotion*. Cambridge University Press.

Russell, J. A. & Bullock, M. (1986). On the meaning preschoolers attribute to facial expressions of emotion. *Developmental Psychology, 29*, 97–102.

Saarni, C. (1989). The control of emotion. In C. Saarni & P. L. Harris (Eds), *Children's understanding of emotion*. Cambridge University Press.

Saarni, C. & Harris, P. L., (Eds) (1989). *Children's understanding of emotions*. Cambridge University Press.

Scherer, K. R. (1984). On the nature and function of emotion: A component process approach. In K. R. Scherer & Ekman, P. (Eds), *Approaches to emotion*. Hillsdale, N.J.: Lawrence Erlbaum Associates Inc.

Schwarz, N. (1988). *Happy but mindless*. Paper presented at the Symposium: Affect and Cognition, 24th International Congress and Psychology, Sydney, Australia, August.

Shaver, P., Schwartz, J., O'Connor, C., & Kirson, D. (1987). Emotion knowledge: Further explanations of a prototype approach. *Journal of Personality and Social Psychology, 52*, 1016–1086.

Shultz, T. (1980). Development of the concept of intention. In W. A. Collins (Ed.), *Minnesota symposium on child psychology: Development of cognition, affect, and social relations, Vol. 13*, Hillsdale, N.J.: Lawrence Erlbaum Associates Inc, pp. 131–164.

Smiley, P. & Huttenlocher, J. (1989). Young children's understanding of facial and situational components of emotion words. In C. Saarni and P. L. Harris (Eds), *Children's understanding of emotion*. Cambridge University Press.

Smith, C. A. & Ellsworth, P. C. (1985). Patterns of cognitive appraisal in emotion. *Journal of Personality and Social Psychology, 48*, 813–838.

Stein, N. L. (1979). How children understand stories: A developmental analysis. In L. Katz (Ed.), *Current topics in early childhood education, Vol. 2*. Norwood, N.J.: Ablex Inc.

Stein, N. L. & Jewett, J. (1986). A conceptual analysis of the meaning of negative emotions: implications for a theory of development. In C. E. Izard and P. Read (Eds), *Measurement of emotion in infants and children, Vol. 2*. Cambridge University Press, pp. 238–267.

Stein, N. L. & Levine, L. J. (1987). Thinking about feelings: The development and organization of emotional knowledge. In R. E. Snow and M. Farr (Eds), *Aptitude, learning, and instruction: Cognition, conation and affect, Vol. 3*. Hillsdale, N.J.: Lawrence Erlbaum Associates Inc. pp. 165–198.

Stein, N. L. & Levine, L. J. (1990). Making sense of emotion: The representation and use of goal-structured knowledge. In N. L. Stein, B. Leventhal, & T. Trabasso (Eds), *Psychological and biological approaches to emotion*. Hillsdale, N.J.: Lawrence Erlbaum Associates Inc.

Stein, N. L. & Policastro, M. (1984). The concept of a story: A comparison between children's and teachers' perspectives. In H. Mandl, N. L. Stein, & T. Trabasso (Eds), *Learning and comprehension of text*. Hillsdale, N.J.: Lawrence Erlbaum Associates Inc.

Stein, N. L. & Trabasso, T. (1982). What's in a story: An approach to comprehension and instruction. In R. Glaser (Ed.), *Advances in instructional psychology, Vol. 2*. Hillsdale, N.J.: Lawrence Erlbaum Associates Inc.

Stein, N. L. & Trabasso, T. (1989). Children's understanding of changing emotion states. In C. Saarni & P. L. Harris (Eds), *Children's understanding of emotion*. Cambridge University Press.

Thompson, R. (1987a). Development of children's inferences of the emotions of others. *Developmental Psychology, 22*, 124–131.

Thompson, R. (1987b). Empathy and emotional understanding: The early development of empathy. In N. Eisenberg & J. Strayer (Eds), *The development of empathy*. Cambridge University Press.

Trabasso, T., Stein, N. L., & Johnson, L. R. (1981). Children's knowledge of events: A causal analysis of story structure. In G. Bower (Ed.), *Learning and motivation, Vol. 15*. New York: Academic Press, pp. 237–282.

Trope, Y. (1982). Inferences of personal characteristics on the basis of information retrieved from one's memory. In D. Kahneman, P. Slovic, & A. Tversky (Eds.), *Judgement under uncertainty: Heuristics and biases*. Cambridge University Press.

Weiner, B. (1985). An attributional theory of achievement motivation and emotion. *Psychological Review, 92*(4), 548–573.

Wellman, H. M. (1988). First steps in the child's theorizing about mind. In Astington, J. A., Harris, P. L., & Olson, D. R. (Eds), *Developing theories of mind*. Cambridge University Press.

Wimmer, H., Hogrefe, J., & Sodian, B. (1988). A second stage in children's conception of mental life: Understanding informational access as origins of knowledge and belief. In Astington, J. A., Harris, P. L., & Olson, D. R. (Eds), *Developing theories of mind*. Cambridge University Press.

Wolf, D. (1982). Understanding others: A longitudinal study of the concept of independent agency. In G. Forman (Ed.), *Action and thought*. New York: Academic Press, pp. 297–328.

Wolf, D., Rygh, J., & Altshuler, J. (1984). Agency and experience: Actions and states in play narratives. In I. Bretherton (Ed.), *Symbolic play*. New York: Academic Press, pp. 195–217.

COGNITION AND EMOTION, 1989, 3(4), 379–400

Young Children's Theory of Mind and Emotion

Paul L. Harris, Carl N. Johnson, Deborah Hutton,
Giles Andrews, and Tim Cooke

Department of Experimental Psychology, University of Oxford, U.K.

In three experiments, children aged 3 to 7 years were tested for their understanding of the impact of beliefs and desires on emotion. Children watched while animal characters were offered various types of container and then predicted their emotional reaction. In Experiment 1, the children (but not the characters) knew that the desirable contents of each container had been removed. The majority of 6-year-olds and a minority of 4-year-olds understood that the characters would be happy with the gift, given their mistaken belief about its contents. In Experiment 2, characters were given containers apparently containing an object they wanted but really containing an object they did not want, or vice versa. Predictions of emotion based on both the desire and the mistaken belief of the characters increased with age. In Experiment 3, characters were given closed containers that might or might not contain an item they wanted. Both 3- and 5-year-olds grasped that the characters' emotional reaction would depend on both their (unconfirmed) beliefs and desires about its content.

The experiments show that preschool children deploy a theory-like conception of mind in predicting emotional reactions. They understand that the emotional impact of a situation depends not on its objective features but on the beliefs and desires that are brought to it.

INTRODUCTION

How do young children predict the impact of an emotionally charged situation on another person? For example, how do they make the prediction that losing a toy will provoke sadness whereas getting a treat will provoke happiness (Borke, 1971)? One plausible explanation is that on the basis of their own experience, children build up a set of emotion scripts in which particular situations are associated with particular emotions. Asked what another person might feel in a specified situation, they retrieve a

---

Requests for reprints should be sent to P. L. Harris, Department of Experimental Psychology, South Parks Road, Oxford, OX1 3UD, U.K.

© 1989 Lawrence Erlbaum Associates Limited

script that includes that situation, or one similar to it, and use it to make predictions about other people (Chandler & Greenspan, 1972). If this explanation is correct, it implies that young children do not take into account the way in which different individuals might appraise the same situation differently; they simply assume that a given situation has a similar impact on everyone. Despite its simplicity, this script-based strategy could account for young children's success both in identifying the emotion that a particular situation will elicit (Barden, Zelko, Duncan, & Masters, 1980; Borke, 1971) and in identifying situations that would be likely to provoke a particular emotion (Harris, Olthof, Meerum, Terwogt, & Hardman, 1987; Trabasso, Stein, & Johnson, 1981).

Recent evidence suggests, however, that young children might be able to make predictions about emotion in a more sophisticated way. When they predict a person's actions, such as where he or she will search for a hidden object, they do not simply attend to the objective situation. Instead, they work with some conception of the mental processes by which the person will appraise the situation. They appreciate that what someone does will depend upon the beliefs and desires that he or she brings to the situation (Astington, Harris, & Olson, 1988). For example, 4- and 5-year-olds correctly predict that a person will mistakenly search for some chocolate in an empty cupboard, if the chocolate has been moved without the person's knowledge (Johnson & Maratsos, 1977; Perner, Leekam, & Wimmer, 1987; Wellman & Bartsch, 1988; Wimmer & Perner, 1983). These results demonstrate that young children can predict a person's actions not in terms of the objective situation facing the person, but in terms of the way that the person appraises it. In particular, they understand that people sometimes act against their own interests (e.g. search in the wrong box) if their beliefs about the situation are mistaken.

Do young children acknowledge the crucial importance of such appraisal processes when they predict emotion? At present, there are only limited data to answer this question. Recent evidence does show that 3-year-olds take desires into account. They understand that the same objective situation may make someone happy or sad depending on whether or not it corresponds to what the person wanted (Stein & Levine, 1985; Wellman & Bartsch, 1988; Wellman & Woolley, in press; Yuill, 1984). However, no experiment has yet examined whether children can take beliefs into account when predicting emotion. This is an important question because, alongside desires, beliefs constitute one of the two key components of our everyday folk theory of the mind (Davidson, 1980; Wellman, 1988). The main goal of Experiment 1 was to find out whether young children predict that a person will feel happy if he or she expects to get something desirable even if that belief is objectively false, and is known to be false by the children making the prediction. If children make such predictions accurately, it would provide strong evidence that they appreciate how an emotion is elicited not by the objective situation itself but by the way a person appraises it.

Children ranging from 3 to 7 years were introduced to a toy monkey who played tricks on each of four other toy animals. For example, they watched while the monkey surreptitiously removed the candy from a familiar candy box, replaced it with stones and gave the closed box to a hungry bear. They were then asked to predict: (1) the bear's normal emotional reaction to such a gift; (2) his reaction to this candy box before his discovery of its actual contents; and (3) his reaction after discovery of its actual contents. Question (2) was the crucial test question. If children simply reason on the basis of the objective situation facing the character, they should deny that the bear will feel pleased since the candy has been replaced by stones. If, however, they acknowledge the way in which the bear appraises the situation, namely that he mistakenly expects to find candy in the box, they should grasp that he will feel happy until he discovers the actual contents.

On the basis of earlier findings concerning children's ability to predict simple actions such as search for an object, it was anticipated that older children would take such appraisal processes into account, whereas younger children would often attend only to the objective situation, ignoring the animal's appraisal of it.

EXPERIMENT 1: METHOD

Subjects

There were 20 younger children (mean 4 years 7 months; range 3 years 10 months to 5 years 0 months) and 20 older children (mean 6 years 5 months; range 6 years 0 months to 7 years 0 months). These two groups will be referred to as the 4-year-old and the 6-year-old group. One additional 4-year-old was tested but replaced because of language difficulties. There were approximately equal numbers of boys and girls in each age group. All children were tested at a local state school recruiting children from a wide range of socio-economic backgrounds.

Procedure

Children were taken from their classrooms to a quiet area of the school. They were introduced to Mickey the Monkey, a toy monkey who is "always playing tricks on the other animals". One of the four other toy animals was then indicated and his or her preference for a particular food or drink was described (e.g. "Bertie the bear is very hungry and his favourite snack is smarties (M&Ms)"). The experimenter then proceeded to explain that the monkey played a trick on him. Thus, pursuing the same example, a smarties box was introduced; the monkey was made to empty out the smarties and replaced them with stones. The narrative continued: "Mickey put the smarties box with the stones inside it on Bertie's table. Bertie came home and saw this smarties box on his table". The bear was then brought toward the box and placed directly beside it.

Following this preamble, the children were asked to make and justify three predictions about the duped character's emotion; in addition, their memory for the actual contents of the container was checked. These questions were posed in the following fixed order. (Bracketed phrases varied depending on the gender and name of the duped character, the type of container, the preferred contents and the substitute contents). *Happy* or *sad* was included in the request for a justification depending on the child's prior prediction.

Question 1: How does (Bertie the bear) feel when (his) Mom gives (him) a (box of smarties)? Does (he) feel happy or sad? . . . Yes, and why does (he) feel *happy/sad*?

Memory check: What is in this (box): (smarties) or (stones)?

Question 2: How did (Bertie the bear) feel when (he) first looked at the (box) on the table, before (he had a look inside it)? Did (he) feel happy or sad? . . . Yes, and why was (Bertie) *happy/sad*?

Question 3: How will (Bertie) feel when (he has a look inside the box) and (finds that there's stones inside instead of smarties)? Will (he) feel happy or sad? . . . Yes, and why will (Bertie) feel *happy/sad*?

Other stories involved an elephant who liked Coke but found water in a Coke can; a horse who liked peanuts but found play-doh in a peanuts packet; and a bird who liked weetabix (a cereal) but found string in a weetabix carton.

Each subject was presented with all four stories; the order of the stories was systematically varied across subjects using a Latin-square design.

Results

Results for the memory check will be presented first, followed by results for the three emotion questions.

Memory Check.   All subjects in each age group answered the memory check question concerning the hidden contents of the container correctly for all four stories. One 6-year-old initially gave the wrong answer for one story, but corrected herself without prompting.

TABLE 1

Number of Subjects Predicting Happy Reactions for 0–4 Stories, as a Function of Age and Question

Age and Question	No. of stories					Mean	No.
	0	1	2	3	4		
4-year-olds							
Question 1	0	0	0	0	20	4.00	20
Question 2	11	0	1	1	7	1.65	20
Question 3	18	1	0	0	1	0.25	20
6-year-olds							
Question 1	0	0	0	0	20	4.00	20
Question 2	5	0	0	1	14	2.95	20
Question 3	20	0	0	0	0	0.00	20

Emotion Predictions.   Table 1 indicates the number of subjects who judged that the story character would feel happy for 0, 1, 2, 3, or 4 stories, as a function of Age and Question.

Inspection of Table 1 indicates that almost all subjects in each age group systematically judged that the story character would be happy when presented with the container under normal circumstances (Question 1), and went on to deny that the character would feel happy after opening the container and discovering the substitute contents (Question 3).

Subjects were split in their predictions about what the character would feel on presentation of the trick container prior to discovery of its contents (Question 2). Among 4-year-olds a sizable minority, and among 6-year-olds the majority of subjects, systematically judged that the character would be happy.

A two-way analysis of Age × Question for the number of happy judgements (out of 4) confirmed the main effect of Question ($F(2,76) = 123.32, P < 0.0001$) and the interaction of Age × Question ($F(2,76) = 5.66, P < 0.005$). Further analysis of the interaction showed that the two age groups did not differ in their expectation that the character would usually feel happy when given such a container (Question 1) but sad after opening it (Question 3) ($F(1,114) < 1, P$ n.s., in each case). However, 6-year-olds were more likely than 4-year-olds to predict that the character would be happy before opening the container ($F(1,114) = 13.265, P < 0.001$).

Emotion Justifications.   Subjects' justifications were divided into three categories: *correct* (i.e. justifications that backed up a correct prediction by an appropriate reference to the apparent contents not the real contents, or

TABLE 2
Mean Number of Correct, Incorrect, and Uninformative Justifications
by Age

Age	Type of Justification		
	Correct	Incorrect	Uninformative
4-year-olds	1.35	2.10	0.55
6-year-olds	2.85	0.95	0.20

by reference to the character's restricted knowledge, e.g. "she had coke"; "he likes smarties"; " 'cos she didn't see what was inside"), *incorrect* (i.e. justifications that backed up an incorrect prediction by an inappropriate reference to the actual contents or to the trick that had been played, e.g. " 'cos it's not coke"; " 'cos it's only water"; "he doesn't like play-doh"; " 'cos of the trick"), *uninformative* (i.e. justifications that failed to back up . a prediction, whether correct or incorrect, e.g. "don't know").

The mean frequencies of the three types of justification are given in Table 2 as a function of Age. As the relative frequencies of each type of reply were not independent, an analysis of Age × Type of Justification could not be carried out. However, t-tests indicated that 6-year-olds offered more correct justifications ($t(38) = 2.703$, $P < 0.01$) and fewer incorrect justifications ($t(38) = 2.150$, $P < 0.01$) than 4-year-olds.

Contingency between Predictions and Justifications.   Finally, we may ask whether children who accurately predicted the character's initial emotion (i.e. Question 2) were also likely to give correct justifications. Among the 4-year-olds, 8 of the 20 children made accurate predictions for a minimum of 3 stories. Six of these 8 children then offered a minimum of 3 correct justifications. By contrast, none of the 12 remaining 4-year-olds (who each made accurate predictions for fewer than three stories) gave a comparable number of correct justifications. A Fisher Exact test confirmed this contingency ($P < 0.005$). A similar pattern was observed for the 6-year-olds; 15 of the 20 children accurately diagnosed that the character would be happy for a minimum of three stories. All of them gave at least three correct justifications whereas none of the remaining five children did so ($P < 0.005$). Thus, within each age group, children who made many accurate predictions were likely to justify them by referring to the apparent contents of the container whereas children who made few accurate predictions were likely to justify them by referring to the objective contents of the container.

Discussion

Experiment 1 shows that a majority of 6-year-olds and almost half the 4-year-olds accurately predicted that the duped characters would be happy on first being given the trick containers; accurate predictions were systematically backed up by appropriate reference to the apparent contents of the container. Subjects made such predictions, even though they were clearly aware of the concealed contents, had just been reminded of those contents by the memory check question (which immediately preceded the key test question), and appreciated that the character's eventual feelings about the actual contents would be negative. The remaining subjects wrongly predicted that the duped characters would be sad on initially being given the trick containers. They typically backed up their predictions by referring to the actual contents of the container, even though these were concealed.

These results fit the predictions set out earlier. Whereas just over half of the younger children attended only to the objective situation facing the story characters, the majority of the older children appreciated that the character's mistaken appraisal of that situation would govern his or her initial emotional reaction to the container. Hence, these results show that some 4-year-olds and most 6-year-olds appreciate that beliefs must be taken into account not just in explaining actions but also in explaining emotions.

EXPERIMENT 2

To accurately predict the emotion of the duped characters in Experiment 1, children needed to consider only the characters' mistaken belief. Having taken that belief into account, they could anticipate the emotion of any particular character by imagining their own reaction to being given an apparently full candy box or coke can. Experiment 2 was more complex. It assessed whether children could predict emotion by coordinating belief information with desire information. To make accurate predictions, children needed to consider not just what the animal character mistakenly expected to obtain, but also whether or not it coincided with what he or she wanted to obtain.

Experiment 2 raises an important but unexplored question namely whether children can simultaneously consider beliefs and desires. Philosophers argued that such belief-desire reasoning is at the core of our everyday theory of mind (Davidson, 1980). In simple terms, desires are assumed to provide a direction for our behaviour, whereas beliefs provide a map with which progress in the desired direction may be assessed. Actions are usually a joint function of beliefs and desires. My search in a particular direction is jointly caused by my desire for a particular goal and my belief that search in that direction will bring me closer to realising my goal. A similar analysis can be applied to emotions. My feeling of satisfaction is jointly caused by my desire for a particular goal, and my belief that I have successfully moved closer to attaining that goal. If children are working with such a theory in assessing how a person will appraise a given situation, they should be able to coordinate the two key components of that theory as well as considering each of them in isolation. For example, they should be able to grasp that if a person is about to obtain X but mistakenly expects to obtain Y, the person's emotion will depend on how that mistaken belief matches up with his or her desire. As long as Y is mistakenly expected, a person who wants Y will feel happy, whereas a person who wants X will feel sad. On the other hand, once the objective situation is revealed, each person should feel the opposite emotion.

The narrative adopted in Experiment 1 was modified in order to depict such interlocking beliefs and desires. First, children were told about a character's preference for one specific type of food or drink over any other. For example, they were told that the elephant liked only one kind of drink—milk. Then, as in Experiment 1, the standard contents of a container were removed. However, another potentially desirable food or drink was substituted rather than something undesirable. For example, milk might be substituted for coke. Children were then asked to predict how the character would feel on first receiving such a trick container, and on discovering its actual contents. To accurately predict the animals' initial emotional reaction, children had to consider both the desires as well as the beliefs of the character. They had to consider what the character believed was in the container and check whether this assumed content did or did not correspond to what the character wanted. Thus, pursuing the above example, if the character only liked milk she would be sad on being offered a container apparently containing coke. If children focused on the actual contents and ignored the animal's mistaken belief, or if they assumed that the animal liked any food or drink, their predictions of the characters' emotional reaction would be inaccurate.

Hitherto, assessments of children's theory of mind have examined their understanding of beliefs or desires in isolation. No experiment has required children to make predictions about story characters whose beliefs and desires are both systematically varied. Nevertheless, since earlier research has shown that even 3- and 4-year-olds are quite accurate in taking desires into account, and since Experiment 1 established that the ability to take beliefs into account is firmly established by 6 years, it was anticipated that predictions of emotion based on belief-desire reasoning would be made with increasing accuracy by children ranging from 3 to 7 years of age.

EXPERIMENT 2: METHOD

Subjects

There were 16 younger children (mean 4 years 3 months; range 3 years 4 months to 5 years 0 months); 16 intermediate children (mean 5 years 3 months; range 5 years 1 month to 5 years 6 months); and 16 older children (mean 6 years 10 months; range 6 years 5 months to 7 years 4 months). For convenience, these three groups will be referred to as 4-, 5-, and 6-year-olds. The 4-year-olds were recruited from a local preschool and the two older groups were recruited from local primary schools. In each case, subjects came from a wide range of socio-economic backgrounds. There were approximately equal numbers of boys and girls in each age group.

Procedure

The procedure was similar to that used for Experiment 1 with the following changes. First, whenever a to-be-tricked character was first indicated, his or her exclusive preference for a given item was described (e.g. "Harry the Horse wants a snack, but he only likes one kind of snack and that is peanuts/chewing gum". Mickey the Monkey would then replace the contents of a familiar packet (i.e. in the case of the horse, he would replace the contents of a peanuts packet with chewing gum).

Subjects were then asked two control questions to check their memory for the character's favourite food (e.g. "What does Harry the Horse like best: chewing gum or peanuts?") and the concealed contents of the container (e.g. "What is in the packet: chewing gum or peanuts?"). Finally, two test questions were posed. Subjects were asked to predict and explain the character's emotion: (1) on first being given the container but before opening it; and (2) after discovering its actual contents.

Other stories involved a bear whose favourite candy was smarties or polos and who found polos in a smarties box; an elephant whose favourite drink was coke or milk and who found milk in a coke can; and a bird whose favourite breakfast cereal was weetabix or cornflakes, and who found cornflakes in a weetabix carton.

Subjects were tested on all four stories, each involving a different animal. The order of the four stories was systematically varied across subjects using a Latin-square design. For half the children in each age group, the animals' favourite food in each story had been removed from its container and replaced by a non-favourite food. For the remaining children, the reverse was true: a non-favourite food had been removed from its container and replaced by the favourite food. Thus, for half the subjects, the correct answers to Questions 1 and 2 was *happy*, and *sad* respectively, whereas for half the subjects, the correct answers were *sad* and *happy* respectively. Nevertheless, for all children a correct answer to Question 1 required a consideration of whether the mistakenly expected content was what the character wanted; by contrast, a correct answer to Question 2 required a consideration of whether the real content was what the character wanted.

Results

All subjects in each of the three age groups replied correctly to both memory check questions.

Emotion Predictions. Table 3 indicates the number of subjects whose prediction of the character's emotion was guided by the real but hidden content of the container for Questions 1 and 2 (i.e. incorrectly guided by the real content for Question 1 and correctly guided by the real content for Question 2). Subjects are entered into the Table in terms of the number of reality-oriented predictions they made across the four stories.

Table 3 shows that in reply to Question 2, each age group usually predicted correctly that after opening the container the characters would feel happy or sad depending on whether their favourite item was really inside or not. In answer to Question 1, such reality-oriented predictions declined with age; instead, children increasingly based their predictions on the apparent content.

To check these conclusions, a two-way analysis of Age × Question was carried out. This confirmed that the number of reality-oriented predictions decreased with Age ($F(2,45) = 4.35$, $P < 0.02$) and that reality oriented

TABLE 3

Number of Subjects giving Reality-oriented Replies for 0–4 Stories, as a Function of Age and Question

Age and Question	No. of Stories					Mean	No.
	0	*1*	*2*	*3*	*4*		
4-year-olds							
Question 1	2	1	2	1	10	3.0	16
Question 2	0	0	1	2	13	3.75	16
5-year-olds							
Question 1	7	0	0	3	6	2.06	16
Question 2	0	0	0	3	13	3.81	16
6-year-olds							
Question 1	9	3	1	1	2	1.00	16
Question 2	0	0	0	0	16	4.00	16

TABLE 4
Mean Number of Correct, Incorrect, and Uninformative Justifications
by Age

Age	Type of Justification		
	Correct	Incorrect	Uninformative
4-year-olds	0.50	2.63	0.88
5-year-olds	1.50	1.19	1.31
6-year-olds	3.19	0.63	0.19

predictions were less frequent for Question 1 than Question 2 (Question, $F(1,45) = 55.85$, $P < 0.0001$); these main effects were qualified by the interaction of Age $\times$ Question ($F(2,45) = 7.04$, $P < 0.002$).

Further analysis of the interaction showed that reality-oriented predictions decreased with Age for Question 1 ($F(2,90) = 11.23$, $P < 0.001$) but not for Question 2 ($F(2,90) = 0.190$, P n.s.). Reality-oriented predictions were marginally less frequent for Question 1 than Question 2 among 4-year-olds ($F(1,45) = 3.12$, $P < 0.10$), and significantly less frequent among 5-year-olds ($F(1,45) = 16.97$, $P < 0.001$) and 6-year-olds ($F(1,45) = 50.21$, $P < 0.0001$).

Emotion Justifications. Justifications for replies to Question 1 were divided into *correct*, *incorrect*, and *uninformative* using the same criteria as for Experiment 1. The mean frequencies of the three types of justification are given in Table 4 as a function of Age.

t-Tests showed that 6-year-olds offered more correct justifications than 5-year-olds ($t(38) = 3.241$, $P < 0.005$) who, in turn, offered more correct justifications than 4-year-olds ($t(38) = 2.055$, $P < 0.025$). Conversely, 4-year-olds offered more incorrect justifications than both 5-year-olds ($t(38) = 2.583$, $P < 0.01$) and 6-year-olds ($t(38) = 3.923$, $P < 0.0005$), although the last two groups did not differ significantly ($t(38) = 1.175$, P n.s.).

Contingency between Predictions and Justifications. Subjects in each of the three age groups are entered in Table 5 in terms of whether or not they gave a minimum of three correct predictions for Question 1. These subjects are further subdivided into those who did or did not proceed to offer a minimum of three correct justifications. Fisher Exact tests confirmed that for each age group, those children who gave predominantly accurate predictions were also those who offered predominantly correct justifications (4-year-olds, $P < 0.025$; 5-year-olds, $P < 0.005$; 6-year-olds, $P < 0.01$).

TABLE 5
Contingency between Predictions and Justifications for each Age Group

Age	Correct Predictions	Correct Justifications	
		3 or more	Less than 3
4-year-olds	3 or more	2	1
	less than 3	0	13
5-year-olds	3 or more	5	2
	less than 3	0	9
6-year-olds	3 or more	12	0
	less than 3	1	3

In summary, all three age groups could remember the characters' favourite item, and whether or not that item was concealed in the container. They also correctly judged that the characters' emotion after opening the container would depend on their desire for that item. Accurate predictions and justifications regarding the characters' emotion prior to opening the container increased with age. Within all three age groups, the ability to make accurate predictions was closely linked to an awareness of the character's mistaken belief: Those children who made predominantly accurate predictions were also likely to refer to the apparent contents of the container rather than the actual contents when giving their justifications.

Discussion

The results of Experiment 2 show that children of 4 to 6 years of age increasingly predict emotion from a joint consideration of someone's beliefs and desires. Although all three age groups were quite accurate in diagnosing the characters' emotional reaction to the actual contents of the container, predictions and justifications of the characters' initial emotional reaction improved with age. Before turning to the implications of these findings, the results of Experiment 3 will be presented. This experiment was intended to counter an important and plausible objection to the findings reported so far.

EXPERIMENT 3

It could be argued that the use of stories that involve deception may lead to an underestimate of children's knowledge of the relationship between beliefs and desires. In Experiments 1 and 2, children had to take into account the fact that the duped protagonist was not only unaware of the actual contents of the container, but had a false belief about the contents, thanks to the machinations of Mickey the Monkey. Young children may be able to predict emotion on the basis of belief-desire reasoning before they can take false beliefs into account. For example, Wellman and Bartsch (1988) have shown that 3- and 4-year-olds successfully predict another person's search even if that person's belief about the location of a hidden object is discrepant from their own belief, provided the actual location of the object remains unknown. If its location is revealed, thereby showing that the other person holds a false belief, these same children make inaccurate predictions. These results suggest that young children can understand that people may hold different (but unproven) beliefs before they grasp that one person may hold a true belief and the other a false belief.

Experiment 3 was designed to include the key components of the earlier experiments, but to omit the potentially problematic necessity for taking false beliefs into account. Instead of witnessing a trick, children were shown closed neutral containers and asked to make two predictions about the character's emotional reaction to each container: If the character believed that it contained: (1) the preferred item; and (2) the non-preferred item. As the actual contents of the container were invisible to subjects, they did not need to set their own knowledge of the contents aside in anticipating the animal's reaction. Nor could they determine at this point in the experiment which of the animal's hypothetical beliefs was true or false. Only at the end of the story was the container opened and children asked about the animal's emotional reaction to the actual contents.

EXPERIMENT 3: METHOD

Subjects

There were 20 younger subjects (mean 3 years 10 months; range 3 years 2 months to 4 years 6 months) and 20 older subjects (mean 5 years 5 months; range 4 years 11 months to 5 years 11 months). These two groups will be referred to as the 3- and 5-year-old groups respectively. The children were tested in preschools and primary schools in Surrey, England. They came from a wide range of socio-economic backgrounds.

Procedure

Children were tested individually in a quiet area of their school. They were first shown the four toy animals and told that they were going to listen to a story about each animal. Each story was based on the following format.

Children were told that the animal wanted a snack or drink but liked only one type and not another (e.g. "Ellie the Elephant wants a drink, but she only likes one kind of drink and that is coke. She doesn't like milk, she only likes coke."). The animal's preference for one or the other of the two items was systematically varied across children. Memory for this initial information was checked (e.g. "What does Ellie like to drink?") and repeated where necessary.

Next, a container was introduced, neutral in shape and colour, that might equally well contain the preferred or non-preferred item. The animal's ignorance of its hidden contents was explicitly stated (e.g. "Now, we're going to give her a drink. It's here in this bottle. Ellie doesn't know what's inside the bottle but she's wondering what's inside.").

Children were then asked to predict the animal's emotion given each of two different hypothetical beliefs about the contents of the container. Specifically, they were asked how the animal would feel if the animal believed the preferred item was inside the container and similarly how the animal would feel if the animal believed the non-preferred item was in the container. The wording of each question was as follows: "What if Ellie thinks there's *item* inside—will she be happy or sad if she thinks we've given her *item*?" Each child heard two stories in which the first question for each story was about the preferred item and the second question for each story was about the non-preferred item, and two stories in which this order was reversed. The order of the two story types was randomised across children.

The next question tested children's continued acknowledgement that the animal still did not know the contents of the container (e.g. "Now, Ellie is wondering what's inside the bottle, but does she really know yet what's inside?").

The child was then asked to open up the container to reveal its contents which were named by the experimenter. The final question tested children's appreciation of the impact of those contents on the animal (e.g. "Oh look, it's *item*. So is Ellie happy or sad?"). For half the children in each age group, the revealed contents always turned out to be the preferred item, and for the remaining half the revealed contents always turned out to be the non-preferred item.

Results

Children's predictions about the animal's hypothetical emotion were analysed first, then their appreciation of the animal's ignorance of the hidden contents, and finally their predictions about the animal's reaction to the actual contents.

Hypothetical Emotion. Children were scored (out of 4) for the number of stories in which they claimed that the animal would be happy. Table 6 shows the number of subjects who claimed that the animal would be happy for 0, 1, 2, 3, or 4 stories as a function of Age and Item Expected (preferred versus non-preferred).

Inspection of Table 6 shows that both age groups judged that the animals would be happier given positive expectations rather than negative expectations (i.e. if they believed the preferred rather than the non-preferred item was in the container). However, the older children distinguished more sharply between these two expectations. To check this conclusion, an Age × Item Expected analyis was carried out. This revealed a main effect of Age ($F(1,38) = 16.46$, $P < 0.0002$), a main effect of Item Expected ($F(1,38) = 127.61$, $P < 0.0001$), and the interaction of Age × Item Expected ($F(1,38) = 25.72$, $P < 0.0001$).

Further analysis of the interaction confirmed that both 3- and 5-year-olds were more likely to judge that the animals would be happy given positive rather than negative expectations [3-year-olds: $F(1,38) = 18.23$, $P < 0.0002$; 5-year-olds: ($F(1,38) = 126.03$, $P < 0.0001$)]. However, although the two age groups were equally likely to claim that the animals would be happy given positive expectations ($F(1,38) = 0.63$, P n.s.), the 3-year-olds were more likely to judge that the animals would be happy even given negative expectations ($F(1,38) = 38.03$, $P < 0.0001$).

Knowledge of the Contents. Table 7 indicates the number of subjects who correctly denied that the animal knew the contents of the container for 0, 1, 2, 3, or 4 stories as a function of Age.

All the 5-year-olds but slightly less than half the 3-year-old children systematically and correctly denied that the animal knew the actual con-

TABLE 6

Number of Subjects judging Animal to be Happy for 0–4 Stories, as a Function of Age and Item Expected

Age and Item Expected	No. of Stories					Mean	No.
	0	1	2	3	4		
3-year-olds							
Preferred	0	0	3	3	14	3.55	20
Non-preferred	5	2	4	2	7	2.20	20
5-year-olds							
Preferred	0	0	0	4	16	3.80	20
Non-preferred	15	5	0	0	0	0.25	20

TABLE 7
Number of Subjects judging Animal Not to Know for 0–4 Stories, as a
Function of Age and Item

Age	No. of Stories					Mean	No.
	0	1	2	3	4		
3-year-olds	2	8	1	0	9	2.30	20
5-year-olds	0	0	0	0	20	4.00	20

tents. A chi-square test confirmed that the proportion of children who were correct on all four stories was greater in the older group than the younger group (χ (1, $n = 40$) = 12.54, $P < 0.001$).

Actual Emotion. At the end of each story, the hidden contents of the container were revealed and children were asked to judge whether the animal felt happy or sad as a result. Table 8 indicates the number of subjects who judged the animal to be happy for 0, 1, 2, 3, or 4 stories as a function of Age and Type of Content (preferred versus non-preferred).

Inspection of Table 8 shows that children typically judged that the animal would be happy if the content turned out to be the preferred item, but not if it turned out to be the non-preferred item. This pattern of prediction was produced by 3- and 5-year-olds alike although it was somewhat more systematic among 5-year-olds. To check these conclusions, an analysis of Age × Item was carried out. This revealed only the main effect of Item ($F(1,36)$ = 66.31, $P < 0.0001$).

In summary, (1) both age groups appropriately adjusted their prediction of the animals' hypothetical emotion depending on whether the animals had positive or negative expectations about getting the item they wanted,

TABLE 8
Number of Subjects judging Animal to be Happy for 0–4 Stories, as a Function of Age and Item

Age and Item	No. of Stories					Mean	No.
	0	1	2	3	4		
3-year-olds							
Preferred	0	0	0	2	8	3.80	10
Non-preferred	5	2	1	0	2	1.20	10
5-year-olds							
Preferred	0	0	0	0	10	4.00	10
Non-preferred	6	2	0	1	1	0.90	10

(2) both age groups adjusted their prediction about the animals' actual emotion depending on whether the contents turned out to match what they had wanted. Nevertheless, the 3-year-olds were less accurate than the 5-year-olds in two respects: they sometimes predicted that the animal would be happy despite negative expectations, and they were less systematic in their assertion that the animal did not know the contents of the container before it was opened.

GENERAL DISCUSSION

The three experiments show that between the age of 3 and 7 years, young children increasingly recognise that a person's emotional reactions to a situation are governed by an appraisal of that situation rather than objective features of the situation itself. Children's sensitivity to the importance of appraisal emerged in three ways. First, they took the character's desires into account; secondly, they took the character's beliefs into account; and finally, they considered the relationship between beliefs and desires.

Children's appreciation of the role of desires emerged in Experiments 2 and 3. Children predicted that the characters would be happy if the eventual outcome was what they wanted and sad if it was not. Thus, children understood that emotional reactions were not dictated by the outcome *per se*; the same outcome was judged to elicit either happiness or sadness depending on the desire that characters brought to it. Moreover, in each experiment, no age change was apparent in the ability to take desires into account. The early emergence of this ability confirms previous findings (Stein & Levine, 1986; Wellman & Bartsch, 1988; Wellman & Woolley, in press; Yuill, 1984).

The two important novel findings were that children can take beliefs into account, as shown by Experiment 1, and can jointly consider beliefs and desires, as shown by Experiments 2 and 3. Children increasingly understand that emotion is governed not by the relationship between desire and actual reality but by the relationship between desire and expected reality, even when the expectation in question is objectively false or remains unproven. Children's ability to take beliefs as well as desires into account was reflected in several ways. First, they made accurate predictions about how the character would feel before opening the container—predictions that required that they consider whether the character expected to obtain what he or she wanted. Secondly, children justified those predictions by referring to what the character believed to be in the container (i.e. its apparent contents) rather than to its actual contents. Finally, despite the overall improvement with age in accuracy of both predictions and justifications, there was a firm relationship between the two responses within each age group: those individuals who often made accurate predictions proceeded to concentrate on the apparent as opposed to the actual contents of the container in justifying their predictions.

Taken together, the results of the three experiments show that young children predict and explain emotion with reference to a theory of mind, or at least with joint reference to the two key components of that theory, namely beliefs and desires. Such belief-desire reasoning has already emerged by 3 years and is well established by 5 or 6 years of age. This conclusion undermines earlier claims that 6-year-olds adopt a situational or behaviouristic theory of emotion (Harris & Olthof, 1982). On the contrary, the present results show that 6-year-olds adopt a relatively mentalistic account of the causes of emotion. They do not assume that an emotional reaction is caused by inherent features of the external situation and they do not simply rely on their recollection of how the objective situation made them feel in the past.

Although even 3-year-olds were quite competent at taking desires into account, as shown by their accurate predictions of the characters' emotional reaction to the actual contents of the container, there was a clear improvement with age when children were asked to predict the characters' emotional reaction to the anticipated contents of the container. How should this improvement be explained? A definitive answer will require further research. For the moment, however, it seems clear that one component of the age change is the marked improvement in the ability to take beliefs into account, particularly when they conflict with the subject's own knowledge. Several pieces of evidence back up this assertion. First, children's justifications varied with age: Young children inappropriately referred to the hidden contents of the container, ignoring the fact that these contents were unknown to the animal character until the container was opened at the end of the story. By contrast, older children were more likely to refer to the apparent contents of the container, acknowledging the false belief of the duped character. Secondly, although it could be argued that young children can understand false beliefs so long as they do not also have to consider desires, a clear age change was observed not just in Experiment 2 where belief-desire coordination was critical but also in Experiment 1, where it was not. Recall that in Experiment 1, the apparent contents were invariably desirable and the hidden contents were undesirable, so that children needed only to consider which item the character believed he or she would get. Thirdly, when children were required to estimate the impact of untested beliefs, as in Experiment 3, rather than false beliefs as in Experiments 1 and 2, even 3-year-olds showed more ability to engage in belief-desire reasoning.

These considerations show that young children's predictions of emotion exhibit remarkable similarities to their predictions of action (Wellman & Bartsch, 1988). Young preschoolers appear to be quite competent in using information about desires to predict what someone will do or feel: They understand that people will engage in actions that move them closer to a realisation of those desires, and that they will react positively or negatively depending on whether they succeed in doing so. Older children grasp that when people estimate where they stand in relation to a current goal, they may rely not on objective information but on untested expectations or even on false beliefs. Paradoxically, therefore, people can engage in actions that actually lead them away from their goal (e.g. they search in the wrong place) or they may feel sad about an event that has actually brought them closer to their goal (e.g. they are sad at being given a trick container with their favourite food concealed inside). This paradox is increasingly acknowledged during the preschool years.

In conclusion, we may speculate about the cognitive processes that children deploy when they engage in belief-desire reasoning. At present, most investigators subscribe more or less explicitly to a rationalistic account (Olson, Astington, & Harris, 1988). Children are credited with a grasp of theoretical entities, notably beliefs and desires, and it is assumed that they reason in a quasi-deductive or computational mode by retrieving theoretical statements embodying causal links between beliefs, desires, and emotions or between beliefs, desires, and actions (Leslie, 1988; Wellman, 1988). Having diagnosed the current mental state of a person (in terms of desires or in terms of desires plus beliefs) children infer the action or emotion that will ensue by reference to the relevant propositions in their theory.

It is worth considering an alternative, less rationalistic proposal (Harris, 1989). A similar proposal has been made within the philosophy of mind (Goldman, in press; Gordon, 1986; 1987), and has been dubbed the "simulation" account, following earlier proposals by Tversky and Kahneman (1982). According to this alternative account, predictions of other people's actions or emotions involve two steps: first, the invocation of a set of pretend or make-believe premises, in which the goals and beliefs of the other person are imagined; and secondly, the running of a simulation in which one's own action or emotion, given such make-believe premises, is estimated. The results of this simulation are then used as a basis for making predictions about the other person. Applied to the results of these experiments, children would first take the desires, or the desires and beliefs, of the animal character as a set of make-believe premises. They would then imagine how they would act or feel in the light of those premises and use their imagined reactions as a basis for making predictions about the story characters. This proposal rests on the assumption that children do not need to have recourse to a theory to imagine how they themselves would react to an imagined situation—any more than they need a theory to produce an actual reaction in an actual situation.

The intuitive appeal of this account is three-fold. First, it avoids imputing a set of theoretical propositions to the preschool child with little explanation of how those theoretical propositions have been arrived at. Instead, it invokes processes that are within the capacity of a 3-year-old. For example, there is considerable evidence from young children's pretend play that they can imagine wanting a particular goal (Wolf, Rygh, & Altshuler, 1984). They frequently attribute such make-believe desires to themselves or to their dolls. Secondly, it provides a plausible explanation of why children in the early preschool years fail to make accurate predictions: The implication is that they fail to entertain the appropriate make-believe premises. Thus, in the case of 3- and 4-year-olds, they may imagine wanting one food item rather than another, but fail to imagine the character's mistaken expectation about what food they are about to get. Five- and 6-year-olds, by contrast, run a more complete simulation by imagining not just what the story character hopes to find in the container, but also what he or she expects to find there. Thirdly, it shows that although children may adopt a fundamentally egocentric strategy (i.e. they ask themselves: "What would I do?" or "How would I feel?") they can nevertheless become more sophisticated in their predictions, as they increasingly take note of critical differences between their mental state and the person whose reactions they are trying to predict; their recognition of those differences is reflected in the increasingly exhaustive recognition of the premises that must be fed in to any given simulation. Thus, younger children concentrate on imagining the other person's goals, whereas older children also take into account the set of beliefs—the mental map—that the other person has about where he or she stands with respect to those goals. In short, the simulation account shows how young children can make predictions about other people that accord with a theory of mind, without necessarily deriving those predictions from a theory.

Finally, it is worth emphasising an important implication of the simulation account for our understanding not just of children's attributions of emotion to other people but also their anticipatory attributions to themselves. Children as well as adults are often asked to indicate their preference for one hypothetical activity or event as compared with another. It seems likely that such decisions are often made by means of a simulation, as outlined above. Thus, people imagine themselves facing each hypothetical alternative and assess whether or not they will enjoy it, fear it, be distressed by it, and so forth. For such simulations to be accurate, it will be necessary to feed into them the expectations and desires that the situation may or may not meet when it is actually encountered. Everyday observation suggests that children and adults alike often have difficulty in running such a simulation accurately. For example, a 3-year-old might eagerly look forward to attending preschool but burst into tears when her father is about to leave her there; in anticipating the situation, the child has not taken into account her desire for a familiar presence. Similarly, prospective parents may fail to anticipate their emotional reactions to childcare. They may find that it thwarts certain unacknowledged desires, yet satisfies other desires that it unexpectedly triggers. The simulation model indicates how we might be able to think more analytically about such gaps between actual and anticipated emotion.

Manuscript received 10 January 1989
Manuscript revised 15 March 1989

REFERENCES

Astington, J. W., Harris, P. L., & Olson, D. R. (Eds) (1988). *Developing theories of mind*. Cambridge University Press.
Barden, R. C., Zelko, F. A., Duncan, S. W., & Masters, J. C. (1980). Children's consensual knowledge about the experiential determinants of emotion. *Journal of Personality and Social Psychology*, *39*, 968–976.
Borke, H. (1971). Interpersonal perception of young children: Egocentrism or empathy? *Developmental Psychology*, *5*, 263–269.
Chandler, M. J. & Greenspan, S. (1972). Ersatz egocentrism: A reply to H. Borke. *Developmental Psychology*, *7*, 104–6.
Davidson, D. (1980). Actions, reasons and causes. In D. Davidson (Ed.), *Actions and events*. Oxford University Press, pp. 3–19.
Goldman, A. I. (in press). Interpretation psychologized. *Mind and Language*.
Gordon, R. M. (1986). Folk psychology as simulation. *Mind and Language*, *1*, 156–171.
Gordon, R. M. (1987). *The structure of emotions*. Cambridge University Press.
Harris, P. L. (1989). *Children and emotion: The development of psychological understanding*. Oxford: Blackwell.
Harris, P. L. & Olthof, T. (1982). The child's concept of emotion. In G. E. Butterworth & P. Light (Eds), *Social cognition*. Brighton, U.K.: Harvester, pp. 188–209.
Harris, P. L., Olthof, T., Meerum Terwogt, M., & Hardman, C. E. (1987). Children's knowledge of the situations that provoke emotion. *International Journal of Behavioral Development*, *10*, 319–344.
Johnson, C. N. & Maratsos, M. P. (1977). Early comprehension of mental verbs: Think and know. *Child Development*, *48*, 1743–1747.
Leslie, A. M. (1988). Some implications of pretense for mechanisms underlying the child's theory of mind. In J. W. Astington, P. L. Harris, & D. R. Olson (Eds). *Developing theories of mind*. Cambridge University Press.
Olson, D. R., Astington, J. W., & Harris, P. L. (1988). Introduction. In J. W. Astington, P. L. Harris, & D. R. Olson (Eds), *Developing theories of mind*. Cambridge University Press.
Perner, J., Leekam, S., & Wimmer, H. (1987). Three-year-olds' difficulty in understanding false belief: Cognitive limitation, lack of knowledge, or pragmatic misunderstanding? *British Journal of Developmental Psychology*.
Stein, N. L. & Levine, L. (1986). *Causal organization of emotional knowledge*. Paper presented at the Psychonomic Society meeting, New Orleans.
Trabasso, T., Stein, N. L., & Johnson, L. R. (1981). Children's knowledge of events: A causal analysis of story structure. In G. Bower (Ed.), *Learning and motivation, Vol. 15*. New York: Academic Press, pp. 237–282.

Tversky, A. & Kahneman, D. (1982). The simulation heuristic. In Kahneman D., P. Slovic, & A. Tversky (Eds), *Heuristics and biases.* Cambridge University Press.

Wellman, H. M. (1988). First steps in the child's theorizing about the mind. In J. Astington, P. L. Harris, & D. R. Olson (Eds), *Developing theories of mind.* Cambridge University Press.

Wellman, H. M. & Bartsch, K. (1988). Young children's reasoning about beliefs. *Cognition, 30,* 239–277.

Wellman, H. M. & Woolley, J. D. (in press). *From simple desires to ordinary beliefs: The early development of everyday psychology.*

Wimmer, H. & Perner, J. (1983). Beliefs about beliefs: Representations and constraining function of wrong beliefs in young children's understanding of deception. *Cognition, 13,* 103–128.

Wolf, D. P., Rygh, J., & Altshuler, J. (1984). Agency and experience: Actions and states in play narratives. In I. Bretherton (Ed.), *Symbolic play,* Orlando, Fla.: Academic Press.

Yuill, N. (1984). Young children's coordination of motive and outcome in judgements of satisfaction and morality. *British Journal of Developmental Psychology, 2,* 73–81.

COGNITION AND EMOTION, 1989, 3(4), 401–419

Understanding the Motivational Role of Affect: Life-span Research from an Attributional Perspective

Bernard Weiner and Sandra Graham

Department of Psychology, University of California, Los Angeles, U.S.A.

A subset of emotions that includes pride, gratitude, guilt, anger, and sympathy are elicited by specific causal ascriptions. In addition, these emotions give rise to distinct behaviours. In this article, two experiments were discussed that examine the attributional antecedents and the behavioural consequences of the five affects listed above. The research participants ranged in age from 5 to 95, so that changes throughout the life span could be examined. Systematic associations as well as developmental trends were found. The picture of the elderly that emerged was one of kindness and altriuism: Pity and helping increased throughout the life span, whereas anger decreased. In addition, relations between attributions, emotions, and judged behaviour did not decrease among the very elderly.

INTRODUCTION

Affective reactions frequently reflect what has happened and provide guides for subsequent actions that might be undertaken. Hence, emotions are the bridge between the past and the future. The general framework of "past outcome–emotion–future behaviour" has been evident in the work of attribution theorists (see reviews in Weiner, 1985, 1986). From an attributional perspective, the historical determinants (the past of emotion) are the perceived reasons why an outcome has occurred, or causal ascriptions for positive and negative events. Different causal interpretations of events are anticipated to give rise to disparate emotional experiences. For example, failure caused by lack of ability is presumed to evoke different feelings than failure attributed by the student to a biased teacher. In a similar manner, success perceived as due to high effort is hypothesised to produce emotions distinct from those elicited by success conceived as due

Requests of reprints should be sent to Bernard Weiner, Department of Psychology, University of California, Los Angeles, California, CA 90024, U.S.A. The second author was supported by a Spencer Foundation grant from the National Academy of Education.

© 1989 Lawrence Erlbaum Associates Limited

to help from others. In sum, for attribution theorists the prior historical determinants of an emotion, or emotional antecedents, include outcome evaluations and their perceived causes.

When distinguishing between perceived causes, their properties or attributes must be considered. Causal beliefs that appear to differ qualitatively, such as ability and effort, or even low ability and a biased teacher, share a small number of underlying characteristics. The causes therefore can be compared and contrasted quantitatively on these basic attributes. For present purposes, two of the properties or dimensions of causality are of prime importance, namely, causal locus and causal controllability. Locus refers to the "position" or the "location" of the cause as internal or external to the actor. Ability and effort as causes of student failure have the same locus—internal to the student. On the other hand, a biased teacher as the cause of student failure is external to the student. The second causal dimension, controllability, denotes the possibility of volitional influence over the onset or offset of the cause. Low aptitude, for example, is not subject to volitional control. Conversely, in most instances effort expenditure can be volitionally increased or decreased. Thus, effort is classified as a controllable cause. Both locus and controllability judgements in part depend on the perspective of the viewer. Thus, failure of a student because of low ability is internal from the perspective of the student but external to him- or herself given the viewpoint of a teacher seeking to understand the failure. In a similar manner, the failing student cannot control the bias of a teacher, but could contend that the teacher can contain his or her biases.

Turning from the antecedents of emotions to their consequences, for researchers examining causal ascriptions the future most often has referred to those behaviours (or judgements about behaviour) that are directly or indirectly instigated by causal perceptions. These actions include withdrawal (given a low ability ascription for failure), expenditure of extra effort (given a lack of effort attribution for failure), aggression (given an attribution for failure to interference from others), and so on.

What emotions have been investigated by attribution theorists, and what are their causal antecedents and behavioural consequences? It is evident that not all emotions are elicited or influenced by causal beliefs. Love and hate, excitement and boredom, and joy and disgust, to mention just a few emotions, are not necessarily (or primarily) mediated by perceptions of causality. The emotions amenable to elicitation by causal ascriptions that have been most studied are anger, gratitude, and guilt, as well as pity (sympathy), pride (self-esteem), and shame (humiliation) (see, for example, Graham, 1984; Weiner, Graham, & Chandler, 1982a; Weiner, Graham, Stern, & Lawson, 1982b). It should be noted that, although an extensive array of emotions has not been (and probably cannot be) incorporated within an attributional analysis, the affects that have been examined are quite prevalent in everyday experience.

Based on empirical evidence, philosophical reasoning, and intuition, the causal antecedents of these emotions and their behavioural consequences, considering for the moment only adults, are given in Table 1. To briefly elaborate on these associations:

Anger given a Negative, Self-relevant Event.   Given a negative, self-related outcome or event, the attributional antecedent for anger is an ascription to factors controllable by others. Thus, anger involves blame and holding others responsible (Averill, 1983). In one illustrative study by Weiner, Graham, and Chandler (1982), respondents were asked to recount instances in their lives in which they experienced anger. Ninety per cent of the recollections involved a controllable action. For example, people are angry when others cheat or lie to them, or when a room-mate fails to clean up the kitchen. These behaviours elicit retaliation, which serves the function of communicating "do not do that again" and therefore helps to maintain social control and social order (Trivers, 1971).

Anger given a Negative, Other-related Event.   Anger and the less intense manifestations of anger such as annoyance and irritation are expressed when negative events impacting on others are controllable by those others. Hence, anger often is experienced when someone is failing because he or she has not tried. We believe that this illustrates that anger may be felt even when the situation does not directly impact on the self. In a similar manner, anger also is elicited by stigmas perceived as controllable, including alcoholism, drug addiction, obesity, AIDS, etc. (Weiner, Perry, & Magnusson, 1988). The person needing help who has not tried, or the individual with a controllability-linked stigma, tends to be neglected and help is withheld. For example, students who state that they need to borrow class notes because they "went to the beach" are reacted to with annoyance and the notes tend not to be lent (see, for example, Reisenzein, 1986). Similarly, it is difficult to collect charity for alcoholics, the obese, drug addicts, and so on.

Gratitude.   Evidence suggests that gratitude toward another is elicited if and only if the act of the benefactor was under volitional control and intended to benefit the recipient (Tesser, Gatewood, & Driver, 1968). Gratitude is a stimulus to return a favour to the other and thus reintroduce balance. Hence, reciprocity is likely when a gift is volitionally rather than forcefully or accidentally given (Goranson & Berkowitz, 1966; Greenberg & Frisch, 1972).

TABLE 1

Antecedents and Consequences of some Affective Experiences

Outcome	Causal Antecedent	Affect	Action Tendency
Negative, self-relevant	Controllable by other	Anger	Retaliation against other
Negative, other-relevant	Controllable by other	Anger (irritation)	Retreat from other (neglect)
Positive, self-relevant	Controllable by other	Gratitude	Restitution; go toward other
Negative, self-relevant	Controllable by self	Guilt	Reproof; go toward task
Negative, other-relevant	Controllable by self	Guilt	Reproof and restitution; go toward other
Negative, other-relevant	Uncontrollable	Pity (sympathy)	Restitution; go toward other
Positive, self-relevant	Self	Self-esteem (pride)	Reward; go toward task
Negative, self-relevant	Self	Self-esteem decrease[a]	Retreat away from task
Negative, self-relevant	Uncontrollable by self	Shame (humiliation)	Recoil; go away from task

[a]There is not a single emotion label comparable to pride in success when the outcome is failure given an internal cause, irrespective of information about controllability.

Guilt given a Negative, Self-relevant Outcome.   Guilt requires an attribution of personal responsibility (see Izard, 1977). That is, the cause of a negative outcome is both internal and controllable by the actor. In achievement-related contexts, ascription of failure to a lack of effort elicits guilt. There is evidence that guilt, when experienced in manageable intensity, is a positive motivator that augments achievement strivings (see Covington & Omelich, 1984). That is, guilt goads the actor to make amends and try harder.

Guilt given a Negative, Other-related Outcome.   One can be responsible for one's own failure or plight, or for harm done to others. As in the case of personal harm, actions involving damage to others also elicit guilt if the harmdoer perceives these actions as controllable by him- or herself (see Weiner et al., 1982a).

Pity (sympathy) given a Negative, Other-related Outcome.   Uncontrollable causes of negative events elicit sympathy. Thus, typical instances of pity and sympathy are sights of the blind, crippled, aged, retarded, and so on. These are stigmas for which the stigmatised person is not held responsible (Weiner et al., 1988). Sympathy instigates approach behaviour to help the needy other. For example, students with eye problems who ask to borrow class notes are reacted to with sympathy and the notes are lent (Reisenzein, 1986). In a similar manner, it is comparatively easy to collect charity donations for individuals with Alzheimer's disease, paraplegia, and other illnesses for which the disabled person is not held responsible.

Pride (Self-esteem).   Pride and increased self-esteem are experienced when a positive outcome is ascribed to the self; lowered self-esteem is experienced when a negative outcome is self-attributed. Thus, success and failure due to ability, effort, personality, etc. have implications for self-worth. This is reflected in the so-called "hedonic bias", which describes the ego-enhancing and ego-defensive tendencies to ascribe success internally and failure externally. Pride is a cue to go toward a situation and recapture the positive affect previously enjoyed, whereas lowered self-esteem propels the individual away from the situation of prior negative affect (see review in Weiner, 1986).

Shame.   Shame (humiliation, embarrassment) appears to be elicited when the cause of a negative event is internal but uncontrollable. Thus, for example, when failure is ascribed to lack of ability, the failing individual feels ashamed (Brown & Weiner, 1984; Jagacinski & Nicholls, 1984). Shame, which often is considered a "public" emotion, implies that a social comparison is being made and that one has not measured up to others.

Hence, being too (tall, uncoordinated, dumb, etc.) tend to elicit shame in the individual possessing these attributes if they resulted in perceived achievement failure, social rejection, etc. (see Wicker, Payne, & Morgan, 1983). Although the data are not extensive, shame apparently leads to withdrawal and removal from the situation; shame makes one want to "curl up in a ball" and "disappear".

Summary. A number of linkages between causal perceptions, emotions, and subsequent actions have been identified. Some of the most salient human emotions are determined by thoughts about causality, and these reactions have far-reaching motivational consequences.

Developmental Considerations

A common theme underlying much of the literature concerned with the development of emotion is the child's growing awareness of the psychological complexity of emotional life (see Harris, 1983; Harter & Buddin, 1987; Saarni, 1979). In this vein, attribution researchers have been particularly concerned with the development of children's understanding of the attribution–emotion–action linkages discussed in the prior sections (see reviews in Graham & Weiner, 1986; Weiner & Graham, 1984). This research has been guided by two fundamental questions:

1. Considering first the hypothesised attribution–emotion linkages, at what age do children understand that particular causal thoughts precede specific emotional reactions? The fact that the emotions under investigation are cognitively determined suggests that there may be age-related changes in the understanding of these linkages.
2. In the "past outcome–emotion–figure behaviour" framework elaborated in Table 1, we have specified a particular set of relations between thinking, feeling, and action. At what age do children perceive this motivational sequence as involving emotion, and what are the age-related changes related specifically to the emotion-action union?

Prior research has provided more answers to the first question than to the second. In a number of studies, attribution theorists have documented that emotional understanding becomes more differentiated with age as particular feelings become more uniquely tied to specific antecedent thoughts (Graham & Weiner, 1986; Weiner & Graham, 1984). Thus, there has been increasing knowledge about the development of attribution–affect bonds, the initial step in the "past outcome–emotion–future behaviour" sequence. However, among both attribution theorists as well as general students of affect, there have been few studies of the development and understanding of the second step in the sequence, that between emotion and action, or of the complete set of relations involving cognition, emotion, and action.

In the remainder of this article, we present two research studies examining growth and changes in judgements regarding cognition–emotion–action linkages. The initial investigation conducted by Graham (1988) involved the affects of gratitude, guilt, and pride among children aged 5 to 11. This investigation has recently appeared in print and will not be presented in detail. However, because the source of the publication may not come to the attention of nondevelopmental emotion researchers, it will be given somewhat more than a cursory review. In contrast, the second investigation has only recently been completed. This study involved the affects of anger and sympathy. Furthermore, respondents ranged in age from 5 to 95, so that a full range of the life span could be examined.

At the outset, we wish to acknowledge that the studies to be presented employ a role-playing methodology. Participants infer how someone else would think or feel in hypothetical situations or how they would behave if they thought or felt a particular way. One may question whether this is a legitimate approach to the study of emotion inasmuch as affects during their states of activation were not examined. There are no definitive answers or rebuttals to this criticism. Nonetheless, this methodology and others relying on verbal understanding of emotion are viewed as reasonable starting points for building conceptual models of affective growth such as the one proposed here. We believe that we are examining both the development of the understanding of cognition–emotion–action linkages, as well as their actual growth.

AN EMPIRICAL STUDY OF PRIDE, GRATITUDE, AND GUILT

Graham (1988) created three story scenarios[1] that had the potential of eliciting pride, gratitude, or guilt in the target children, who ranged in age from 5 to 11. The scenarios were as follows:

Pride

This is a story about a boy named Chris. Chris's teacher gave a spelling test and he got all the words right. Chris received an 'A' on the test.

---

[1]See Graham (1988) for complete reporting of the story scenarios and other methodological information.

It was revealed that the child received an "A" either because he or she studied all the words the night before (internal cause) or because the teacher gave a very easy test (external cause). Only the former cause elicits pride among adults.

Gratitude

This is a story about two boys, Bob and Tim, who are in the same class. Bob is the captain of the baseball team and he is just now choosing players for the team. Tim is new in the school. He wants to be picked, but no one knows how well he plays. Bob picks Tim to be on the team.

One causal condition indicated that the team captain voluntarily chose the target child as a gesture of kindness (controllable cause). The second condition revealed that the team rules required selection of the target child (uncontrollable cause). Only the former elicits gratitude among adults.

Guilt

This is a story about a boy named Jason. One day Jason was riding his bike in the park. Suddenly, he crashed into another boy named Tommy who also was riding in the park. Tommy fell off his bike and broke his front wheel.

In the controllable condition, Jason was portrayed as negligent. In the uncontrollable condition, Jason was described as making a quick stop to avoid hitting an inattentive small child and that caused the crash. Only the former condition elicits guilt among adults.

Following each scenario, children first rated the given cause on degree of locus in the pride scenario and the degree of controllability in the gratitude and guilt scenarios. The children then made judgements about the affects appropriate to each story. In addition, ratings were made about an intended action that might follow each outcome (see Table 1). The pride scenario assessed the magnitude of self-reward following success on the test; in the gratitude scenario, participants judged the likelihood that the target child would reciprocate the action of the team captain by giving him a gift; and in the guilt scenario involving damage to another child's bike, the subjects were asked whether Jason would contribute some portion of his own money toward repairing the bike.

Affective ratings as a function of the causal condition are shown in Fig. 1 (top half). Based on prior research, it was anticipated that affects would be more uniquely tied to their antecedent causal thoughts as children increased in age.

This is what the data in the top half of Fig. 1 reveal. Even though all children indicated some awareness that emotions varied in the two causal

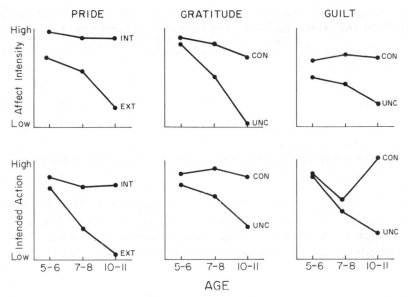

FIG. 1.   Affect and intended action ratings in three emotion conditions, by age group (from Graham, 1988).

conditions, as children grew older, pride was less elicited by externality and gratitude and guilt was less evoked given an uncontrollable cause.

There was an even greater developmental shift observed for intended action, as shown in the bottom half of Fig. 1. The youngest children were consistently committed to rewarding themselves, reciprocating another's choice, and making reparations regardless of the causal information. But, among 10-year-olds, these actions were judged as less appropriate given externality (for pride) and uncontrollability (for gratitude and guilt).

The correlations between the causal, emotional, and behavioural judgements are shown in Table 2. As children grew older, causal thoughts, affects, and intended actions became more interrelated. Among the 10-year-olds, Table 2 reveals positive relations between internality, pride, and self-reward; controllability in others, gratitude, and reciprocation; and between personal controllability, guilt, and reparation. Among the youngest children these relations are greatly modulated.

To examine more directly the mediational role of affect within our attribution–emotion–behaviour framework, the partial correlations between causal thoughts and intended actions, controlling for the intensity of reported emotions, were determined. A low or substantially reduced correlation would indicate that emotion mediates the relation between attribution and action. Table 2 reveals that within each emotion there is increasing evidence of affective mediation as children increased in age. For example, the gratitude data among the 5-year-olds showed no differences in the

TABLE 2
Correlations among Thoughts, Affects, and Intended Action in 3
Emotion Conditions, by Age Group

	Age		
	5–6	8	10–11
Emotion	($n = 34$)	($n = 46$)	($n = 39$)
Pride			
Thought × Affect	0.03	0.57[d]	0.58[d]
Affect × Action	0.36[b]	0.32[b]	0.53[d]
Thought × Action	0.32	0.54[d]	0.56[d]
Partial[a]	0.30	0.46[b]	0.36[b]
Gratitude			
Thought × Affect	0.07	0.45[b]	0.60[d]
Affect × Action	0.34	0.56[d]	0.72[d]
Thought × Action	0.48[c]	0.61[d]	0.64[d]
Partial	0.48[c]	0.48[d]	0.38[c]
Guilt			
Thought × Affect	0.03	0.28	0.57[d]
Affect × Action	0.19	0.15	0.61[d]
Thought × Action	−0.30	0.07	0.46[c]
Partial	−0.31	0.02	0.17

[a]Indicates partial correlation between thought and action, controlling for the influence of affect. [b]$P < 0.05$; [c]$P < 0.01$; [d]$P < 0.001$.
The data are from Graham (1988).

zero-order and partial correlations (both r's = 0.48). For these young respondents, one chooses to reciprocate with the purchase of a gift when a benefactor's actions are perceived as controllable, and this relation is not influenced by feelings of gratitude. With the oldest children, in contrast, the strong correlation between controllability and reciprocating behaviour decreased markedly once feelings of gratitude were held constant (from $r = 0.64$ to $r = 0.38$). This reveals that with increasing age, more of the relation between what we think and intended behaviour can be accounted for by how we feel. That is, thoughts tell us what to feel and feelings tell us what to do. This is the motivational sequence we believe emerges with age. However, it will be seen that this sequence is not equally apparent for all attribution-linked emotions and actions.

A LIFE SPAN EXAMINATION OF ANGER AND SYMPATHY

Do other emotions that fit within the attributional conception follow this same developmental course? This question guided our next developmental study. Even in the research reported by Graham (1988), there were differences between emotions such that, for example, attribution–guilt relations developed more slowly than the relations between causal thinking and the other two emotions. In the study we are about to report, we conducted the same attribution–emotion–action analysis with anger and sympathy, relating these emotions to perceived controllability and the commitment to offer or withhold help (see Table 1). Furthermore, as already indicated, the range of participants was extended to include the entire life span, from 5 to 95. Thus, we became concerned about the effects of ageing on the postulated motivational sequence. Studies of the psychological effects of ageing have to a great extent concentrated on two broad consequences: cognitive functioning, with particular attention paid to intelligence and memory; and mental health, particularly depression and suicide. This respective focus on rationality and emotionality is consistent with the general scaffold of the present research, concerned as it is with developmental changes in causal reasoning and affective as well as behavioural reactions.

There are two classes of developmental modification pertinent to the proposed attribution–affect–action scheme. On the one hand, there might be mean changes in causal beliefs about controllability, intensity of emotional responding, and/or behavioural tendencies that are exhibited over the life span. We already know from the study by Graham (1988) that young children report relatively high emotional intensities and behavioural intentions irrespective of causal considerations. In contrast, there are descriptions of the elderly as self-involved, emotionally spent, and in the process of disengagement. Thus, one might anticipate lower emotional intensities or behavioural commitments on the part of the oldest age groups. At present, there are virtually no empirical life span data regarding changes in the magnitude of emotions such as anger and sympathy that are experienced in particular contexts.

In addition to possible changes in the magnitudes of causal inferences, emotions, and behavioural inclinations, there also might be differences across the life span in the relations between these variables (see Table 2). It is evident from Table 2 that associations between these factors do increase with development. Equally interesting questions concern potential changes in these linkages for the elderly. Perhaps among the elderly reason without emotion (or emotion without reason!) determines the subsequent course of action. Or perhaps the linkages involving anger and pity decline overall in old age. For senior citizens, the nonattributional determinants of a behaviour such as helping may be quite important, so that there will be a "regression" to a less differentiated developmental stage when considered from an attributional perspective. Indeed, as one poses these questions it becomes evident that by focusing attention on abstract intellectual capacities and aberrant emotions such as depression among the elderly, there has been a vast neglect of everyday motivational sequences that include thinking and affective components.

To determine the relations between attributions, emotions, and judged actions involving anger and sympathy, as well as the absolute magnitude of these judgements, we gave subjects vignettes concerning a person in need of aid. The vignettes differed in the controllability of the cause of the need. For each causal scenario, perceptions of controllability, reactions of anger and sympathy, and the likelihood of helping the needy person were ascertained.

Subjects

There were six age groups: 5–6-year-olds ($M = 5.2$; $n = 42$); 10–12-year-olds ($M = 10.7$; $n = 39$); college students ($M = 19.2$; $n = 119$); 35–45-year-old adults ($M = 39.2$; $n = 70$); 60–75-year-old seniors ($M = 69.6$; $n = 55$); and 75–95-year-olds ($M = 79.8$; $n = 45$). The two groups of children were selected from a university-affiliated elementary school; college students participated in partial fulfilment of an introductory psychology course requirement at the University of California, Los Angeles (UCLA); the adult participants were volunteers from two large shopping malls in greater Los Angeles; and finally, both groups of elderly participants were recruited from a senior citizen's community centre located near UCLA. The centre is a daytime facility with organised senior citizen activities and patrons had to be in reasonably good physical and mental health to attend. Within each age group, the participants were approximately evenly distributed across the two sexes.

Stimuli and Procedure

We designed two story themes that potentially could elicit either pity or anger in the respondents. The themes involved common experiences that pilot testing indicated were readily understood by, and were applicable to, all age groups. The story themes were written as brief scenarios, appropriately varied across the age groups, that manipulated the controllability of the cause of an outcome. A "waiting in line" theme was presented to the two groups of children as follows:

> Let's pretend that you and some friends are waiting in line to see a special movie. It's a long line because this is a movie all the kids your age have been waiting for. Now let's pretend that the kid in back of you, we'll call him Chris, suddenly falls forward, causing both of you to fall down, and you hurt yourself. Let's pretend that Chris knocked you down because he was fooling around in line, not paying attention to what he was doing [alternate uncontrollable cause: because he had a cast on his leg and just then lost his balance].

In the second vignette, participants imagined that a neighbour had agreed to care for their plants (or goldfish, for the children), yet failed to keep her promise. The causal information revealed that the neighbour did not fulfil the agreement because she became ill (uncontrollable condition) or because she was busy and forgot about it (controllable condition).

For each causal condition, the participants rated the cause of the outcome on the degree of controllability. With adult subjects, ratings were marked on seven point scales anchored with "not at all controllable" and "entirely controllable". For children, the ratings were drawn to represent a horizontal road along which they could move their pencil, stopping whenever they wished and marking an X to indicate their answer. We operationalised perceived controllability as "made it happen" and "couldn't stop it from happening".

The participants then judged the degree of pity and anger they would feel toward the falling person and the neighbour, as well as the likelihood that they would help these persons. The helping behaviour involved picking up some of the other person's packages in the falling scenario, or taking in the mail when the other person was away in the plant (goldfish) scenario. An incomplete within-subjects design was used, with each subject presented with two of the four possible vignettes (2 story themes × 2 causal conditions). Subjects rated one controllable and one uncontrollable causal scenario across the two story themes in counterbalanced order. Because of possible attention and fatigue problems for the very young and very old, it was decided not to use a complete within-subjects design.

Results and Discussion

As previously indicated, both the mean ratings and the correlations between the variables have significant implications. The mean ratings of the four dependent variables, combined across story themes, are shown in Fig. 2. It is evident from the ratings of causal controllability (top left) that the manipulation had its intended effect: The cause in the controllable stories was perceived as more controllable than the cause in the uncontrollable stories. In addition, given the controllable cause, greater anger and less pity were elicited, and less help was rated as being provided. Conversely, of course, uncontrollable stories elicited less anger, more pity, and higher judgements to help. Thus, for example, fooling around as the cause of falling was perceived as more controllable than falling due to a leg cast, and the negligent person evoked less sympathy, more anger, and help was less likely to be extended as compared with the injured individual. For all four dependent variables, differences as a function of the causal manipulation were highly significant, all Fs $(1,364) > 100$, all $Ps < 0.0001$. This pattern

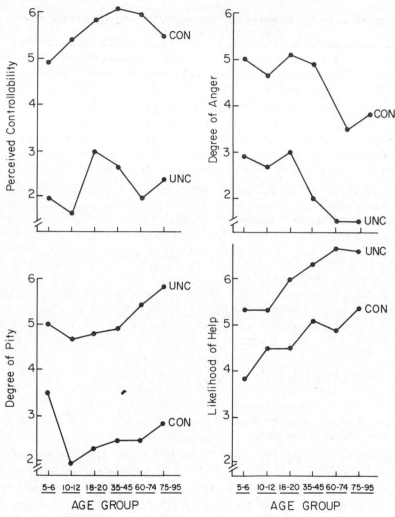

FIG. 2.   Mean ratings on controllability, affects of anger and pity, and commitment to help as a function of age group and causal condition.

of relations for anger and sympathy is consistent with a myriad of prior research studies and confirms the associations shown in Table 1.

Turning next to the age effects, analyses revealed that none of the Age × Cause interactions reached a significance of $P < 0.01$. Hence, only the main effects of age will be considered (see Table 3). A multivariate main effect of age revealed mean differences over the life span independent of the causal manipulation, $F(20,361) = 7.94$, $P < 0.0001$. Table 3 shows that ratings of controllability were influenced by age, $F(5,364) = 7.94$, $P <$

TABLE 3
Mean Ratings on the Dependent Variables in the Pity–Anger Themes, combined
across Causal Conditions

		Variable			
Group	M age	Control	Pity	Anger	Help
Young children	5.2	6.8_a	8.5_{ac}	8.0_{ab}	9.2_a
Older children	10.7	7.1_a	6.7_b	7.4_{ab}	9.9_{ab}
College	19.2	9.0_b	7.1_b	8.0_a	10.5_{bc}
Middle-aged	39.2	8.8_b	7.4_{ab}	6.9_b	11.5_{cd}
Seniors	69.6	8.0_a	7.8_{abc}	5.1_c	11.6_d
Elderly	79.8	7.9_a	8.6_c	5.3_c	11.9_d

Note. Means in each column of numbers that do not share a common subscript are significantly different at $P < 0.01$.

0.0001, with college students and middle-aged adults perceiving the causes as more controllable than did the younger or older age groups. Turning next to pity, with the exception of the youngest children who reported relatively intense feelings of this emotion in the controllable condition (see Fig. 2), the intensity of pity tended to increase with age, $F(5, 364) = 4.36$, $P < 0.001$. Life span changes were even more evident with ratings of anger, $F(5, 364) = 14.75$, and with commitment to help, $F(5, 364) = 7.02$ (both $Ps < 0.0001$). With increasing age, and particularly among the two elderly populations, there was less reported anger and more willingness to help the person in need, regardless of the cause of the need.

Trend analyses were performed on the pity, anger, and helping data shown in Table 3 to more systematically describe how each variable changed with age. The function relating pity to age group was primarily quadratic, $F(1,364) = 14.76$, $P < 0.001$. This quadratic trend explains the decline in feelings of pity from the younger to the older children, followed by a steady increase over the remaining age groups. For both anger and help, the linear trend components were highly significant: for anger, $F(1,364) = 52.85$; and for help, $F(1,364) = 33.15$ ($Ps < 0.0001$), indicating that the intensity of anger decreased steadily across the life span whereas commitment to help increased in the same manner. This paints a very positive picture of the elderly as relatively forgiving and altruistic. Thus, the stereotype of the elderly as comparatively self-involved and "cranky" certainly is not consistent with our data. Of course, one must be careful in reaching premature conclusions because of the limited sample of participants, particularly given that these are the healthy elderly relatively able to help; the small sample of story themes; and the absence of cohort comparisons.

TABLE 4
Correlations between Controllability, Affects of Pity and Anger, and Judgements of Help, within Each Age Group

	Age Group					
	5–6 (n = 42)	10–12 (n = 39)	18–20 (n = 119)	30–45 (n = 70)	60–74 (n = 55)	75–95 (n = 45)
Contol × Pity	−0.49	−0.58	−0.68	−0.67	−0.50	−0.43
Control × Anger	0.34	0.53	0.58	0.66	0.58	0.40
Control × Help	−0.30	−0.12	−0.19	−0.32	−0.40	−0.24
Pity × Help	0.51	0.25	0.27	0.41	0.43	0.43
Anger × Help	−0.58	−0.28	−0.33	−0.41	−0.51	−0.29

Next we turn to the correlational data, which are shown in Table 4. A glance at Table 4 reveals that, for all age groups, the correlations are as outlined in Table 1. That is, controllability relates negatively with pity, positively with anger, and negatively with help. Furthermore, pity promotes helping, whereas anger generates neglect. There also seem to be some differences between age groups in the magnitudes of the correlations, but these are not systematic and unambiguous trends are not revealed.

We then examined more closely the proposed attribution–emotion–action sequence. As previously intimated, this ordering implies that if

TABLE 5
Zero-order and Partial Correlations between Controllability, Affects of Pity and Anger, and Judgements of Help, within each Age Group

	Age Group					
	5–6 (n = 42)	10–12 (n = 39)	18–20 (n = 119)	30–45 (n = 70)	60–74 (n = 55)	75–95 (n = 45)
Control × Help[a]	−0.30	−0.12	−0.19	−0.32	−0.40	−0.24
Control × Help.P[b]	−0.07	0.04	0	−0.07	−0.24	−0.07
Control × Help.A[c]	−0.13	0.04	0.01	−0.08	−0.15	−0.14
Pity × Help[a]	0.51	0.25	0.27	0.41	0.43	0.43
Pity × Help.C[d]	0.44	0.22	0.20	0.28	0.29	0.37
Anger × Help[a]	−0.58	−0.28	−0.33	−0.41	−0.51	−0.29
Anger × Help.C[e]	−0.54	−0.26	−0.27	−0.27	−0.37	−0.22

[a]Zero-order correlation.
[b]Partial r between control and help, holding pity constant.
[c]Partial r between control and help, holding anger constant.
[d]Partial r between pity and help, holding control constant.
[e]Partial r between anger and help, holding control constant.

affect is partialled from the attribution–action (i.e. controllability–help) correlation, then that relation should be greatly modulated. On the other hand, if attribution is partialled from the affect–help relation, then little reduction in the magnitude of this correlation should be exhibited. The partial correlation data, shown in Table 5, support this line of reasoning across all age groups. Among the very youngest and very oldest age groups, for example, controllability–help correlations of $r = -0.30$ and $r = -24$ respectively are reduced to $rs = -0.07$ when pity is held constant and approximately $rs = -0.13$ when anger is held constant, suggesting that affect mediates the relation between causal controllability and intended action. But note that when perception of perceived control is partialled from the two affect–help correlations, these correlations are only minimally reduced. In sum, emotions rather than thoughts appear to be the main direct determinants of action. Furthermore, no meaningful developmental trends can be discerned in these data. Indeed, what is most impressive about Table 5 is the clear replication and consistency across the life span.

GENERAL DISCUSSION

At the beginning of this article, a taxonomy of emotions based on causal thinking was proposed. It also was suggested that particular attributions give rise to feeling states, and that these emotions then guide specific actions. The data that have been presented here are very supportive of these positions. Thoughts about causal locus (for pride) and causal controllability (for gratitude, guilt, anger, and pity) in part determine feeling states for the indicated emotion. In addition, pride is associated with self-reward, gratitude with reciprocity, guilt with reparation, anger with neglect, and sympathy with help. These relations are evident across the life span, although the strengths of the specific associations do vary with the emotion under consideration and the age of the respondent. The data we have presented intimate that the social emotions of anger and sympathy are understood quite early and undergo little developmental shift over the life span. Elsewhere we have speculated that anger and sympathy might be emotions with evolutionary significance (Graham & Weiner, 1986; also see Trivers, 1971). On the other hand, pride (which is an achievement-related emotion), gratitude (which is a pro-social emotion), and guilt (which is a moral emotion) appear to be more complex and show considerable developmental change up to adolescence. Whether these emotions exhibit further shift across the life span is a question we are currently pursuing.

It also is evident from the two research studies that relations between emotion and action are amenable to investigation, and surely are just as important to psychologists as are linkages between antecedents and affects. The imbalance between the antecedent–affect versus affect–action unions is in part due to the dominance of cognitive development, rather than emotional development. We see this imbalance lessening in the future with the increasing interest in affects, which bridge cognitive and motivational psychology.

Finally, we demonstrated that conceptions concerning the affective life of the elderly are subject to experimental investigation. The limited data that we have collected indicates that linkages between thinking, affect, and behaviour do not decline among the healthy elderly, which certainly corresponds with other data revealing that declines in intelligence and memory primarily are due to illness, rather than to ageing *per se*. But above that, growing social concerns and tolerance are displayed across the life span. Perhaps a greater understanding of the perils in life makes one more compassionate. Whatever the reason or mechanism of change, we leave this research with a very positive conception of the elderly. We hope that affective researchers will continue with this line of inquiry, broadening research problems from suicide and depression among the elderly to the more typical affective states experienced in everyday life.

Manuscript received 7 October 1988
Manuscript revised 3 January 1989

REFERENCES

Averill, J. A. (1983). Studies on anger and aggression. *American Psychologist, 38*, 1145–1160.

Brown, J. & Weiner, B. (1984). Affective consequences of ability versus effort ascriptions: Controversies, resolutions, and quandaries. *Journal of Educational Psychology, 76*, 146–158.

Covington, M. V. & Omelich, C. L. (1984). An empirical examination of Weiner's critique of attributional research. *Journal of Educational Psychology, 76*, 1214–1225.

Goranson, R. E. & Berkowitz, L. (1966). Reciprocity and responsibility reactions to prior help. *Journal of Personality and Social Psychology, 3*, 227–232.

Graham, S. (1984). Communicated sympathy and anger to black and white children: The cognitive (attributional) consequences of affective cues. *Journal of Personality and Social Psychology, 47*, 40–54.

Graham, S. (1988). Children's developing understanding of the motivational role of affect: An attributional analysis. *Cognitive Development, 3*, 71–88.

Graham, S. & Weiner, B. (1986). From attribution theory to developmental psychology: A round-trip ticket? *Social Cognition, 4*, 152–179.

Greenberg, M. S. & Frisch, D. M. (1972). Effect of intentionality on willingness to reciprocate a favor. *Journal of Experimental Social Psychology, 8*, 99–111.

Harris, P. (1983). Children's understanding of the link between situation and emotion. *Journal of Experimental Child Psychology, 36*, 490–509.

Harter, S. & Buddin, B. (1987). Children's understanding of the simultaneity of two emotions: A five-stage developmental acquisition sequence. *Developmental Psychology, 32*, 388–399.

Izard, C. E. (1977). *Human emotions*. New York: Plenum.
Jagacinski, C. & Nicholls, J. G. (1984). Conception of ability and related affects in task involvement and ego involvement. *Journal of Educational Psychology*, 76, 909–919.
Reisenzein, R. (1986). A structural equation analysis of Weiner's attribution-affect model of helping behavior. *Journal of Personality and Social Psychology*, 50, 1123–1133.
Saarni, C. (1979). Children's understanding of display rules for expressive behavior. *Developmental Psychology*, 15, 424–429.
Tesser, A., Gatewood, R., & Driver, M (1968). Some determinants of gratitude. *Journal of Personality and Social Psychology*, 9, 233–236.
Trivers, R. L. (1971). The evolution of reciprocal altruism. *Quarterly Review of Biology*, 46, 35–57.
Weiner, B. (1985). An attributional theory of achievement motivation and emotion. *Psychological Review*, 92, 548–573.
Weiner, B. (1986). *An attributional theory of motivation and emotion*. New York: Springer.
Weiner, B. & Graham, S. (1984). An attributional approach to emotional development. In C. Izard, J. Kagan, & R. Zajonc (Eds), *Emotion, cognition, and behavior*. Cambridge University Press, pp. 167–191.
Weiner, B., Graham, S., Chandler, C.C. (1982a). Pity, anger, and guilt: An attributional analysis. *Personality and Social Psychology Bulletin*, 8, 226–232.
Weiner, B., Graham, S., Stern, P., & Lawson, M. E. (1982b). Using affective cues to infer causal thoughts. *Developmental Psychology*, 18, 278–286.
Weiner, B., Perry, R. P., & Magnusson, J. (1988). An attributional analysis of reactions to stigmas. *Journal of Personality and Social Psychology*, 55, 238–248.
Wicker, F. W., Payne, G. C., & Morgan, R. D. (1983). Participant descriptions of guilt and shame. *Motivation and Emotion*, 7, 25–39.

Subject index

Affect *see* emotion
Affective primacy, 279
Amnesia, infantile, 279-281
Amygdala, 273-281
Anger, 346-348, 403, 410-417
  causes of, 357-361, 370-372
  consequences of, 372-373
Anticipation of emotions, 258, 262-263, 379-399
  beliefs, 395-396
  empathy, 397-398
  prediction, 379-381, 395-397
  study, 381-395
Attributions as causes and explanations of emotions, 258, 264, 401-418

Brain, cognitive-emotional interactions, 257-258, 259-261, 267-284
  early neurobiological theories of emotion, 268-269
  independence of emotion and cognition, 278-281
  neurologising emotional experience, 281-284
  psychological theory, 269-272
  stimulus evaluation, 271-277
  system interactions, 277-278

Causal organisation of emotional knowledge, 258, 263-264, 343-375
  causes of emotions, 355-361
  consequences of emotions, 362-368
  developmental differences in understanding, 373-375
  study, 349-368
Causes, and attributions of emotions, 258, 264, 401-418
Central theories of emotion, 270-271, 282-283
Cognition
  influence on emotion, 277-278
  influenced by emotion, 278, 279
  see also emotion-cognition relations
Cognitive theories of emotion, 270-271
Consciousness of emotional experience, 281-284

Development
  dissociation of emotion and cognition, 279-281
  empathy, 258, 262-263, 379-399
  language, 316-317
  language for emotional expression, 336-337

and understanding emotions,
373-375

Emotion
  causal organisation of knowledge,
  258, 263-264, 343-375
  influence on cognition, 278, 279
  influenced by cognition, 277-278
  language of, 335-336
Emotion-cognition relations,
257-265
  anticipation and empathy, 258,
  262-263, 379-399
  brain, interactions, 257-258,
  258-259, 267-284
  causal organisation, 258,
  263-264, 343-375
  expectations and, 258, 259-261,
  291-309
  linguistic and behavioral
  expression, 258, 261-262,
  313-337
  and motivation, 258, 264,
  401-418
Empathy, 258, 262-263, 379-399
Expectations and enjoyment of
play, 258, 259-261, 291-309
  study, 295-308
Expression of emotions
  and expectations, 258, 259-261,
  291-309
  and language, 258, 261-262,
  313-337

Feedback theories of emotion,
270-271, 283-284

Gratitude, 403, 408-410, 417
Guilt, 405, 408-410, 417

Happiness, 346-348
Hippocampus, 269, 276-281
Hypothalamus, 268, 270

Infants
  expectations and enjoyment of
  play, 258, 259-261, 291-309
  language development, 316-317
  memory, 279-281
  verbalisation of emotions, 258,
  261-262, 313-337

Labelling of emotions, 258,
263-264, 343-375
Language, development, 316-317
Language, and expression of
emotions, 258, 261-262, 313-337
  acquisition of language for
  expression, 336-337
  allocation of cognitive resources,
  332-335
  language of emotion, 335-336
  study, 318-337
Limbic system hypothesis,
268-269

Memory
  and emotional responses in
  infants,   258, 259-261, 291-309
  infancy, 279-281
  working, 281-284
Motivation and emotion, 258, 264,
401-418
  life-span research, 410-419

Negative vs. positive emotions, 355-370
Neocortex, 274-275
Neural processing *see* brain

Pity, 405, 417
Play, expectations and enjoyment, 258, 259-261, 291-309
Positive vs. negative emotions, 355-370
Pride, 405, 407-410, 417

Regulation of emotional experiences, 258, 262-263, 379-399

Sadness, 346-348
  causes of, 357-361, 370-372
  consequences of, 372-373
Shame, 405-406
Stimuli, evaluation of, 271-277
Studies in emotion-cognition relations, 257-265
  attributions of emotions, 264, 401-418
  development and applications of

emotional knowledge, 262-264, 343-375, 379-399
  infants' behavior and verbalisations, 261-262, 313-337
  infants' expectations, 259-261, 291-309
  separate neural basis, 258-259, 267-284
Sympathy, 410-417

Thalamus, 274-275
Theory of emotion
  central, 270-271, 282-283
  children's, 258, 262-263, 379-399
  cognitive, 270-271
  early neurobiological theories, 268-269
  feedback, 270-271, 283-284
  psychological theory, 269-272

Verbalisation of emotions, 258, 261-262, 313-337

Working memory, 281-284